D1224191

"A must-read for any American thinking of moving to Canada, not to mention an American already living there."

"The revised second edition of *The American in Canada* is an invaluable guide to the complexities of financial and lifestyle planning spanning two countries with their attendant tax laws, estate planning rules, customs and immigration issues, and a tax treaty sitting on top of all of these. The book is also an invaluable practical guide to dealing with the everyday issues of relocating, traveling, and dealing with quirky government agencies and cultural complexities between the two countries. The second edition has been expansively updated and is an invaluable resource. The book is ideally a starting point for the layperson and professional to grasp the complexities of the issues and the complex relationships between planning, legal, and regulatory regimes in order to ask intelligent questions of an expert in this area. Brian should be commended for providing this valuable information to the public and profession."

The American in Canada

Real-Life Tax and Financial Insights
into Moving to and Living in Canada

REVISED 2nd Edition

Brian D. Wruk

ecw press

Published by ECW Press
2120 Queen Street East, Suite 200, Toronto, Ontario, Canada M4E 1E2
416-694-3348 / info@ecwpress.com

Library and Archives Canada Cataloguing in Publication

Wruk, Brian D., author
The American in Canada : real-life tax and financial insights into moving to and living in Canada / Brian D. Wruk. — Updated and revised second edition.

Includes bibliographical references and index.
ISBN 978-1-77041-089-3
also issued as: 978-1-77090-647-1 (PDF); 978-1-77090-648-8 (EPUB)

1. Americans—Canada—Finance, Personal. 2. Americans—Taxation—Law and legislation—Canada. 3. Americans—Legal status, laws, etc.—Canada. 4. United States—Emigration and immigration. 5. Canada—Emigration and immigration. I. Title.

HG179.W775 2015   332.024'008913071   C2014-902585-8
C2014-902586-6

Cover design: Tania Craan
Cover images: suitcase © terex/iStockphoto; tag © alexsl/iStockphoto; Canada flag © hazimsn/ iStockphoto
Printed and bound in Canada at Friesens   5   4   3   2   1

ECW Press acknowledges the financial support of the Government of Canada through the Canada Book Fund for our publishing activities.

I dedicate this book to my wife, Kathy, my American in Canada,
and Corrine and Emily, my Canadians in America.
You made my dream come true.

PROVERBS 18:22
He who finds a wife finds what is good
and receives favor from the Lord.

PSALM 127:3
Sons are a heritage from the Lord,
children a reward from Him.

In memoriam to J. Pierre Lacroix, my very first manager and mentor.
You took this newly minted university graduate and taught me how to write.
Thank you for making me the author I am today.

CONTENTS

3 | O CANADA! 39

ACKNOWLEDGMENTS

Given the vast complexities and issues surrounding our own moves to Canada, we are unashamed to say we don't know everything! However, we view ourselves as the quarterback of a team of people to effectively coordinate your move. To that end, our firm relies on a large network of trusted, competent professionals to assist with the variety of issues our clients have. We view our knowledge as being a mile wide and a foot deep, but we have experts in all areas whose knowledge is a foot wide but a mile deep. We have drawn on these experts to review various parts of this book and want to thank them individually for their assistance in making this large undertaking possible.

Richard Brunton, a fabulous Canada-U.S. tax accountant in Boca Raton, Florida, thank you for imparting your wisdom and knowledge whenever needed.

Bruce Cohen, author of *The Pension Puzzle* and *The Money Advisor*, thank you for your review of the pension and saving alternatives in Canada.

Ed Northwood, a one-of-a-kind and much-sought-after Canada-U.S. estate planning attorney in Buffalo, New York, who reviewed the highly complex estate planning section.

Veronica Choy, an excellent immigration attorney with Miller Thompson in Calgary, Alberta, who helped this Canadian citizen to better understand the alternatives for immigrating to Canada.

Mitch Marenus, our chief investment officer, my partner, my friend. Thank you for helping me through the difficult times and keeping our clients and my investment strategies focused on the long term.

Eva Sunderlin, our Canada-U.S. paraplanner and a cherished associate, thank you for all the work you did to make this book possible. Thanks for all you do for our clients and us!

Jorge Alonso, our Canada-U.S. investment associate and a cherished associate, thank you for all you do in implementing our unique investment approach.

Our clients in Canada and the United States, without whom our firm would not exist — we enjoy our relationships with you and appreciate your excitement about this project.

Our friends in the United States and Canada, who have lent their support to this project and encouraged us along the way, thank you for your useful insights and comments.

My family, especially Dad and Mom, thanks for all you have done for me over the years and your support of whatever I did (including moving to the U.S., which I know caused you to worry). I appreciate the home cooking, your prayers, and the wisdom you imparted along the way.

And finally my wife, Kathy, and our daughters, Corrine and Emily (my little Americans) — I love you and thank you for your support in this endeavor. Again, I apologize for underestimating the time I'd be away from you during the revision of this book. You'd think I would have learned by now.

And to our readers, thank you for buying the first edition of this book. We trust you will find it a useful reference for those of you who are already "Americans in Canada" or as you begin, undertake, and complete your move to Canada. Thanks to all of you who have purchased *The Canadian in America* (coming in our third edition) as well. Our hope is this book will save you more time, money, and frustration than we experienced in our Canada-U.S. moves. If you have any questions, comments, edits, or things you'd like to see in later editions, please email us at book@transitionfinancial.com and tell us what is on your mind. For more information, articles, and other publications, or to chat with us live, please visit our website at www.transitionfinancial.com.

INTRODUCTION

I want to start by thanking all of you who made the first edition of this book such a success. I knew there was a need for this information, but I am truly overwhelmed by your kind comments and great suggestions. I have incorporated many of them along with all the law changes that have occurred (the latest changes to the Canada-U.S. Tax Treaty, the host of new disclosure and tax regulations as a result of FATCA for American tax filers living abroad) to continue making this book the definitive resource available for those in America considering moving to, or already located in Canada. The complexities associated with moving to Canada are astounding, yet, according to the Association of Canadian Studies in the U.S., more than 9,000 people moved from the United States to Canada in 2012 to become permanent residents. Citizenship and Immigration Canada approved 34,185 temporary and permanent visas for U.S. residents in 2011, just short of the record in 2010 of 35,060. The question is "How many moved with little or no idea of these complexities?" In addition, there are hundreds of thousands of U.S. citizens and green card holders already living in Canada with no idea of the Canadian and U.S. tax and estate planning issues that apply to them. Interestingly enough, fewer than 20,000 Canadians moved to the U.S. over the past two years . . . the lowest number in nearly a decade. What causes people to move to another country without understanding the financial impacts or opportunities a move presents? We believe it is the similarities in culture, currency, language, and goods consumed between the United States and Canada that lead people to think their situations are simple. In fact, the differences in taxation, investing, health care, wills, and estates are profound. It was mind-boggling, the complexities I had when I moved back to Canada in 1992 with my American-born wife before moving back to the United States permanently in 1996, as the following story illustrates.

MY STORY

My fascination with the U.S. started in high school when I took a bus trip to Portland to participate in a school band competition. I became interested in U.S. culture, geography, and so on. Then I took another bus trip with Campus Life that went through Montana, Idaho, Utah, and Las Vegas to Los Angeles. There I experienced Disneyland, Knott's Berry Farm, Magic Mountain, and Universal Studios. These experiences combined with the oceans, beaches, and warm weather had me hooked. From that point on, I decided I would eventually live in the U.S. My goal was to get a green card and have the ability to move, live, and work anywhere in Canada and the U.S.

In 1990, I decided a master of business administration degree would help my telephone career, so with the support of my employer I began applying to business schools across the U.S. and Canada. I maintained that, if I was accepted at any of the U.S. schools I applied to, I was going to the U.S. Fortunately, I was accepted by two programs and responded to the invitation from the MBA program at the University of Arizona. As I neared graduation, I began the application process and was getting interest from prospective employers when I gained the affection of a young lady while in Tucson. After graduating, Kathy and I got married, and we decided to move to Calgary to resume my telephone career while she began training as a nurse. To this day, I am not sure why we did that other than to resume my career in the telephone business. It wasn't until four years later that I realized I was "waking up next to a green card every morning," and escape from the cold winters and punishing taxes was just an application form away. I applied for and obtained a green card through the sponsorship of Kathy, and in April of 1996 I was finally able to realize my lifelong dream of residing in the United States. I became a naturalized U.S. citizen in 1999.

My migrations between Canada and the U.S. came with much frustration and complexity even though I thought my financial situation was simple. The following examples illustrate how the simple situation of a single, poor student can become incredibly complex when moving back and forth across the border.

- Applying for and receiving a student visa required a lot of paperwork and coordination with the University of Arizona.
- I received an assistantship from the university that caused no end of grief in figuring out the payroll and income tax implications in both Canada and the United States because there was so little information to be found on the subject.
- Getting married in the U.S. and moving to Canada created untold difficulties with the Canada Border Services Agency when we brought our car, personal effects, and wedding gifts across the border.
- Clearing Canadian immigration with my wife, despite months of paperwork and phone calls beforehand, we were told we had broken five immigration laws when our plane landed. Thankfully, immigration officials issued a minister's permit to allow Kathy into the country until we figured out our mess.
- We had to file U.S. income tax returns for my U.S. citizen wife each year we lived in Canada.
- We had to go through the green card application process when we decided to move to the United States and had to make at least two trips to Vancouver (now it's Montreal only) and wait in unbelievably long lines to get fingerprinted, complete the medical (including X-rays), and be interviewed.
- We had to complete paperwork to expedite U.S. Customs and Border Protection processing with our automobile and combined personal effects.
- We had to figure out what income to declare on which tax

return and when to file in the year we left Canada and took up residency in the United States (including the tax implications of our RRSPs).

- We collapsed our RRSPs, endured the terrible currency exchange at the time, suffered the Canadian government's withholding tax, and moved our money to the United States.
- Finally, we had to apply for a Social Security card, write the test to get our Arizona driver's licenses, and coordinate our health-care coverage during our move.

Now, let me be clear: I will always be Canadian, will always love Canada, and will always visit as long as God gives me the health and strength to do so. However, I have settled in the U.S., become a dual citizen, love this country and what it has to offer. In particular, the weather of Arizona is much better for my health than Canada's winters, and I find I can remain active year-round — biking, swimming, and golfing.

And that's the starting point for any move to Canada, the desired lifestyle you are trying to achieve. You should never consider a move for monetary or tax reasons alone. I have witnessed many times a couple with young kids move to Canada because one spouse has a great job opportunity in the oil patch and will make incredible money. It doesn't take long for the other spouse to become disenchanted when there is no family nearby, no friends, no support structure, and the working spouse is at the office or traveling all the time in the new career. Good planning should help you to document your desired lifestyle, see the pros and cons of your move, and consider more than just the financial rewards or taxes.

• • •

I have written this second edition of *The American in Canada: Real-Life Tax and Financial Insights into Moving to and Living in Canada* to equip you with the up-to-date information you need to consider when making the transition to life in Canada or if you are a U.S. citizen or green card holder, make you aware of the U.S. ties you still have. However, this book has been questioned as to why it is not a step-by-step guide for those who do not want to spend money on good advice, or why they cannot prepare their own tax returns with this book. The reason a step-by-step book is impossible to write is that each person has an individualized fact pattern that requires individualized advice, so it is impossible to write a "how to" guide that would specifically apply to your situation (the real-life examples throughout this book illustrate this). The information provided has to be general enough that you will still become aware of what applies to your situation and issues. It is akin to writing a procedural manual for taking out your appendix; it just can't be done. Further, many CRA and IRS forms that are required to be filed have detailed instructions on their respective websites. Finally, this is why I started Transition Financial Advisors Group — to provide you with an experienced helper to assist you in making this transition or sorting out the issues. Our goal is to ensure our clients have a smooth transition to Canada from the U.S. versus an abrupt move and all the connotations that come with it. The constantly changing rules and their application to your unique financial situation require the right professional help.

CANADIAN 1
ASPIRATIONS

A simple man believes anything,
but a prudent man gives thought to his steps.
— PROVERBS 14:15

So, you've decided to move to Canada (or maybe you are already there). It may be because of a great job offer, a spouse, or to return to your roots, but you have decided to leave the U.S. and move to Canada. How do you prepare for such a major transition? On the other hand, maybe you are an American or U.S. green card holder living in Canada and have heard all the horror stories about your tax filing obligations with the IRS or that you are subject to U.S. estate taxes.

You have entered our world . . . the world of Canada-U.S. transition planning. With the laws and regulations of two countries such as Canada and the U.S., such planning quickly becomes complex. This unique niche has been termed "cross-border" planning by some, but we prefer to call it Canada-U.S. transition planning. We caution you now that you shouldn't proceed with your move to Canada without allowing yourself enough time to understand all the nuances of your unique situation and then having enough time to take all the necessary actions before leaving the United States. If you are reading this book, you are off to a good start.

WHAT IS TRANSITION PLANNING?

You have your stuff packed and the moving company selected, but suddenly you think, "How do I move my financial affairs to Canada?" Or you are an American citizen and have seen article after article about how the IRS is coming to get you, and it is leaving you feeling very uncomfortable, particularly when you are clearing customs for a trip to the U.S. Financial planning is the core of transition planning, but we clearly define which border we are talking about and, in particular, how to smoothly transition your finances from the United States to Canada while saving time, aggravation, professional fees, and every tax dollar you possibly can.

According to the College of Financial Planning, comprehensive financial planning is "the process in which coordinated, comprehensive strategies are developed and implemented for the achievement of the client's financial goals and objectives." According to the Financial Planners Standards Council (the licensing organization for the Certified Financial Planner™ designation in Canada), financial planning consists of the following six distinct steps.

1. Establish the client–planner relationship.

2. Gather client data and determine the client's goals and objectives.

3. Clarify the client's current financial situation and identify any problem areas or opportunities.

4. Develop and document the financial plan and present it to the client.

5. Assist the client with implementing the plan.

6. Monitor and update the financial plan.

You will notice that financial planning is a process, not a transaction or an end in itself. The same applies to transition planning. Since the financial planning industry is only about 40 years old, a brief history might help. The industry started as a transaction-based business with life insurance agents selling policies over the kitchen table or mutual fund salespeople coming to your door. It has since evolved into a technically based business in which people manage an investment portfolio, analyze your insurance needs, or provide tax advice. Today the industry has realized that you can't make decisions with a person's money and ignore the person — the two are integrated. As a result, the industry is rapidly moving toward a relationship-based model where "Money is a means to an end, not an end in itself."

Comprehensive financial planning begins by understanding what you are trying to achieve in terms of lifestyle now, and in the future. This is driven by your values and beliefs about money and what you have observed during your lifetime. It is akin to taking off in an airplane with a flight plan in hand. Once our firm knows where you are trying to go (documented goals and objectives), we can develop a specific plan to test the feasibility of your goals and objectives and then figure out how to get you to your destination. Other factors constantly affect your ability to achieve your goals, such as changes in tax and estate laws, your income and expenses, death, disability, and investment performance. Therefore, our firm views transition planning as a lifelong process, not an event or a transaction. Without a flight plan, how do you know which direction to go when you take off from the airport?

It is important to note the difference between a goal and an objective. A goal is a desired end state, such as "I want to simplify my life" or "I want a better understanding of my financial situation." Only you will know whether you have accomplished that goal or not. An objective is clearly measurable, and everyone knows whether it has been achieved or not. For example, "I want to move to Canada by December 31st of this year." Once in place, your plan provides the overall context in which to place the individual, day-to-day decisions. When people struggle with individual financial decisions, it is usually because they do not have a plan. They are stuck in the individual decisions and have lost the overall perspective in which to place each decision. For example, a popular question we field is "Should we withdraw our IRAs?" The answer is "What are you trying to achieve?" The tax implications are one small part of the answer. Why do you want to take them out? When do you need the funds? What will you do with the funds when they are available? Will you move the funds to Canada? How? Do you understand the pros and cons of doing so? Will you invest them? If so, how? For what purpose or objective?

Table 1.1 depicts the elements of Canada-U.S. transition planning. Based on this table, our firm's transition planning includes the comprehensive analysis of eight specific areas in any move to Canada.

TABLE 1.1
LIVING DESIRED LIFESTYLE

Values, Beliefs, Goals, Objectives			
Client (Spouse, Children, Family, Relatives, Friends)			
Transition Financial Advisors Group			
Comprehensive Overview			
Cash Management Planning	Income Tax Planning	Independence/ Education Planning	Risk Management
• Mortgage broker	• U.S. Accountant	• Pension plan	• Insurance agents:
• Banker	(CPA)	administrator	- Property/
• Currency	• Cdn Accountant	• Actuary	Casualty
exchange firm	(CA)	• RRSP, LIRA,	- Disability
• Realtor	• Enrolled Agent	RRIF, IRA, 401(k)	- Long-term care
• Auto Dealer	• Bookkeeper	• Social Security	- Health
	• Tax Attorney	Administration	- Life
	(Cdn, U.S.)	• Human Resources	• Social Security
	• Canada Revenue	Development	Administration
	Agency	Canada (Canada	(Medicare)
	• Provincial taxing	Pension Plan/Old	• Provincial Health-
	authority	Age Security)	care provider
	• Internal Revenue	• College savings	
	Service/ U.S. Dept.	plan administrator	
	of Treasury	• RESP custodian	
	• State taxing		
	authority		

1. **Customs planning** addresses issues in relocating your physical assets to Canada. The transportation of items such as pets, guns, cars, or a wine collection across the border has unique issues that need to be dealt with in advance.

2. **Immigration planning** looks at the legal ways of moving to, working in, and residing in Canada either temporarily or

Values, Beliefs, Goals, Objectives			
Client (Spouse, Children, Family, Relatives, Friends)			
Transition Financial Advisors Group			
Comprehensive Overview			
Estate/Charitable Planning	Investment Planning	Immigration Planning	Customs Planning
• Estate planning attorney	• Stock broker	• Immigration attorney	• U.S. Customs
• Charities	• Mutual fund manager/company	• Immigration & Naturalization Services	• Canada Customs
• Trust administrator	• Brokerage firm		• Moving Company
• Estate/gift/trust tax accountant	• Investment manager		
• Custodian	• Securities and Exchange Commission		
• Trustee	• Provincial/State Regulator		
• STEP member			

permanently. You need some legal means of entering Canada because, despite popular opinion, Canada is another country, not another state in the union!

3. **Cash management planning** includes the development and review of your net worth statement and a review of your cash inflows/outflows during your move. From there, our firm can analyze the ownership of your assets between spouses and between the U.S. and Canada (for U.S. estate tax issues), and we can calculate various financial ratios to determine if any opportunities or issues exist. The net worth statement serves as a benchmark to evaluate the effects of your move over time. We also address the movement of cash from the U.S. to Canada and how to simplify your life prior to your move.

4. **Income tax planning** is a comprehensive review of your current and projected tax situation with an eye for opportunities to reduce your current and future tax liability both before and after your Canadian move. It is important to note the difference between tax preparation and tax planning. Tax preparation is a purely historical perspective and simply takes what has happened (your tax slips) and records it on a tax form for the Canadian and U.S. governments. At that point, whatever tax liability or refund results is what you must adhere to. Tax planning, on the other hand, tries to optimize your tax situation by reviewing any tax avoidance techniques that may apply to your situation in advance of any tax preparation. There is nothing illegal about proper tax planning or tax avoidance, but it must be differentiated from tax evasion, which is the intentional defrauding of government authorities of the tax dollars they are due.

5. **Independence/education planning** develops detailed projections out to age 100 using current assets, income, and expenses to determine the feasibility of your financial independence and lifestyle objectives in Canada. Alternative

scenarios and sensitivity analysis are conducted to provide insights into which actions, if any, may be necessary to achieve your goals. For example, do you need to save more and be more aggressive with your portfolio, or can a more conservative approach be taken? Education planning determines how much is required, at what point in time, and what you need to do to fund these future education liabilities. It also provides a review of your education saving options in Canada and what to do with your education savings in the U.S. before moving.

6. **Risk management** examines your current situation for risk exposures and determines the best course of action in addressing them. For example, illness, fire, theft, accident, disability, death, etc. are potential catastrophic events that could devastate what has taken a lifetime to accumulate. There are many differences in managing risk between the U.S. and Canada that need to be addressed to ensure you are fully covered.

7. **Estate planning** helps you to arrange your affairs so you can **(1)** continue to control your property while alive, **(2)** provide for the needs of loved ones in the event of disability, and **(3)** give what you have, to whom you want, when you want, the way you want, at the lowest overall cost. The focus is on control first and on saving tax dollars, professional fees, and court costs second.

8. **Investment planning** determines your investment objectives as derived from your financial plan and then designs an investment portfolio to achieve your required rate of return while managing your tax liability. Ongoing monitoring, reporting, and rebalancing of your portfolio in both Canada and the U.S. are required over the long term to ensure that it achieves your goals and meets your risk tolerance.

BEFORE YOU GO!

The two items you must have thought out and in place before you even consider a transition to Canada are adequate health-care coverage and a legal means of residing in Canada (valid immigration status).

1. Health-Care Coverage

    You may not be aware, but despite its socialized health-care acclaim, you may not automatically be eligible to join the health-care system in Canada immediately when you move there. Further, your current U.S. group or individual health insurance policy will most likely consider you "out of network" for any benefits, resulting in direct costs to you if you need health care in Canada. The rules are different for each province, but you should have some form of U.S. travel medical insurance to cover yourself in the event of illness or injury in Canada until you are eligible for provincial benefits. This coverage is best secured just before you make the transition to Canada to minimize your liability and costs. There are several options to cover you and your family that are discussed in more detail, along with items such as life, auto, and homeowner insurance, in Chapter 2.

2. Residing in Canada

    Despite popular opinion, you must have a legal means (i.e., a valid permit or Canadian citizenship) of entering and remaining in Canada for any period of time. To work there requires the appropriate authorization as well. No matter what, you have to fit into one of the immigration categories outlined by Citizenship and Immigration Canada. Unfortunately, many Americans go to Canada to visit and mistakenly believe they can work there just like they can in any state. This misconception comes in part because Americans do not need a visa to cross the border into Canada (you don't even need a passport, just a valid form of identification, such as a birth certificate). Even though you don't need a visa to cross the border into Canada, some people believe they can stay or work as long as they want. In fact, if you are caught working in Canada without a valid work visa, you will be considered an illegal immigrant and could face deportation and banishment from Canada. There are numerous legal options you can use to enter Canada, and you can review them in Chapter 3, "O Canada!" Once you have these two essentials in place, the following must also be considered.

CUSTOMS

This is where most people spend the bulk of their time, to the jeopardy of most everything else. No doubt the movement of your physical assets to Canada is time consuming. You have to make travel plans for yourself, your spouse, and your children whether you are going to fly or drive. There is also coordination of the visa applications for your spouse and children that can cause havoc at the border if not done correctly. Then there is packing your household goods, selecting a moving company, filling out all the requisite forms for Canada Border Services, and so on. When you get down to your final destination, you have to coordinate the arrival of your moving truck with the closing on your house. Then there is unpacking and putting everything away. We offer some considerations in Chapter 4, "Moving Your Stuff."

INCOME TAXES

CANADA

There is much work to be done in optimizing your tax situation before taking up tax residency in Canada. If you choose not to do it, you can face unnecessary taxes and compliance issues that can be punishing. The Canada-U.S. Tax Treaty and the relevant provisions in the U.S. Internal Revenue Code and Canadian Income Tax Act are your protection from double (and triple) taxation in both countries. Obviously, a thorough understanding of these rules and their application to your situation is the key.

An analogy may help. Imagine you are the owner of a dinner theater, and CRA is sitting in the audience. You have one chance to "set the stage" before the curtains open, and CRA has a full view of your "financial stage." As soon as you become a tax resident of Canada, you open your entire "financial stage" for CRA to see. At that point, you can no longer set the stage to present your tax and financial situation in the best light possible to optimize your tax liability, and maximize your opportunities. Interestingly enough, you can become a tax resident of both Canada and the U.S. and have to look to the Canada-U.S. Tax Treaty to avoid double taxation and determine to which country you belong for tax purposes. All of this is explored in greater detail in Chapter 5, "Double Taxes, Double Trouble." As a side note, Canadian citizens, properly severing their tax ties with Canada, no longer have to file any tax returns with CRA.

Social Insurance Number: To work or live in Canada, everyone in your family must have a Social Insurance Number (SIN). It is required by your employer, and you need it to file your Canadian tax return or open a bank account. See Chapter 5 for further details on obtaining a SIN.

UNITED STATES

Based on popular opinion, many people just stop filing U.S. tax returns when they leave the U.S. for Canada. The rationale is usually "I don't live there anymore, so I don't have to file taxes there anymore." In fact, there are filing requirements with the IRS that could increase your tax bill unexpectedly. This is doubly true because U.S. citizens, derivative citizens, and green card holders living in Canada must file U.S. income tax returns annually! Ensure that you do the requisite planning before your departure to understand how to mitigate the taxes in your unique financial situation.

The bottom line: if you haven't done proper planning prior to your departure, many planning opportunities may be lost forever, and you'll find yourself in a situation where you have to pay many financial professionals on both sides of the border to get yourself back in compliance with both governments in addition to paying higher taxes.

CURRENCY EXCHANGE

Along with moving yourself, your spouse, your family, and your physical goods, you have to move some or all of your financial assets to Canada. Doing so can be confusing, and most folks are unsure about how to tackle it. There are many misconceptions about currency exchange, and people often leave assets in the United States because they believe they will "lose" money in moving them to Canada, but other risks can be incurred by leaving everything in the United States. These myths and facts are addressed in Chapter 6, "Show Me the Money."

ESTATE PLANNING

In our experience, the area most often neglected is wills and estates. Unfortunately, many Americans go to an attorney to "update" their U.S. last wills and living trusts before moving to Canada to make sure they have it in order. What they don't realize is it may be a complete waste of time and money because their U.S. estate planning attorney typically doesn't know the Canadian rules on trusts and may be subjecting them to the punishing Canadian trust tax rates. Further, you can have a valid will in the U.S., but the provisions contained in the document may not be executable in Canada (i.e., domestic laws, disinheriting heirs, etc.). The complexities of estate planning for such citizens are considered in Chapter 7, "Till Death Do Us Part."

INDEPENDENCE PLANNING

Our firm avoids the term "retirement" because it conjures up images of an unscheduled, unproductive life pursuing leisure activities. In our experience, this pursuit of leisure is short-lived, and it doesn't take long before people look for more meaning in life, including returning back to work! As a result, our firm prefers the term "financial independence" because it prompts the question "Independent to do what?" Associated with becoming financially independent are the issues of saving for the future with company pensions, U.S. Social Security (SS), Canada Pension Plan (CPP), Old Age Security (OAS), etc. Typically, a move to Canada means the start of a new phase in your life. But now that you live in Canada, it may not make sense to invest in a 401(k) or Roth IRA, so you need to understand the alternatives for saving in Canada. These issues are dealt with in Chapter 8, "Financial Freedom."

EDUCATION PLANNING

Once people have left the U.S. for Canada, many wonder how they will be able to save for their children's education and what happens to the savings they have accrued so far in the United States. Can these savings be used at a Canadian educational institution? If you save for education in Canada, can the funds be used at an American educational institution? There are some landmines to be aware of here, and these issues are addressed in Chapter 9, "Smarten Up!"

INVESTMENT PLANNING

Many people have established a nest egg for their financial independence, but how do you manage it in Canada? Can you move your current investments and IRAs there? If so, how? Can they remain in the U.S.? How do you invest in Canada? Which financial institutions or mutual funds should you use? How are the various types of investment income taxed in Canada? It is a whole new ballgame in Canada, and there are several things of which to be aware. They are addressed in Chapter 10, "Money Doesn't Grow on Trees."

BUSINESS ENTITY PLANNING

If you have a small business in the U.S., it can afford you some unique opportunities in your move to Canada. Your business may be used to get you permanent residence in Canada and help you to establish a CPP retirement benefit and allow you to get disability coverage. There are many planning opportunities available and potential landmines to contend with for small-business owners, and they are discussed in Chapter 11, "The Business of Business."

OWNING A SECOND HOME

For some, living in the United States but escaping the heat of the summer months is appealing, particularly to those living in the southern states. To that end, these "sunbirds" prefer owning a second home in Canada for recreation, vacation, or investment purposes. There are many tax and estate planning issues that arise with owning property in Canada while remaining a resident of the United States, and they are highlighted in Chapter 12, "Northern Exposure."

SELECTING THE RIGHT PROFESSIONALS

When it comes to planning your move, we don't recommend you do it yourself, even in the "simplest" of situations (which are rare). Trust me, I tried with my simple situation, and it didn't go well. That is why I started this firm! To us, it's like giving yourself a haircut — you might do fine on your front bangs because you can see them in the mirror, but what about the sides and the back? The complexities associated with a Canada-U.S. transition are far too complex, and based on our experiences it is in your best interests to pay for the right assistance. When you look at your time, aggravation, lost opportunities, and costly mistakes, it should be an easy justification to hire someone to provide the information you need, when you need it, to make informed decisions. The key benefit of doing so is that you get an outside, unbiased understanding of your entire financial situation and the obstacles and opportunities it presents when moving to Canada. That is the benefit of good advice! With that in mind, Chapter 13 presents some of the things you should look for in any qualified Canada-U.S. transition planner.

SIMPLIFY YOUR LIFE

This is probably one of the most neglected areas in making the transition to Canada. Before you move, take the opportunity to consolidate all of your investment, IRA, Roth, and 401(k) retirement accounts with one brokerage firm. Also, maintain only one checking account and one savings account in the United States where possible. Once you are in Canada, the management of your financial affairs in the United States will be greatly simplified (i.e., one call to manage all of your accounts, one checking account to deal with, etc.). If you are a small-business owner, typically it is best to sell or wind up your entity if possible prior to moving to Canada, but it depends on your individual circumstances and how your business entity might be used for immigration purposes, qualifying for CPP, etc. Either way, you should try to set up your affairs so you are not required to manage the day-to-day operations of the entity from another country. There are also many cultural differences, and variations in the postal system, of which you should be aware. There is a brief overview of some of the major differences in Chapter 14, "Realizing the Dream."

COVER YOUR 2 ASSETS

*Therefore, a man cannot
discover anything about his future.*
— ECCLESIASTES 7:14

There are many risks in everyday life that can have devastating effects on what has taken you a lifetime to accumulate. Unfortunate events such as a sudden illness, the death of a working spouse, an auto accident, or the disability of the primary breadwinner can cause severe problems. These risk exposures must be reviewed in light of your transition to Canada to ensure that your current risk management strategies remain appropriate and that new strategies are selected as required. Consider the following questions.

- When making the transition to Canada, what coverage will your current company or government health-care insurance provide? Are you out of network? Do you need it?
- Does U.S. Medicare cover you in Canada? If not, are you automatically eligible for the universal health-care system in Canada?
- You may have sufficient life insurance coverage in the United States; however, if your death benefits pay in American dollars, what effect will the exchange rate have on how much you receive in Canada? Are your life insurance needs higher or lower in Canada than in the United States?
- Have you considered the same issues with your disability

insurance as well? Will your policy still pay benefits if you live and are employed in Canada?

- Will your American auto and homeowner insurance cover you in Canada? What differences in homeowner and auto insurance need to be considered if you get Canadian policies?
- What do you do in Canada if you can no longer perform some of the activities of daily living and require skilled nursing care around the clock?

As these questions illustrate, there is the potential for new risk exposures when making the transition to Canada that were previously covered. The following attempts to establish the facts and dispel some of the myths surrounding the major risk exposures when moving to Canada.

MEDICAL COVERAGE IN CANADA

There are a number of rumors and opinions about the health-care systems in both Canada and the United States. In our opinion, both systems offer some of the best care in the world, but there is a greater availability of services and specialists in the United States. There is more flexibility in scheduling various tests and in getting elective, non-emergency procedures, and there are more professionals available in a particular specialty. The main reason is that the medical system in the United States is primarily "for profit." This means there is competition for patients and group health insurance contracts that leads to a clearer "customer/patient" service orientation. This is particularly acute now that "Obamacare" has passed and "health insurance exchanges" have been set up to compete for your health insurance business. The Canadian medical system has been criticized for being a good medical diagnosis system but not a good treatment system. We often hear from clients who have been placed on a waiting list for treatment that may come many months later. I have personally experienced hospitalization and medical treatment on both sides of the border. In my experience, the hospitals and physicians in Canada take the view that you are there for them to practice medicine on, while in the United States the view is that they are there to get you better to live your life again. U.S. hospitals conduct patient surveys and base compensation on the outcome of these surveys, which is unheard of in Canada. The drawback of the U.S. system compared with Canada's system is the lack of universal coverage . . . which is changing with the passing of the landmark Patient Protection and Affordable Healthcare Act (affectionately known as Obamacare). Several people have come into our practice for pro bono budget counseling whose finances have been depleted because of high medical costs, co-pays, and prescription costs in the United States. It is interesting to note that approximately 62% of all bankruptcies in the United States in 2007 were due to medical expenses (2009 Harvard study published in the *American Journal of Medicine*). In Canada, "socialized medicine" means everyone pays (through higher taxes), and as a result no individual's health-care problems can leave them bankrupt. It is basically a nation-wide health maintenance organization (HMO). According to the Canada Health Act (1984), "The primary objective of the Canadian health care policy is to protect, promote, and restore the physical and mental well-being of Canadian residents and to facilitate reasonable access to health services without financial or other barriers." Unfortunately, that is not the case in the United States, and you have probably seen a bucket at a local cash register asking for donations to help an employee who was in an accident or needs a heart transplant because he or she can't keep up with the out-of-pocket medical expenses. I am curious to see if they disappear with the advent of Obamacare, under which everyone can get health insurance. In 2008, the World Health Organization came out with the results of a three-year study that showed major inequalities in health and life expectancy continue worldwide. Its recommendation? Universal health care worldwide.

Despite popular opinion, the medical system in Canada does function fairly well, and medical treatment is available if you need it. Some have termed it a medical diagnosis system versus a medical care system because, after you are diagnosed as needing treatment, it is often difficult to get that treatment. "Elective" surgeries cause the most controversy. When you are in pain and need a knee replacement, no doubt it is difficult to wait six months to see a specialist and another 12 months or more to have your surgery. In the 2012 study by the Fraser Institute on wait times for health care in Canada, the average wait time is 17.7 weeks from referral to treatment for an elective medical issue. Surprisingly, this has fallen from 19 weeks in 2011. The longest wait is for orthopedic surgery (knee/hip replacements and the like), at 39.6 weeks, while the shortest treatment is for medical oncology (cancer treatments) at 4.1 weeks. Likewise, if you need noninvasive testing such as an MRI or CT scan, the wait can be frustrating at an average of 8.4 and 3.7 weeks respectively, but our understanding is that, if the test is urgent (e.g., to diagnose cancer), you get priority status. Furthermore, if you are in a car accident and need emergency services, you will get top-notch care promptly. And if you are a hockey player and need medical attention, you can jump the queue in the public system and get it right away, while others have to wait. Now, the hockey teams would argue that they have their own physicians, but isn't that "private health care," which is against the law in Canada? Interestingly enough, physicians believe that current wait times are three weeks longer than is clinically reasonable for elective treatment *after* an appointment with a specialist.

Another misnomer you will have to contend with is that "universal" health care does not mean "free" health care. As outlined below, there are monthly medical premiums in some provinces, and often there are co-pays for splints, medical equipment, orthopedic shoes, and other medical devices as well as user fees. And universal health care does not cover items such as prescription drugs, vision care, or dental work. They must be paid for out of pocket unless you have group coverage through your employer's benefit package or obtain an individual policy. One interesting thing we have seen in the U.S. is that the cost associated with a hospital stay, surgery, doctor visit, etc. is far more transparent than in Canada. In our opinion, Canadians should be presented with a statement showing the cost of the surgery they are about to have or see what the doctor charges for a visit to start to understand the costs associated with the medical system in Canada in order to better manage it. As outlined in Chapter 5, "Double Taxes, Double Trouble," the health-care system is supported through increased income taxes. Co-pays, user fees, and higher taxes don't sound free to us!

The government-run health-care system has become a political "hot potato" because Canadians are fed up with the socialized system and demanding private alternatives to get prompt service. In fact, Dr.

Chaoulli and his patient, George Zeliotis, successfully sued the government of Quebec in 2005 in the Supreme Court of Canada. "Quebec's health-care regulations were an infringement of individual rights under the Quebec Charter. Access to a waiting list is not access to healthcare," the court proclaimed in its decision. The court went on to say that, "as long as the government was unable to provide effective health services, it could not prevent its citizens from obtaining these services elsewhere (private health care)." This has led to laws in Quebec that permit health-care payments from the government to be paid to private health-care providers for certain medical services. In fact, Dr. Chaoulli has now set up a private health-care clinic in Quebec and charges patients directly to see a physician. Similar lawsuits in Ontario, BC, and Alberta are before the courts and Alberta's case for a two-tier system recently went down in defeat. In some cases, patients want to be reimbursed by their provincial health-care provider for procedures paid out-of-pocket in the U.S. and England. It will be interesting to see how it all plays out and who is going to pay for it all in Canada or the U.S. It is hard to deny that there is much better access to health care in the U.S. given the number of Canadians crossing the border to pay for an MRI and even "elective" surgeries. This has led to many U.S. hospitals along the border offering services and packages to Canadians for elective surgeries with no wait times! Port Huron Hospital in Michigan, for example, is one such hospital doing this (www.porthuronhospital.org/Canada). It offers package deals for weight-loss surgery, joint replacement, MRI tests, and wound care. Given where we live and practice, we have had occasion to visit with Canadians who specifically come to Arizona to seek and pay for their health-care treatment at the Mayo Clinic in Scottsdale. Once they have experienced the level of care available at the clinic and the beauty of Arizona, it's not uncommon for these folks to contact our firm to look at the opportunities to move to Arizona, particularly since the M.D. Anderson Cancer Center has expanded to Mesa, AZ.

In a public health-care system, cost is the main factor in the care you receive. For example, I went in for an X-ray that required a dye injection. The X-ray technician told me that the dye has a tendency to cause an allergic reaction but is less expensive than another dye that has a much lower rate of allergic reactions. As he informed me of the symptoms to notify him of (e.g., difficulty breathing, feeling flush or faint, etc.), he began squeezing the dye into my blood veins as my heart began to race. Thankfully, I had no reaction. Another example is using less expensive artificial hips and knees that are made from less durable material and don't last as long. When the government of Canada has to pay for thousands of them every year, it chooses not to buy the best ones available.

In our opinion, a combination of the Canadian and U.S. medical systems is probably the ideal scenario. The United States seems to be moving toward universal coverage on a more formalized basis with the passing of Obamacare so that individuals and families are no longer devastated financially, while Canada appears to be moving toward a private, "pay-as-you-go" or "co-pay" system so that those who can afford it can shoulder more of the costs and get treatment right away. This approach is evident in the private eye clinics and MRI machines popping up all over the place (particularly in Alberta). As both countries continue with increasing austerity measures to deal with the ballooning debt, health care will be a topic hotly debated and likely tinkered with given the amount of money it costs annually.

PROVINCIAL/TERRITORIAL COVERAGE

When you move to Canada and become a tax resident, you become eligible for the socialized health-care system there. You are required to notify the provincial health-care agency that you have moved into the province so that you can receive a health-care card. However, you may not be eligible on the date you arrive, and you may have to make other arrangements to cover this risk exposure for the interim.

ALBERTA

The Alberta Health Care Insurance Plan (AHCIP — www.health.alberta .ca) coverage commences the date you arrive as long as you apply within three months of arriving in Alberta and it is your intention to stay in Alberta for at least 183 days in the next 12 months. Your eligibility will be determined by the information on the document you use to enter Canada. This means you need to have a valid work permit to reside and work in Alberta, unless you are a Canadian citizen. No one is required to pay any monthly premiums for coverage. There are supplemental plans that you can purchase to cover all the other items AHCIP does not, such as extended health coverage for ambulance services, prescriptions, dental work, and the like. Alberta Blue Cross, for example, provides three different individual plans that offer basic medical, dental, and drug prescription for its Personal Plan "A" to more comprehensive coverage that includes vision and extensive dental, including orthodontics, for its Personal Plan "C." There are also plans for seniors ranging from Seniors Plan "A" through "D." The premiums are very reasonable and range from C$250 annually for individual coverage to C$500 for family coverage.

BRITISH COLUMBIA

Health Insurance BC manages the Medical Services Plan (MSP — www.gov.bc.ca/health/), which provides coverage after a waiting period of the balance of the month you arrive plus two months. This means the waiting period can be up to three months if you arrive in British Columbia on the first of the month. You should apply for MSP as soon as you arrive in the province to ensure that your application is processed in time for when you become eligible. This waiting period means that you will have to make other arrangements to cover this risk exposure in the event you need coverage in the interim. Premiums are very reasonable. For example, 2014 premiums for single coverage were C$69.25 per month (C$831 annually), C$125.50 per month (C$1,506 annually) for a family of two, and C$138.50 per month (C$1,662 annually) for a family of three or more if your income exceeds $30,000. There are premium assistance programs for those in lower income brackets. PharmaCare provides subsidized prescription drug and medical supplies coverage to eligible BC residents based on income. The higher your income, the higher your deductible for PharmaCare and the higher your maximum out-of-pocket costs will be. These qualifiers change annually, so you will need to see which of them applies to your unique situation.

MANITOBA

Manitoba Health coverage (www.gov.mb.ca/health/) is available the day you arrive in Manitoba. You will be required to show proof of Canadian citizenship or residence status to be eligible for health coverage (customs form showing the settling of your personal effects). Even better, there are no premiums for this coverage. There is a Pharmacare program in Manitoba as well to subsidize prescription drug and medical supplies. As in British Columbia, the higher your income, the higher your deductible, but unlike in British Columbia there is no cap on your deductible.

TABLE 2.1
PHARMACARE DEDUCTIBLES

Total Family Income (C$)	Deductible (C$)
Less than 15,001	Greater of $100 or 2.85%
15,001–21,000	4.05%
21,001–22,000	4.09%
22,001–23,000	4.17%
23,001–24,000	4.23%
24,001–25,000	4.27%
25,001–26,000	4.32%
26,001–27,000	4.37%
27,001–28,000	4.41%
28,001–29,000	4.45%
29,001–40,000	4.48%
40,001–42,500	4.87%
42,501–45,000	4.99%
45,001–47,500	5.09%
47,501–75,000	5.16%
75,001+	6.46%

NEW BRUNSWICK

Medicare (www.gnb.ca) is available after a waiting period of the balance of the month you arrive plus two months. Again, this means the waiting period can be up to three months if you arrive in New Brunswick on the first of the month. However, if you resided in New Brunswick previously and are returning to live there, you are entitled to Medicare coverage on the first day you establish residency again. You should apply for Medicare as soon as you arrive to ensure that your application is processed in time for when you become eligible. This waiting period means you will have to make other arrangements to cover this risk exposure in the event you need coverage in the interim. There are no premiums for this coverage. The New Brunswick Prescription Drug Program provides prescription drug benefits to eligible residents of New Brunswick based on various beneficiary groupings. Each group is listed below and has a different formula for eligibility, deductibles, and co-payments, so you will need to confirm your individual situation.

A — Seniors
B — Cystic fibrosis
E — Adults in licensed facilities
F — Social development clients
G — Special needs children and children in the care of the minister of social development
H — Multiple sclerosis
R — Organ transplant recipients
T — Human growth hormone deficiency
U — HIV/AIDS
V — Nursing home residents

Unfortunately, the Fraser Institute study shows that New Brunswick has the longest wait times in Canada for elective surgeries, seeing a specialist, and receiving treatment from a specialist.

NEWFOUNDLAND AND LABRADOR

The Medical Care Plan (www.health.gov.nl.ca/health) is available after a waiting period of the balance of the month you arrive plus two months. Again, this means the waiting period can be up to three months if you arrive in Newfoundland and Labrador on the first of the month. You should apply for the Medical Care Plan as soon as you arrive to ensure your application is processed in time for when you become eligible. This waiting period means you will have to make other arrangements to cover this risk exposure should you need coverage in the interim. There are no premiums for this coverage. Like programs in the other provinces, there is a Newfoundland and Labrador Prescription Drug Program available to those with lower incomes. There is also a child's preventative dental program available to everyone under the age of 13 and a social assistance component for those between the ages of 13 and 17.

NORTHWEST TERRITORIES

Health care (www.hlthss.gov.nt.ca) is available after a waiting period of the balance of the month you arrive plus two months. Again, this means the waiting period can be up to three months if you arrive in the Northwest Territories on the first of the month. You should apply for health insurance as soon as you arrive to ensure your application is processed in time for when you become eligible. This waiting period means you will have to make other arrangements to cover this risk exposure in the event you need coverage in the interim. However, if you are a returning Canadian citizen, coverage begins your first day of residency in the NWT. There are no premiums for this coverage. There are also drug prescription, dental, and vision benefits offered through Alberta Blue Cross (see Alberta).

NOVA SCOTIA

If you are moving to Nova Scotia, you are eligible for the province's Medical Services Insurance Programs (novascotia.ca/dhw/msi/) the day you arrive. You have to sign a declaration that you are planning to live in Nova Scotia for at least one full year after your arrival, and if you are a worker you can't be absent from the province for more than 31 days except as required by your employer. Again, you will have to show proof of your work or study permit to qualify when you register for Medical Services Insurance. The other good news is that there are no premiums required for your health-care coverage since the cost of providing these services is met through the general revenues of the province. Similar to other provinces, Nova Scotia has a Pharmacare Program for eligible residents. If you don't have private drug coverage, you can apply for the Pharmacare Program. It has a 20% co-payment up to the annual family deductible, which is based on your income. Thankfully, the Nova Scotia government has a calculator online to assist you in figuring out the specifics of your situation. Once you reach the age of 65, your Pharmacare coverage is completely paid for by the government of Nova Scotia.

NUNAVUT ("OUR LAND" IN THE INUKTITUT LANGUAGE)

Health insurance (www.gov.nu.ca/health) is available after a waiting period of the balance of the month you arrive plus two months. Again, this means the waiting period can be up to three months if you arrive in Nunavut on the first of the month. You should apply for health insurance as soon as you arrive to ensure your application is processed in time for when you become eligible. Incomplete or incorrect application forms will be returned and could delay your eligibility. This waiting period means you will have to make other arrangements to cover this risk exposure should you need coverage in the interim. There are no premiums for this coverage.

ONTARIO

The Ontario Health Insurance Plan (OHIP — www.health.gov.on.ca) is available after a waiting period of three months after your arrival date. You should apply for OHIP as soon as you arrive to get the clock running and ensure your application is processed in time for when you become eligible. This waiting period means you will have to make other arrangements to cover this risk exposure in the event you need coverage in the interim. There are premiums for this coverage depending on how much you earn. If you make less than C$20,000 (like most children), there are no premiums. However, as your income increases, you pay a higher premium to the Ministry of Finance (not OHIP); the maximum annual premium per person earning more than C$20,000 will be C$900, which doesn't occur until your income exceeds C$200,900. This premium is generally withheld through your paycheck as part of your income tax withholding.

Through the Ontario Drug Benefit Program (ODB), you can get coverage for the cost of prescription drugs if you are over the age of 65 or in a long-term care facility. If you are single and have annual income in excess of C$16,018 or married with a combined income in excess of C$24,175, you have a C$100 deductible per person and up to C$6.11 dispensing fee each time a prescription is filled.

It is interesting to note that OHIP is now issuing photo health cards to stem fraud in the health-care system, similar to a government-issued ID required to receive services here in the U.S.

PRINCE EDWARD ISLAND

You are eligible for a PEI health card (www.gov.pe.ca/health/index.php3) the day you arrive in Prince Edward Island. You are required to show proof of Canadian citizenship or residence status to be eligible for health coverage (customs form showing the settling of your personal effects). Even better, there are no premiums for this coverage. There is also a Family Health Benefit Program that assists those with a family income of less than C$22,000. The PEI Pharmacare Programs are available to reduce the cost of drugs for select groups of people. Again, there are different formulas of eligibility, deductibles, and co-pays depending on which group you are in and where you obtain your prescription drugs (hospital, provincial pharmacy, or retail pharmacy).

QUEBEC

You are eligible for the Quebec Health Insurance Plan (www.msss.gouv. qc.ca/en/index.php) after a waiting period of three months following registration. That is why it is vital to submit your application to Régie de l'assurance maladie as soon as you arrive to get the clock started on your waiting period. This waiting period is waived if you are from Belgium, Denmark, Finland, France, Greece, Luxembourg, Norway, Portugal, or Sweden because Quebec has signed social security agreements with these countries to facilitate mobility between them. There are no premiums for this coverage. There is also a Public Prescription Drug Insurance Plan available for those over age 65, welfare recipients, those with no access to a private plan, or children of persons covered by a public plan. For those under age 65 and not eligible for a private drug plan, the monthly deductible is C$16.25 with a 32% co-insurance and a monthly maximum of C$82.66. The public plan premium is calculated based on your income and remitted when you file your Quebec tax return. The annual premium can range from C$0 to $579 per adult. If you retain a private plan (group insurance or employee benefit plan), there is basic and supplemental coverage, so ensure you understand your options and get the coverage appropriate for your family. Similar to Ontario, the Régie issues a health insurance card that contains your picture and a unique barcode.

SASKATCHEWAN

Health benefits (www.health.gov.sk.ca) are available after a waiting period of the balance of the month you arrive plus two months. Again, this means the waiting period can be up to three months if you arrive in Saskatchewan on the first of the month. You should apply for health benefits as soon as you arrive to ensure your application is processed in time for when you become eligible. This waiting period means you will have to make other arrangements to cover this risk exposure should you need coverage in the interim. There are no premiums for this coverage. There is a drug plan available for lower-income seniors with a flat C$20 dispensing fee for any prescription (or less if the prescription costs less than C$20). In addition, there are family health benefits for low-income families that include dental services, eye exams, basic medical supplies, and prescription drugs with a variety of formulas for eligibility, deductibles, and co-pays.

YUKON

Health Care Insurance Plan (www.hss.gov.yk.ca) coverage becomes effective three months after the date you establish residency in Yukon. You should apply for coverage as soon as you arrive to get the clock running and ensure your application is processed in time for when you become eligible. This waiting period means you will have to make other arrangements to cover this risk exposure in the event you need coverage in the interim. There are no premiums for this coverage. There is a Pharmacare plan available for those aged 65 or older or married to a Yukon resident aged 65 or older. There is also an extended health-care plan that will provide coverage for hearing aids, dental care (including dentures), eye exams, and glasses. There is also a Children's Drug and Optical Program available to assist low-income families for children under the age of 19. There is a maximum deductible of C$250 per child and C$500 per family.

First-time users of the Canadian health-care system will experience a few differences from the American system. For example, there are fewer forms to fill out and less administrative burden to get in and see a physician or be admitted to a hospital. And it is rare that someone will ask you "Will that be cash, check, or credit?" when you are done your doctor's visit, lab session, X-ray, or emergency care. Fewer co-pays and deductibles will be a welcome change for those experiencing the Canadian health-care system for the first time, but be aware that these costs are embedded in the higher income and property taxes you pay in Canada. Another thing you will notice is there are fewer urgent care, regional, lower-level, health-care centers available. The tendency among Canadians is to just go to the emergency room and wait, particularly on weekends when physicians' offices are closed, but this is slowly changing. However, the big difference you will notice between the American and Canadian health-care systems is the amount of time it takes to see a specialist or get the medical care you need, as it is much longer in Canada than in the United States.

COVERAGE WHILE IN THE UNITED STATES

When you travel back to the United States for a visit or adopt a "snowbird lifestyle" (see our companion book *The Canadian in America*) to spend the winters, your provincial health-care coverage may be good for up to six months depending on your province of residence (some terminate it sooner). However, there are several problems in relying on your provincial coverage in the United States that make it virtually of no use to you. First, your provincial health care will only pay "table" rates. For example, the table rate for a hernia operation in Canada may be C$4,000 — and that is all that will be paid. If you need a hernia operation while resident in the United States and it costs U$4,990, your provincial health care will pay only C$4,000, and you will be billed by the U.S. hospital for the balance. Second, there are limits on the daily rate paid for hospitalization; this rate covers a very small portion of what is required (Alberta pays C$100 per day) and includes the room, bandages, food, medicines, etc. In the United States, however, there is one fee for the room, another for the physician, another for the nurse, and each bandage, pill, and syringe is tracked separately. Needless to say, this system leaves you with a potentially large balance to pay personally for almost any hospital stay in the U.S.

The solution is travel insurance, which can cover any balance owing. These policies may require underwriting, so if you have a "preexisting" condition you may not be able to get insurance coverage for it. Likewise, the insurance company may attempt to attribute any illness to the pre-existing condition so that it doesn't have to pay benefits. Therefore, it is always prudent to do the requisite planning beforehand to solidify your health-care coverage if you are going to visit the United States. If you are getting travel insurance, you should apply for it before you leave the safety of Canada's health-care system in the event you are "uninsurable." The ideal situation is — if you qualify for U.S. Medicare — to use those medical benefits when you snowbird in the United States and to use the socialized health-care system in Canada when you are there.

U.S. MEDICARE

Canadians living legally in the United States for at least five years at some point in their lives become eligible to pay for U.S. Medicare starting at age 65. U.S. citizens (naturalized, derivative, or naturally born in the United States) and their spouses (non-citizens included) are generally automat-ically eligible at their own age 65, provided the qualifying spouse reaches 65 (newlyweds have to be married for one year to their U.S. citizen/resi-dent spouse before the Canadian spouse is eligible for Medicare through the U.S. spouse and only at the Canadian's age 65). This can be a great situation because, if you end up on a waiting list in Canada, you can go to a city in the U.S. for treatment, noninvasive testing, etc. Furthermore, if you end up living a snowbird lifestyle (see our companion book *The Canadian in America* for more details) for some period of time in the U.S. during the year, you can use your U.S. Medicare coverage during your stay in the United States to get your treatment before heading back up north to the universal health-care system in Canada.

Medicare is currently made up of four parts: Part A, Part B, Part C, and Part D. Part A is hospital insurance and helps to pay for the cost of care while in a hospital. Part B is medical insurance and helps to pay for the doctors, outpatient hospital care, and a variety of other medical services not covered by Part A. Part C is a Medicare advantage plan that combines Parts A, B, and D and is offered by private insurers through a Health Maintenance Organization (HMO) or Preferred Provider Organization (PPO) plan, but Obamacare is likely to eliminate these plans. Part D is the drug prescription plan. With the passing of Obamacare in the U.S., there are many changes taking effect in Medicare. For example, there are no longer any out-of-pocket co-pays or deductibles for preventive-care services. In addition, there are incentives to keep patients in their homes longer and out of hospitals by encouraging in-home Medicaid services and "Care Transitions" projects in which a nurse goes to the patient's house after discharge.

In 2015, Part A costs U$407 per month (U$4,884 annually) per person. However, to qualify for free Medicare Part A at age 65, you must have "earned" income that you paid Social Security taxes on in excess of the required amount (U$4,880 in 2015) for at least 10 years. Once you have established the required 40 quarters of Medicare-eligible earnings, you qualify for free Medicare Part A coverage. Another important aspect of qualifying for U.S. Medicare is the disability benefits you can receive (see section on Disability Insurance later in this chapter). Once 30 quarters have been established, the premium for Part A drops 45% to U$224 per month (U$2,688 annually). Canadian spouses who have not paid one nickel into the U.S. Social Security system do not qualify for free Medicare Part A coverage under the qualifying spouse unless they have lived in the United States for at least five years or have qualified under their own earnings record. Another wrinkle that has been added is, if you don't qualify for free Part A and don't enroll in it as soon as you are eligible at age 65, your monthly premium increases 10% for twice the number of years you should have had Part A but didn't sign up. It is important to understand your benefits and sign up as soon as you are eligible, or it could be costly.

Part B coverage for doctors and outpatient hospital care costs U$104.90 per month in 2015 (U$1,258.80 annually) per person, and everyone pays it no matter how many quarters of eligibility you have. The monthly premium for Part B is now "means tested" which means the more you make, the more you pay and is broken down in the following table. To determine your premium, Medicare uses your income tax return from two years earlier, and your premium is automatically deducted from your Social Security payments.

TABLE 2.2

MEDICARE PART B PREMIUMS, 2015

If Your Yearly Income in 2013 Was . . .			
You Pay (U$)	Single	Filing Married	Filing Separate
104.90	85,000 or less	170,000 or less	85,000 or less
146.90	107,000 or less	214,000 or less	
209.80	160,000 or less	320,000 or less	
272.70	214,000 or less	428,000 or less	129,000 or less
335.70	above 214,000	above 428,000	above 129,000

Similar to Part A, you must enroll in Part B as soon as you are eligible at age 65, or your monthly premium increases 10% for each 12 month period you delay in signing up after becoming eligible. This penalty is permanent and must be paid for the balance of your life, so it can get expensive. The intent of Congress with this policy passed with Obamacare is to get everyone medical coverage as soon as they are eligible.

A problem arises when you move to Canada, turn 65, and become eligible for Medicare Part B but don't sign up because you don't need it in Canada. Medicare does not provide much coverage in Canada except to get you across the border back into the U.S. for treatment. However, if you don't sign up, you are subject to the penalty unless you can show you have coverage elsewhere (like a group plan through a spouse). It is uncertain if you show coverage through your Canadian health plan if that will be accepted as valid coverage by the Medicare folks but it is worth trying as the penalty is punitive.

The Part C "Medicare Advantage Plans" are offered by a variety of private health insurance companies in all different states. These plans tend to be less expensive than Medicare with a supplement, but they tend to be more restrictive in terms of which doctors, hospitals, and other facilities you use (must be in network). They are generally all-inclusive plans that include drug coverage (see below), so they can be quite economical. However, with the passing of Obamacare in 2010, the future of Medicare Advantage Plans is unknown because the payments to these types of plans are gradually being reduced to be more in line with average fee-for-service payments. These payment reductions started in 2012 and will reach the full amount in 2016. As a result of these reductions, it is likely that Part C plans may go the way of the dodo bird.

The Part D drug coverage can cost as little as six to eight dollars per month in some states and goes up from there (depending on which state you reside in and which plan you select). In addition, Part D is now "means tested" as well, as outlined in the following table.

TABLE 2.3

MEDICARE PART D PREMIUMS, 2015

If Your Yearly Income in 2013 Was . . .			
You Pay (U$)	**Single**	**Filing Married**	**Filing Separate**
Plan premium	85,000 or less	170,000 or less	85,000 or less
+12.30	107,000 or less	214,000 or less	
+31.80	160,000 or less	320,000 or less	
+51.30	214,000 or less	428,000 or less	129,000 or less
+70.80	above 214,000	above 428,000	above 129,000

Everyone eligible for the drug plan must enroll as soon as they are eligible at age 65, or penalties are added on a permanent basis in the amount of 1% per month of the "national base beneficiary premium" ($33.13 in 2015). There is a maximum U$320 deductible in 2015, and then annual prescription expenses from U$325.01 to U$2,970 are shared through a co-insurance plan specific to which plan you subscribe to. After that, you enter the Part D "donut hole," where you pay 45% for brand-name drugs and 65% for generic drugs. Once you have spent $4,700 out-of-pocket for the year, you are out of the donut hole, and you automatically get "catastrophic" coverage that kicks in. With the passing of Obamacare, discounts and other benefits begin to kick in within the donut hole, and there are provisions that will gradually eliminate the donut hole by 2020, and the costs of all drugs will simply be 25% of the total drug cost.

While Medicare provides good base coverage, it cannot be relied on to cover all of your medical expenses. In addition to the premiums listed above for Part A, there is a deductible in 2015 of U$1,260 that must be paid for a hospital stay of from 1 to 60 days (U$0), U$315 per day for days 61–90, and U$630 per day for days 91–150, while hospital stays greater than 150 days are not covered at all! For Part B, there is a deductible of

U$147 per year, plus you pay 20% of the Medicare-approved amount after that. You'll need to purchase a Medicare supplement policy to cover the expenses not covered by Medicare. These supplements have 10 government-defined types of policies, ranging from basic (A) to comprehensive (J). They are all the same no matter who provides them, so it becomes a matter of price. Your Medicare supplement does require underwriting, but it is very lenient, and we have not heard of an instance of anyone being turned down. Medicare supplements cost approximately U$1,500 per year per person.

LIFE INSURANCE IN CANADA

Another area often overlooked when making the transition to Canada is the appropriate amount of life insurance to cover the risk exposure if the primary breadwinner dies prematurely or estate liquidity to pay Canadian and/or U.S. estate taxes. All of your policies should be reviewed to ensure you have the right type and amount of coverage as well as the correct ownership to avoid potential U.S. income/estate tax issues (see Chapter 7 for more details). For example, your life insurance coverage could increase as soon as you take up residency in Canada. How? If you need U$500,000 in the United States to cover your needs and you move to Canada and need C$500,000, you could be underinsured because, at a U$1=C 85¢ exchange rate, you have only C$425,000 in coverage. This amount will leave you underinsured by C$75,000 in covering your risk exposure in Canada. Another important aspect is to reevaluate your life insurance needs in Canada to see if you need more, the same, or less insurance than you did in the United States based on the change in your financial circumstances. For example, if your lifestyle goes up and you now need C$750,000 in life insurance in Canada (see Chapter 7 on the deemed disposition tax at death in Canada), relying on your U.S. life insurance policy alone could leave you underinsured by C$325,000. If you decide to collapse your life insurance policies in the United States and take out the cash value as a tax resident of Canada, you'll be subject to tax in both Canada and the United States. Another complication is that the cash values inside life insurance policies in Canada must be reported to the IRS if the total of all assets outside the U.S. is greater than U$10,000 (see Chapter 5 for the tax implications). As you can see, the complexities surrounding a simple item such as life insurance can often be overlooked.

DISABILITY INSURANCE

If you are under the age of 40, statistics say you have a higher probability of becoming disabled than dying. If you are a young, high-income worker, becoming disabled and no longer being able to earn the income you are accustomed to can be devastating to your finances. In addition to losing the high earning potential for the balance of your life, your medical expenses tend to increase dramatically at the same time because you are temporarily or permanently disabled and need additional nursing care, medical equipment, etc. To cover this risk exposure, a disability insurance policy can be invaluable in insuring your future income.

There are generally two types of disability insurance: Own Occupation ("Own Occ") and Any Occupation ("Any Occ"). With Own Occ, the policy pays benefits if you are unable to return to the occupation held prior to your disability. If you were a brain surgeon prior to your disability and you are unable to return to your occupation as a brain surgeon, the policy will pay you benefits (generally up to 60–66% of your salary). With Any Occ, the policy pays benefits only if you are unable to return to any occupation. If you were a brain surgeon prior to your disability and you are unable to return to any job (e.g., Welcome to Walmart! How can I assist you today?), the policy will not pay any benefits. Obviously, an Own Occ policy will be more expensive than an Any Occ policy.

In Canada, the federal government offers disability benefits through the Canada Pension Plan. To qualify, you must have contributed to CPP in four of the past six years or three of the past six years if you have contributed to the system for a minimum of 25 years. If you fail to meet these requirements, the Canada-U.S. Totalization Agreement can be used to get you qualified for partial disability benefits. The agreement allows your time in the U.S. to be used to qualify for disability benefits in Canada. To understand what your disability benefit is, you should log on to your

Service Canada account (www.servicecanada.gc.ca/eng/home.shtml) and view your statement at least annually. Likewise, if you have qualified for U.S. Social Security disability benefits, you are eligible to continue them even when living in Canada. If you are not collecting, you are eligible to apply. The Social Security Administration has a great "payments abroad screening tool" that you can use to determine your U.S. Social Security benefits at www.ssa.gov/international/payments_outsideUS.html.

In the U.S. and Canada, most major employers will have a group disability insurance policy, and you are well advised to get the most disability insurance possible through them. If you own an individual policy in the U.S. and move to Canada, it is likely your insurance company will continue to pay benefits based on your employment in Canada, but you should confirm the details before paying any more premiums. If you have no group policy benefits available through your employer, you should seriously consider obtaining an individual disability insurance policy provided you are insurable. Whether you secure a Canadian or U.S. policy depends on where you are going to live in the longer term and whether you need the policy to be portable and follow you to employment in the U.S., where you will need to insure a U.S. dollar income.

Disability insurance policies can be issued for short-term disability (generally six months) and long-term disability (anything over six months up to age 65). Obviously, long-term disability carries the biggest risk exposure, as short-term disability needs can be covered with saved-up vacation time and savings. One tax note: you need to understand whether you are paying for your disability insurance premiums or if your employer is paying for them, as it can make a dramatic difference to your benefits. If your employer pays your premiums, any benefits the policy pays will be fully taxable to you, giving you a significant haircut in the benefits available for your care. However, if you pay your premiums with after-tax dollars, your benefits will not be taxable to you.

LONG-TERM CARE INSURANCE

One of the largest issues facing the federal governments in both Canada and the United States is providing long-term care to the aging boomers and baby boomers. Long-term care consists of home care, assisted living, or skilled nursing care in a qualified facility for those who are unable to maintain the five activities of daily living (dressing, eating, continence, transferring, and bathing). With today's medical advances, people are living longer but generally sicker (Alzheimer's, dementia), and as a result these costs can quickly become very expensive. The average cost across the U.S. for a private room in a nursing home is U$230 per day. These costs will be higher in Hawaii, Alaska, and New York but less in Wyoming. In Canada, the government subsidizes long-term care costs in nursing homes (residential facilities) as part of its socialized medical system, so the average out-of-pocket co-payment amount across the country for a private room in a nursing home is about C$76, but it is "means tested," so you may pay less depending on your after-tax income. As in the U.S., this may be higher in places such as Nova Scotia and New Brunswick and lower in places such as Alberta. The government-subsidized facilities can have unusually long waiting lists, and the quality is not as good as in some of the private facilities, which you will have to pay more for out-of-pocket. Furthermore, if you require home care or assisted living, the availability of services is not as good as it is in the U.S. The long-term care insurance industry is not as developed in Canada as it is in the United States, but policies are still available. If you have a long-term care insurance policy issued by a U.S. company, you need to determine if your policy will pay benefits to a Canadian facility (otherwise you should consider a "cash pay" policy) and, if so, determine the effects of the exchange rate on your benefits.

Another insurance you will see in Canada that you won't see in the United States is critical illness insurance. It will pay you cash to use as you wish if you are diagnosed with a terminal or severe illness such as Parkinson's, paralysis, Alzheimer's, cancer, stroke, heart attack, etc. We believe that this insurance is expensive for the benefits received, so you should look at your risk exposure and even consider self-insuring some of these risks if you have sufficient assets. Another alternative, if you have a life insurance policy and acquire a terminal illness, is to sell your life insurance policy for cash you can use (called a viatical settlement) but be careful who you deal with. Furthermore, make sure this isn't duplicate coverage of your existing disability benefits.

OTHER INSURANCE

AUTO INSURANCE

Private companies run all auto insurance in the United States; however, when you move to Canada, British Columbia (icbc.com), Saskatchewan (sgi.sk.ca), and Manitoba (mpi.mb.ca) have government-run auto insurance that is the only source for the mandated auto insurance required. You can check your insurance options for all provinces at the Insurance Bureau of Canada at ibc.ca. If you are unhappy with your claim or customer service, there is little recourse, so this can be a big adjustment for those used to the privately run, competitive property/casualty insurance industry in the United States. This also means there are fewer lawsuits and much smaller payouts in Canada than in the United States. In Manitoba, a victim of a catastrophic injury has no right to sue for economic losses, lost wages, etc. over a predetermined amount. Another difference is that auto insurance is generally quoted on a six-month basis in the United States versus annual premiums in Canada. Auto insurance also tends to be less expensive in Canada than in the United States. Provincial governments have mandated a minimum liability insurance of C$200,000 in all provinces except Quebec, where it is only C$50,000. Remember to register your vehicle in the province you are relocating to, and get a provincial driver's license within the required time frame for each province (see Chapter 4 on "Moving Your Stuff").

HOMEOWNER/CONDOMINIUM INSURANCE

Just like banks in the United States, Canadian banks require you to have homeowner insurance if you have a mortgage on your home (the bank wants to protect its investment!). This coverage is fairly standard, and it is best to consolidate your auto and homeowner policies with the same firm since you can usually save on premiums. But beware . . . if you are running a small business out of your home, your homeowner insurance typically won't provide the coverage you need.

LIABILITY

In Canada, there are more laws to prevent the big liability payouts possible in the United States, and as a result it is a less litigious society. Tort reform is being called for here in the U.S., but with Congress in such a deadlock it is uncertain when anything will be done. In Canada, you will still find injury attorneys in the phone book and on TV and radio advertising for those who may have been injured in a car accident. We don't recommend you try to use your American liability or auto insurance policies when making the transition to Canada — they just don't provide the coverage you need as a resident there.

O CANADA! 3

From far and wide, O Canada,
We stand on guard for thee.
God keep our land . . .
— JUSTICE ROBERT STANLEY WEIR

According to Citizenship and Immigration Canada, over 9,200 Americans moved to Canada in 2010. For some Americans, singing "O Canada!" in a Canadian citizenship ceremony someday is the ultimate dream, while for others it is considered the utmost in treason against the United States. It is a personal issue that each person must wrestle with and come to a conclusion on. The issue of immigration to, and citizenship in, Canada can be confusing, and this chapter aims to provide you with a basic understanding of the options you have for living and working in Canada on a long-term basis. However, it is not a substitute for a good immigration attorney. To live year-round or work at any time in Canada, you must have the appropriate non-immigrant or immigrant status or be a citizen of Canada. If you are not a Canadian citizen, your long-term objectives should determine whether you pursue a temporary work permit, permanent residence, or citizenship, because there are tax implications, healthcare risks, the cost of living, and lifestyle issues to consider with each option. Again, a thorough analysis of your unique situation is required to determine the best immigration strategy for you and how to best achieve your goals. For example, if you hope to move to Canada and remain there for the balance of your life, you need to ask your immigration attorney for the road map to get you from where you are now (American citizen) to where you want to be (dual American-Canadian citizen). Likewise, if you want to move to Canada for a short-term job opportunity and then return to the U.S., a different road map is required.

A lack of planning in this area can result in some negative consequences. One scenario we often see is one spouse gets a job offer and a work permit for a Canadian employer, while an immigration strategy for the accompanying dependent spouse or common-law partner is not addressed. In many situations, if a person receives a work permit, there are provisions allowing the spouse or common-law partner to also receive an open work permit. However, if this issue is not properly addressed, one spouse may end up working in Canada while the other is left at home in a strange city because he or she cannot work, and there may be no family or support structure in place. This situation tends to raise tensions in the non-working spouse and create a longing to go back to the United States. In one client situation we witnessed, the husband accepted an academic position in Canada, but his wife was unable to work, even temporarily, and was driven stir crazy by her two rambunctious boys at home with no support structure around her. It was only eight months later, after completing his first year, that they contacted our firm to assist them with their move back to the United States (see our companion book *The Canadian in America*). It is also useful to consider that spouses with differing citizenships may encounter different methods by which they can apply for their work permits. This may result in one spouse not obtaining his/her work permit until several months after the primary applicant applies for and obtains his/hers. We encourage you to start this part of your transition early by meeting with a competent immigration lawyer who can assist you in designing your Canadian immigration strategy from start to finish and achieving your goal of temporary or permanent residence or citizenship if that is your desire.

STATUS IN CANADA

Broadly speaking, there are three types of "status" in Canada: temporary residents, permanent residents, and citizens. Temporary residents consist of anyone who is not a permanent resident or citizen and include all visitors, foreign workers, and international students. Permanent residents can work and study without restriction in Canada and have the right to enter and remain in Canada indefinitely. A child born in Canada will, in most cases, be a Canadian citizen, regardless of the parents' status. A child born to a Canadian citizen outside Canada *may* also have immediate claim to Canadian citizenship. Otherwise, a person must first become a permanent resident before being eligible to apply for Canadian citizenship. Canada currently permits dual citizenship, which means that a person can become a Canadian citizen without relinquishing his or her U.S. citizenship or passport.

TEMPORARY RESIDENTS

VISITORS

Despite the close relationship between Canada and the United States, anytime you cross the border you mustn't forget you are crossing into another country. Therefore, you must have the proper documentation to prove your origin and identity. For American citizens and green card holders (permanent residents) entering Canada to visit, no visa is required. You must have your U.S. green card with you (or other proof that you are a permanent resident of the U.S.), demonstrate your intent to return to the U.S., as well as your passport. Unless otherwise specified, a visitor is allowed to stay for a maximum of six months in Canada per calendar year. In fact, you don't need a visa if you are an American since America is one of the few countries whose citizens don't need a visa to visit or transit Canada. You need to demonstrate to the immigration officer that you intend to return to the United States after your stay in Canada and that you have sufficient funds to support yourself without working for your intended stay in Canada (unless you have a work permit). If you are not able to establish the purpose of your stay in Canada, you may incur some inconvenience if you are sent to secondary screening/questioning upon seeking entry to Canada.

We have stated many times that 9/11 changed/will change many things between Canada and the U.S. To that end, the United States and Canada issued on December 7, 2011, an agreement to a Joint Border Action Plan "designed to speed up legitimate trade and travel, improve security in North America, and align regulatory approaches between the two countries." One key initiative coming out of this plan is that "Entry-exit verification will be put in place so that both countries can count people coming in and going out to enforce immigration and other programs." On June 30, 2014, this initiative became a reality.

One "gotcha" you need to be aware of is Canada's stance in barring entry to those with criminal records — regardless of your intended purpose for entering Canada or whether you have been admitted to Canada previously. You can be denied entry into Canada, even for a visit, if you are known as "inadmissible" under Canada's Immigration and Refugee Protection Act. This means, if you have a criminal record, even for some seemingly minor offences such as theft and driving under the influence (DUI), your vacation plans could be ruined. If you or the person(s) accompanying you have one of those tucked away in a dark closet somewhere, you should deal with it well in advance of your travels to Canada to avoid any inconvenience. You should speak with an immigration lawyer about any criminality — even if it seems minor — to verify whether you may be deemed inadmissible. In many cases, there are options to overcome criminal inadmissibility on either a temporary or a permanent basis, but it is important to identify them up front before an application is filed. Either way you will need to satisfy an immigration officer that you have met the legal requirement to be "deemed rehabilitated," have applied for or been granted "rehabilitation," were granted a pardon, or have a Temporary Resident Permit (see below).

Being "deemed rehabilitated" depends on the crime committed, how serious your crime was, how much time has passed since completing the sentence for your crime, whether you committed more than one crime, and whether the crime is punishable in Canada by a maximum prison term of less than 10 years. You can be "assessed" at a Canadian port of entry but only if you have the appropriate documentation to show evidence of all the above factors. You can make a formal application to a Canadian visa office in the U.S. (i.e., a Canadian consulate in the U.S. that can process immigration-related applications), but generally it will not take the time to complete informal inquiries/assessments.

Individual rehabilitation means you have led a stable life and are not likely to commit new crimes (at least five years have passed since you completed all elements of your sentence, including probation). This process requires you to submit an application (along with a processing fee, of course) to a Canadian visa office in your area. This can take close to two years to process, so you will have to plan well in advance of your travels to ensure that your rehabilitation application is approved by the time you get to the border.

In rare cases, an application for rehabilitation may be adjudicated at the port of entry by Canada Border Services Agency. However, this practice is not encouraged, and you may be simply told to submit your application to a visa office anyway. If you have been granted a pardon or discharge in Canada for your conviction, you will have no problem at the border. However, if your pardon or discharge originated in the U.S., you should check with Canada Border Services Agency at a port of entry or with a visa office in the U.S. to determine if the pardon is considered valid in Canada.

TEMPORARY PERMITS

A temporary resident permit is another alternative for those who do not meet the criteria of the Immigration and Refugee Protection Act and are refused processing or entry into Canada but have compelling reasons to travel to Canada. This permit is issued at the discretion of the authorities when exceptional circumstances justify it. This occurred when I tried to bring my American wife to Canada after we got married in Arizona. We had made many calls to Citizenship and Immigration Canada (CIC) and filled out much paperwork, yet as soon as we landed in Canada the border agent informed us that we had just broken five immigration laws and were sent to secondary screening! We had to explain we were newlyweds, show our marriage certificate, and give details about our marriage ceremony to prove it was "substantive." At that point, my wife was issued a temporary resident permit (a minister's permit back then) to enter Canada, with clear instructions to get the required paperwork filed as soon as possible to get right with the world!

Another situation that often causes confusion involves "seasonal residents." The reason for the confusion is that CIC has no immigration category for such residents; rather, this is a Customs Canada category that allows a tax and duty exemption on personal goods brought into Canada to furnish a seasonal home or those who have signed a long-term lease on a dwelling in Canada. This does not include those traveling with a motor home to stay at their timeshare or mobile home, or those who own a property with a Canadian resident. In most cases, people claiming the customs exemption as seasonal residents are entering Canada as temporary residents (visitors). See Chapter 12 for details on owning recreational property in Canada and living the "sunbird" lifestyle.

Once U.S. Citizenship and Immigration Services (U.S. CIS) implemented the Western Hemisphere Travel Initiative, all travelers to the U.S. are required to have a passport . . . period. As many have found out, no exceptions apply, and the State Department now has expedited processing (for an extra fee of course) on passports for those who don't realize their passport has expired before embarking on a trip or their passport will expire will traveling abroad. This is now the "new way of the world" for travel to the U.S. and most anywhere, so be sure to check the expiration date on your passport or put an alert on your smartphone a few months before it expires so you can avoid any potential problems.

STUDENTS

According to CIC, close to 100,000 students entered Canada to study in 2013, with over 4,500 being from the U.S. For those students to enter, they need a study permit. It is generally easy to get once you have been accepted at a recognized institution of learning in Canada. You need to prove that you have enough money to pay all of your tuition fees and sustain your living expenses during your intended stay. You also need to prove that you will have sufficient funds to transport yourself (and your family) back to your originating country. Again, be careful of any criminal record abroad that could come back to haunt you as you will be denied a study permit if this record is discovered. It is best to deal with these matters well in advance of your planned enrollment, as outlined previously.

Visitors can enroll in a program of study that is less than six months without a study permit. However, even if you are seeking to study in Canada for less than six months, you will likely need to provide evidence of your financial ability to pay your fees and live in Canada for this time period without working, as you will not have the legal ability to work in Canada without a work permit. To apply for a study permit, you can go online to cic.gc.ca/English/index-int.asp and fill out Form IMM 1294 — Application for Study Permit Made Outside of Canada (plus supplemental forms), provide the list of required documents, and even see the current application processing times. There is a C$125 filing fee, and applications from the U.S. are taking approximately two to three months to process when applying from within the U.S. Processing times for applications submitted from within Canada are taking approximately one to two months. As always, good planning in advance of your studies is always recommended.

If you wish to change your studies or transfer to another educational institution, nothing further is required as this falls under your original study permit. You are eligible to work at the institution where you are studying without a work permit as long as you are a full-time student. However, if you want to extend your studies or change the conditions of your stay, you will need to submit an Application to Change Form IMM5709 — Application to Change Conditions, Extend My Stay, or Remain in Canada as a Student. While study permits may be issued for all types of educational institutions, the type of school you attend and your program of study may impact your "off campus" work opportunities or those of your spouse in Canada as well as your opportunities to become permanent residents after you graduate. If you want to remain in Canada after your studies, there are a number of programs available for you to apply to in order to get a work permit to remain in Canada. Ensure you are equipped with the right information beforehand.

TEMPORARY WORKERS

As a rule, anyone who is not a permanent resident or Canadian citizen will need a work permit to work in Canada. There are some exceptions, such as clergy, emergency workers, properly accredited foreign representatives, some performing artists, athletes, coaches, public speakers, judges and referees of sports and cultural competitions, expert witnesses, crew members, and business visitors, to name the major ones. For the other 40,000 foreign workers entering Canada from the U.S. in 2013 (according to CIC) to work in temporary jobs in areas where there are skill shortages, a work permit is needed.

To apply for a work permit, you will need to fill out Form IMM 1295 — Application for Work Permit Made Outside Canada (plus supplemental forms), provide a list of documents, and pay the C$150 application fee. If you are filing for employment in Quebec, you need to meet all of the federal requirements plus get a Certificate of Acceptance from the province of Quebec. Processing times when applying from within the U.S. or from within Canada are taking approximately two months.

This permit is an immigration document that specifies the terms and conditions under which you can work in Canada. There are numerous categories under which one can apply for a work permit, but with each category comes a specific set of requirements. Almost all work permits must be supported or "sponsored" in some way by a Canadian employer and are issued to a specific position, employer, location, and period of time. The work permit itself does not grant you the automatic right to re-enter Canada (for those who may still be required to apply for a visa to enter Canada) or remain in Canada permanently.

In many cases, the Canadian employer will often be required to obtain a Labour Market Opinion (LMO) from Service Canada verifying that there are no qualified and available Canadians or permanent residents available for the position. There is a C$275 non-refundable LMO processing fee per position, and overall this is generally a lengthy and labor-intensive process. Employers are required to advertise their open positions in three or more locations (some specified) for a minimum of four weeks and continue to "actively" seek qualified Canadian candidates during the period when the LMO application is being processed (approximately eight or more weeks).

Immigration attorneys are often able to assist employers with the LMO process or, even better, determine if there are any other work permit categories that might apply where the employer does not have to obtain an LMO. For example, work permits exempt from needing a Labour Market Opinion include NAFTA work permits, entrepreneurs, intra-company transferees, spouses of work permit holders, certain academics, current students, and recently graduated students.

Additional programs recognize the dire need for temporary workers in particular industries in certain geographic regions. As such, there may be special "pilot" programs lasting for one year or less (and may or may not be renewed) that greatly simplify the process for Canadian employers to obtain work permits for prospective temporary foreign workers in these categories.

Another well-known program is for live-in caregivers in Canada to provide care for children, the elderly, or the disabled in private homes without supervision. In these cases, the prospective Canadian employer can obtain an LMO and show that he/she is unable to hire sufficiently qualified and able Canadians/permanent residents for the position. The applicant must also demonstrate the ability to meet certain requirements, which include (but may not be restricted to) living in the private home in which he or she is working, producing a written contract, completion of secondary school, possessing sufficient English- or French-language skills to work unsupervised, and proof of at least six months of formal training or a full year of relevant experience to qualify.

NAFTA WORK PERMITS

NAFTA (North American Free Trade Agreement) permits citizens of the United States and Mexico to obtain work permits for certain types of jobs in Canada without the need for a Labour Market Opinion. In other words, U.S. and Mexican citizens can get work permits for qualifying NAFTA jobs even if there are qualified Canadians available. One of the categories is NAFTA professionals, which includes over 60 professions eligible for work permits if they meet the specified minimum educational and/or experience requirements for a specific occupational category. The list includes specific professions, including doctors and nurses, scientists, engineers, computer programmers, accountants, and management consultants. Generally, you must have a bachelor's degree related to your field of work, and your work permit may be issued for a period of up to three years.

People who have been granted work permits (under NAFTA or otherwise) often forget that this is a document that allows for only a temporary stay in Canada. As such, remaining in Canada past the expiry date of your work permit is entirely dependent on whether your Canadian employer will sponsor/support the application to extend or renew your visa. We have seen poorly conceived immigration strategies in which people have moved to Canada under a temporary work permit but in reality intend to stay permanently. The key thing to remember is that a work permit may be issued for up to a three-year period, but it will expire and does not automatically convert to permanent resident status. You are well advised to plan accordingly. For example, work with your employer when negotiating the terms of your employment to include the employer's support in potentially sponsoring you for permanent resident status in Canada. You can apply for permanent status while in Canada on a temporary work or study permit, but you need to take the necessary steps to maintain your legal temporary status in Canada while you await the processing of your application for permanent residency.

PERMANENT RESIDENTS

There are six main categories through which you can apply for permanent residency in Canada: (1) Family Sponsorship, (2) Federal Skilled Workers and Trades, (3) the Start-Up Visa Program (previously Investors and Entrepreneurs), (4) Canadian Experience Class, (5) Provincial Nominees, and (6) Quebec-Selected Skilled Workers. Generally, people qualify for permanent resident status either under the family class or one of the economic-based categories. Under the Family Sponsorship class, Canadian citizens and permanent residents may sponsor certain family members to become permanent residents in Canada. Members of the family class include, but may not be restricted to, spouses, common-law partners, conjugal partners, dependent children, parents, and grandparents. Other family relationships may also be recognized under certain circumstances, such as orphaned siblings or nieces and nephews under 18 years of age.

Economic immigrants may qualify under any of the other described categories and may require support or sponsorship by a Canadian employer or may apply on their own. If either spouse or common-law partner qualifies under any of the economic categories, the spouse or common-law partner and all dependent children may be "carried along" on an application for permanent resident status submitted by a primary applicant.

As you have seen throughout this book and on our website at transitionfinancial.com, we recommend that you seek competent immigration legal counsel to assist you in developing your immigration strategy from start to finish. Be prepared for the regular government procedures of completing lengthy application forms (many are now available to submit online), paying the appropriate application fees, completing criminal record checks, and enduring a medical examination and language testing. We now turn our attention to each of these six categories in greater detail.

1. FAMILY MEMBERS

CIC wants to keep families together, and if you are a citizen or permanent resident of Canada you can use that status to sponsor your family under the Family Class. Family is generally defined as your spouse, common-law partner, conjugal partner, dependent (adopted) child(ren), parent(s), or grandparent(s). Your family member(s) will have to go through the same medical and security checks as you did when you applied for permanent resident status. To be considered a sponsor, you must fulfill several requirements as well. For example, you must be at least age 18 and sign a sponsorship agreement that ensures you will provide for your children for 10 years or until each child turns 25, whichever comes first. You need to provide support for your spouse for at least three years, and all of your family members have to commit to supporting themselves.

With a broad definition of spouse in Canada, it is important to define this relationship up front. Your spouse is considered the person to whom you are legally married, including a same-sex partner. Your marriage must be legal in the country where it is performed and not contrary to public policy in Canada (i.e. marriage to a minor). In the case of a same-sex marriage, your marriage must have occurred in Canada (where same-sex marriage is legal) or in another jurisdiction where such marriage is legally recognized. At this writing, these jurisdictions include Belgium, the Netherlands, Norway, South Africa, Spain, Sweden, and the States of Connecticut, Delaware, Iowa, Maine, Maryland, Massachusetts, Minnesota, New Hampshire, New York, Rhode Island, Vermont, Washington, the District of Columbia, and possibly California, where these states have legalized same-sex marriage in some form. Common-law partners can be either the same sex or the opposite sex.

For immigration purposes, a common-law relationship is defined as living together in a "marriage-like" relationship for at least one full year. Immigration officers will look at how intertwined your lives are financially and socially. Proof can include shared children, joint ownership of property, rental agreements, bank accounts, credit cards, both names on utility bills, or listing your partner as a beneficiary on a life insurance policy, in a will, or on a health plan.

A conjugal partner applies to both same-sex and opposite-sex "marriage-like" relationships of at least one full year in which there are reasons why a couple has been unable to live together or get married. For example, a couple may not have been able to live together for a full year because of immigration restrictions, or they may have been unable to get married because one partner is waiting for a divorce, or in the case of same-sex couples same-sex marriage is not recognized in the country or state where they reside. Conjugal-partner sponsorships are applied in exceptional circumstances, are recognized rarely, and should be used only where spousal or common-law sponsorships aren't possible.

To curb the large amount of immigration/marriage fraud that occurred when people started using marriages of convenience to get into Canada, the government passed a conditional permanent residence measure for spouses and partners. This new measure applies if you are being sponsored by someone with whom you have been in a relationship for two years or less and have no children in common. The government now requires you to live together in a legitimate relationship with your sponsoring spouse/partner for two years from the day you receive your permanent residence status in Canada.

To sponsor your spouse from outside Canada, use Form IMM 1344 — Application to Sponsor, Sponsorship Agreement and Undertaking (plus supplemental forms). There is a Guide to Immigrating (IMM 3999) for those sponsoring a spouse from outside Canada that you can get from Citizenship and Immigration Canada's website at www.cic.gc.ca/ English/. If you sponsor your spouse from within Canada, use the IMM 1344 form and follow the specific instruction guide (also available on CIC's website). The sponsorship application fee is C$75, and the principal applicant has an application fee of C$475. You will also be required to pass a background check, pass a medical examination, and submit biometric identifiers, and you may be required to attend an interview with a CIC officer (with all of those attendant fees and costs). The processing time for sponsored spouses is approximately one month.

Your particular circumstances may dictate *how* you submit your application for spousal sponsorship, or you may be able to choose the method that works best for your situation. There are advantages and disadvantages to submitting a spousal sponsorship application from inside or outside Canada. They include retaining or losing the right to appeal a negative decision, faster processing times, and the ability of the sponsored spouse to legally work in Canada before being granted permanent resident status. It is important to consult with legal counsel to obtain a comprehensive understanding of all the options you might have and the advantages and disadvantages of each before selecting a particular method or path. If you have naturally born or adopted children (19 or under), you can sponsor them (provided they are not married or not in a common-law relationship) using Form IMM 1344 (Type A dependant, with an application fee of C$75). If your children are 19 or older, they can no longer be sponsored even if they are full-time students and financially dependent on you. If they are reliant on you due to a disability (Type C dependant), they continue to be eligible for sponsorship. Type B and Type C dependants have an application fee of C$550. The current processing time for sponsored dependants can be found on CIC's website.

Other family members who can be sponsored include your parents or grandparents and their dependent children using Form IMM 1344 as well. Due to the large backlog of applications for parents and grandparents (about four years), CIC has temporarily stopped taking new applications at this time. Instead, the government has created a parent and grandparent "super visa" that allows them to come to Canada for a period of up to 10 years and remain for up to two years without having to renew their applications. There is only a C$150 entry visa for multiple people or C$400 for entire families. The problem with this visa is obtaining health insurance for this length of time. Travel insurance may be purchased for six months to a year, but the super visa does not make one automatically eligible for socialized medicine in Canada. Other family relationships may also be recognized under this category, but their eligibility will be dependent on the specific circumstances surrounding the sponsoring family member. If a family member is not included in the family class, you might have to see whether he or she can qualify as an economic immigrant. As usual, each situation is unique and should be reviewed by someone with a professional eye before you submit your application.

2. SKILLED WORKERS AND TRADES

The Federal Skilled Workers and Trades classes are two of the most straightforward and predictable of the economic immigrant categories, but only 5,000 applications will be accepted annually for processing and no more than 300 applications per eligible occupation. Eligibility is based on the applicant having a permanent job offer from a Canadian employer for a position classified as being "skilled" or higher, or an individual applicant's professional education, expertise, and experience.

Qualifying employment generally includes managerial, professional, technical, or skilled trades. Jobs within these areas are categorized in the Canadian National Occupation Classification (NOC).

Skill Level O

This includes senior management occupations, middle, and other management positions.

Skill Level A

Occupations at this level usually require university education at the bachelor's, master's, or doctorate level.

Skill Level B

Occupations at this level usually require education obtained at a college or vocational institute, apprenticeship training, or three to four years of secondary school followed by more than two years of on-the-job training, specialized training courses, or specific work experience.

Although we have provided a brief list under each skill level, the NOC is a huge list of skill sets that you can research at the Employment and Social Development Canada website at esdc.gc.ca/eng/jobs/lmi/noc1. Applications for permanent residency under these categories can be submitted from within Canada (by temporary residents with current legal status in Canada) or at a Canadian visa office located outside Canada. For American citizens and those with legal status in the United States, applications from outside Canada will be processed by the Canadian visa offices in Los Angeles or New York. Like the consideration you need to give to *how* you apply to sponsor a family member under the Family Class, consideration of your options needs to be given under one of the economic classes — particularly if you are currently and legally working in Canada with a valid work permit. When contemplating your options, you should consider not only the estimated processing time of each option but also factors such as the place where you may be required to attend an interview (requested at the discretion of CIC).

Under the Federal Skilled Worker category, once applicants find themselves eligible to apply (fall under a specific NOC or have a permanent job offer in a NOC O, A, or B position), they need to qualify under the category based on a point system that allots points for age, education, work experience, linguistic ability, and factors that will increase their ability to establish themselves successfully as permanent residents in Canada. In addition to meeting the points pass mark, you must meet the minimum requirements of having at least one year of continuous, full-time (or equivalent) qualifying work experience in the past 10 years and sufficient settlement funds for you and your accompanying dependants. Entry into Canada at this point is based on a somewhat objective point system that considers six factors in a "selection grid" (see Table 3.1).

TABLE 3.1
SKILLED WORKERS AND TRADES SELECTION GRID

Factor	Points
English/French: points are based on proficiency in speaking, listening, reading, and writing. Up to 6 points each (max. 24), with a minimum of 4 points each (max. 16) for first language (English/French), and up to 6 points each (max. 4) for your second language to count (English/French). Unless English or French is your native language, you should take one of the authorized language tests to establish that you have basic, moderate, or high proficiency.	Max. 28

Education: this is a combination of the highest educational credential obtained and the number of years of study. Give yourself 5 points if you completed high school and up to 25 points for a PhD.	Max. 25
Experience: these points range from 9 for one year of experience to 15 for six years or more of qualifying work in the past 10 years.	Max. 15
Age: 12 points maximum are awarded for anyone between 18 and 35. Subtract 1 point for each year outside this range.	Max. 12
Arranged Employment: you can get points for verified employment arranged or if you are already working in Canada under certain work permits.	Max. 10
Adaptability: if you or your accompanying spouse/ partner has worked one full year in Canada under a work permit (5 points); studied two full years in Canada under a study permit (5 points); a close relative living in Canada (5 points); or your spouse has a command of the English or French language level (5 points).	Max. 10
Total	**Max. 100**
Current Points Needed to "Pass"	**67**

To apply as a Skilled Worker/Trade, you will need Form IMM 0008 — Generic Application Form for Canada (plus supplemental forms) and the C$550 per person processing fee. Depending on where your application is filed and/or on the immigration category you are applying under, your application will go through either the regular process or the misnamed Simplified Application Process (SAP). If possible, avoid SAP since it is an extra step in the process created in anticipation of extra-long processing times. The good news is that American citizens, regardless of where they live, can file permanent resident applications through the Canadian visa office in Buffalo, New York, making them exempt from SAP. Applications filed through any other Canadian visa post outside Canada will be subject to SAP, except the following:

- provincial nominees (see below);
- Quebec Selection Certificates (see below);
- those with arranged employment; and
- anyone admitted to either Canada or the United States with authorization to stay for at least one full year (you can submit your application through the visa office in Buffalo and thereby avoid SAP, and you aren't required to have been in the United States or Canada for one year prior to filing).

3. START-UP VISA (NEW)

In 2011, Citizenship and Immigration Canada placed a moratorium on accepting any applications for permanent residency under the Investor and Entrepreneur categories. For nearly two years, no one could enter under this category until CIC launched the Start-Up Visa program, newly designed to link immigrant entrepreneurs with experienced private sector organizations that have expertise in working with start-ups. This is a pilot program for now and will be available for the next five years (through 2018). CIC expects that, because of the initial narrow focus of the program, applications will be limited. However, if this pilot program proves successful, CIC may formally introduce it as a new economic class in the Immigration and Refugee Protection Regulations.

Partnering with Canada's Venture Capital and Private Equity Association and the National Angel Capital Organization, this pilot program requires foreign entrepreneurs to obtain the support of a designated Canadian angel investor group or a venture capital fund before they can apply to the Start-Up Visa program. The minimum financial investment, which the foreign entrepreneur must secure, is C$75,000 from an angel investor group or C$200,000 from a venture capital fund. It is expected that CIC will eventually designate Canadian "business incubators" that will be eligible to participate in the Start-Up Visa program as potential investors.

In addition to securing the support of a Canadian investor, the foreign entrepreneur will be required to:

- meet minimum language ability in either French or English;
- demonstrate completion of at least one year of study at a postsecondary institution; and
- demonstrate possession of sufficient funds to settle and provide for the cost of living prior to earning an income.

Additional information on the Start-Up Visa can be found on the CIC website at http://www.cic.gc.ca/english/immigrate/business/start-up/index.asp.

4. CANADIAN EXPERIENCE CLASS

The Canadian Experience Class (CEC) category allows foreign workers who have acquired one year of work experience in Canada to apply for permanent residency. The foreign worker must be able to provide evidence that:

(a) the experience was acquired during a period in which he/she was legally able to work in Canada in the position specified;
(b) that the experience was acquired in a NOC A, B, or C position; and
(c) that the experience is from having worked in a full-time capacity (defined as 30 hours per week or more).

The CEC category, like the Federal Skilled Worker category, also possesses minimum language proficiency requirements in English or French. Work experience acquired as part of an academic program, such as an internship or a co-op placement, *does not* qualify under the CEC. Part-time work completed *during* studies similarly cannot be used to meet the requirements under this category. Additional information on the CEC category can be found on the CIC website at www.cic.gc.ca/english/resources/publications/cec.asp. CEC is not available to foreign workers who intend to reside in the province of Quebec (see Quebec-Selected Skilled Workers later in this chapter).

5. PROVINCIAL NOMINEES

This category is for those people who have been identified as possessing the requisite skills, education, and work experience to make an immediate economic contribution to the province or territory from which the nomination originates. Currently, every province and territory participates in this program except Quebec (see below), the Northwest Territories, and Nunavut. Participating provinces and territories set out their own selection criteria depending on provincial/territorial needs. To be clear, the government of Canada still has the final say on your immigration, but participating provinces and territories have an agreement with the federal government that allows them to nominate a certain number of immigrants to help address regional employment needs.

The first step is to get a Certificate of Provincial Nomination in the province you wish to reside in. Of course, each nomination procedure is different. Once you get your certificate, you apply using Form IMM 0008 — Generic Application Form for Canada (and supplemental forms) and pay the C$550 application fee. Check CIC's website for current processing times. Even if you have been granted a nomination from a province, the federal government still retains the right to request criminal checks and medical examinations and set other requirements for you and your dependent family members before granting permanent residence status. Many of these programs are employer driven and require an employer within that province to sponsor the intending immigrant employee. However, some Provincial Nominee Programs also have categories for entrepreneurs and investors as well as international students who have completed postsecondary studies in the province or territory.

With the oil boom, Alberta has been one of the busier provinces using this program. It continues to give priority to skilled workers, international graduates, semi-skilled trades workers, and self-employed farmers, and it has both an employer-driven and a strategic recruitment stream (in which the individual possesses a certain education and specific background). Refer to www.albertacanada.com/immigration/immigrating/ainp.aspx to see the latest skill sets in demand.

6. QUEBEC-SELECTED SKILLED WORKERS

Under the Canada-Quebec Accord on Immigration, Quebec (as usual) administers its own immigration program. Again, this category is for those who have skills, education, and work experience needed to make an immediate economic contribution to Quebec. It is a fairly straightforward process that starts with applying for a Certificat de sélection du Québec to show that Quebec has accepted you for immigration. Once your certificate is in hand, you make a separate application to CIC for permanent residence. Many of the same criteria are used to evaluate your application, including the medical and security requirements and proof of funds. However, you aren't subject to the selection grid as outlined in the other categories.

Quebec offers almost the same immigration categories as the federal government and offers an online assessment tool to evaluate your chances of entering Quebec as a worker. Check www.immigration-quebec.gouv .qc.ca for more details.

APPLYING FOR THE PERMANENT RESIDENCE CARD

To apply for permanent residence in Canada, you will need to fill out the requisite CIC form related to your immigration class and submit it along with the C$475 processing fee. Once your application for permanent resident status is approved, you and your family members will be issued permanent resident visas that permit you to travel to Canada to become a permanent resident. Your visa and documents will be reviewed at a port of entry, and you will be asked to provide an address in Canada to which your permanent resident card will be mailed.

The permanent resident card (see sample in figure 3.1) is valid for five years. Your permanent resident status doesn't expire — only the card. You should plan well in advance if you are going to travel when your card will expire as you can only apply for a renewal of your card from within Canada and, if you find yourself outside Canada after the expiry of your card, you will need to apply for a travel document to return to Canada. You can apply for a new permanent resident card once you have met the residency obligation of living in Canada for at least 730 days (two years) within the previous five-year period. In many cases, new immigrants may qualify for and submit their applications for Canadian citizenship before their first permanent resident cards even expire. You can remain a permanent resident indefinitely without ever applying to become a Canadian citizen. However, if you choose to become a Canadian citizen, you will hand in your permanent resident card and be granted a Certificate of Naturalization that can be used to obtain a Canadian passport. Permanent residents cannot vote, and their status can be lost if they fail to meet the residency obligation or are deemed inadmissible because of a serious criminal offense.

FIGURE 3.1

PERMANENT RESIDENCE CARD

If you do need to apply for another permanent residence card, the starting point is the CIC website to obtain an application kit and supplemental forms and to pay your fees. You start by filing CIC Form IMM 5444 — Application for a Permanent Residence Card along with your receipt for C$50 (per person) and two color photographs. As usual, there is a host of supplemental forms and fees required as part of your overall application "package." Before undertaking this yourself, seek good counsel to save yourself time and ensure that you are filling out the right forms and submitting them in their entirety to the right location. If all of these requirements aren't met, CIC may reject your application — not only delaying the process itself but also potentially affecting your travel plans. Most importantly, make sure you clearly meet the residency obligation before submitting any new application since the consequence of not meeting it could lead to the loss of your permanent resident status.

FACTS AND MYTHS

There are both facts and myths surrounding immigration to and remaining in Canada for an extended period of time. Here are some common ones we have dealt with.

MYTH: SPECIAL CIRCUMSTANCES APPLY

As a general rule, you are required to apply for a temporary visa, work permit, or permanent resident visa before coming to Canada. While there are options for exceptional circumstances, you shouldn't rely on them, and you should consult with an immigration attorney in advance. A relatively straightforward application can become seriously delayed, or fail altogether, if you are simply unaware of or ignore immigration requirements. Although Americans can travel as visitors without a visa to Canada, there are still restrictions on what you can do and how long you can stay in Canada. If your passport is not stamped at the border, you can remain in Canada for only up to six months at a time without applying to extend your stay. However, there is no automatic right to stay six months, and an immigration officer can restrict your stay to some shorter period or even prevent you from entering the country if he or she is concerned about the reason for your trip, whether you appear ready to return to the U.S., or believes you are inadmissible. We have witnessed well-intended children bring an ill non-Canadian citizen parent to Canada to live with them for an extended period of time because there was no other family in the United States. Unfortunately, the parent is likely to be considered inadmissible because of potentially being a significant strain on the Canadian health-care system, despite the good intentions of the family. Furthermore, U.S. Medicare is of no use in Canada (see Chapter 2), and travel insurance policies have finite time limits and limited coverage, leaving the ill parent stuck with a huge medical bill that could devastate what has taken a lifetime to accumulate.

MYTH: RETIRE IN CANADA

Canada no longer has an immigration category for retirees. Someone who is retired may still qualify to become a permanent resident under either the economic or the family class, but there is no category for retirees per se. We have seen people who own vacation property in Canada travel back and forth without incident for years while they are working and/or own a home in the United States. Many new retirees run into trouble at the border after they sell their home in the United States and plan to "live" in their Canadian "vacation" home without any status in Canada and without ongoing ties to the United States. Border officials may determine that they are not really "visitors" but de facto long-term residents in Canada because the retiree has stronger ties to Canada than the U.S. In this scenario, you may be turned away or permitted to enter for a much shorter period of time.

FACT: YOU WILL GET CAUGHT

Some people, with little regard for the laws of the land, have asked, "How will the government know?" or "How will I get caught?" Scrutiny in this area has increased significantly since the unfortunate events of 9/11 and reached its culmination when Canada and the U.S. announced the Beyond the Border — A Shared Vision for Perimeter Security and Economic Competitiveness initiative on February 4, 2011. Since Canada and the United States are the largest trading partners in the world, Canada has been working with the United States on a policy of "secure borders, open doors." On December 12, 2012, officials from Canada and the U.S. signed the U.S.-Canada Visa and Immigration Information-Sharing Agreement. The main purpose of this agreement is to enable a systematic and automated means of sharing immigration and visa information between the two countries on third country nationals applying for a visa or citizenship. This means the other country will automatically be consulted to see if this person has any history or has applied for entry into the other nation. The government stated initially that no information will be shared about citizens or permanent residents in both countries at this time, in accordance with Canadian and U.S. laws, as many people have privacy concerns. In addition, a coordinated Entry/Exit Information System has been developed, and, despite assurances to handle information on travelers "responsibly," both governments are now tracking, and sharing, information about who enters and exits either country from a third country but apparently not citizens or permanent residents of either country. Sure enough, on June 30, 2014, both governments announced that all land travelers entering one country will automatically create an "exit" record with the other country to track that traveler. This is part of the final implementation phase of the entry/exit initiative as part of the Perimeter Security and Economic Competitiveness Action Plan. They are trying to track potential acts of terrorism and those collecting social benefits such as unemployment insurance from one country when they are not entitled to do so because they are not resident there.

With Canada and the IRS cracking down on international tax cheats and the IRS going after U.S. citizens living abroad, it is logical that the countries' entry/exit databases will become integrated. With the economic downturn in the U.S., there have been documented cases of Canadian citizens living in the U.S. going to Canada, applying for unemployment insurance benefits using a Canadian address, and then going back to their homes in the U.S. (you are ineligible for most Canadian benefits, including UIC, if you are a non-resident of Canada). To stop this type of abuse, both countries will be comparing the border entry/exit dates to catch the perpetrators, including snowbirds and sunbirds overstaying their welcome.

Overall, "beyond the border" policies are intended to build systems to expedite the passage of legitimate travelers but make it much more difficult for illegitimate travelers (i.e., those whose stated purpose may not be consistent with their travel and behavioral patterns) to cross the border. To achieve these goals, both countries are creating, maintaining, and sharing a database of biometric identifiers using the latest in technology to identify the wrong people and prohibit them from entering Canada or overstaying their visas while enhancing traffic flow for those crossing the border for legitimate purposes. Furthermore, the IRS (part of the Department of Treasury) and the United States Citizenship and Immigration Services (U.S. CIS, part of the Department of Homeland Security) appear to be working more closely together, similar to Canada Revenue Agency and Citizenship and Immigration Canada. It appears they are combining tax slips with visa records to ferret out tax evaders and illegal aliens. An American citizen client living in Canada recently traveled to the United States for a visit. To our amazement, the U.S. CIS agent asked him if he has been filing U.S. income tax returns, to which he replied "yes." We are uncertain what would have happened to him if he had not been in compliance with the IRS (see Chapter 5 for the tax filing requirements of U.S. citizens). Whatever you do, don't enter Canada illegally or overstay the temporary period of time that has been granted to you on your passport or your work/visitor/student permit. The likelihood of getting caught increases with each passing day. Besides, for anyone who is not a Canadian citizen, entering Canada is a privilege, not a right. To that end, respect the laws of the land.

MYTH: CANADA-U.S. MARRIAGE IMMEDIATELY GRANTS THE SPOUSE THE RIGHT TO LIVE IN CANADA

With the advent of the Internet and increased Canada-U.S. travel, many Americans are finding love in Canada. And, since Canada now legally recognizes same-sex common-law relationships and marriages, there has been more interest in the same-sex community to reside in Canada to live their chosen lifestyle. Our firm has seen a large increase in inquiries (and horror stories) from Americans getting married to Canadian citizens. Many of these brides-to-be are in tears when they realize their wedding plans are in jeopardy due to the unanticipated long immigration processing times. The difficulty starts when deciding where to get married. If you are getting married in the United States, the Canadian resident approaches the U.S. CIS officer, who asks, "The purpose of your visit?" If you reply "To get married," you will be asked for your K-1 fiancé/ée visa. If you don't have it, you will need to prove to the border agent that you have the intention of returning to Canada after you are married so you can be issued a B-2 — visitor's visa. It is important to be truthful since the officer may document the conversation, and if you are caught lying you could be banned from entering the United States for five years or more. Needless to say, you will likely be barred from entering the United States at that time unless you can convince the officer that you intend to return to Canada. Likewise, if you are getting married in Canada, the American resident approaches the Canadian Border Services agent, who asks, "The purpose of your visit?" If you reply "To get married," you will be asked for your permanent residence card under the Family Sponsorship class. If you can't produce it, your entry into Canada will be up to the discretion of the border official and whether he or she will grant you temporary residence so you can get married.

At the heart of the confusion and heartache is the concept of "dual intent." If you are an American seeking entry into Canada and have no other legal basis for doing so (i.e., you have not been approved for a student or work permit or do not possess Canadian permanent resident status), you essentially have no choice but to seek entry into Canada as a "temporary visitor." By definition, a visitor is someone who will leave the country within a specified period of time. However, if you indicate to CBSA that your intention is to live in Canada with your Canadian spouse, then that indicates your intention to remain in Canada *permanently* — and thus conflicts with your temporary visitor status. The same goes for a Canadian who has recently married an American and now seeks to move to the United States but has not filed for any other status with the U.S. CIS beforehand. This conflict of intent is called "dual intent" and can be sufficient cause for officers on either side of the border to refuse the "intending immigrant" entry into their respective countries.

Canadian immigration laws and policies allow for officers to exercise a bit more discretion when encountering situations of dual intent. Officers are permitted to allow someone to enter as a temporary visitor (even though that person has declared the intention to file for permanent residence in Canada) if they are satisfied that the individual will, in fact, leave Canada if the permanent residence application is denied or the individual is at the end of the term of authorized temporary stay (whichever happens first). American immigration laws regarding dual intent are much stricter and more straightforward in their wording and application, and most CBP officers will require a significant amount of evidence from the intending immigrant of his/her ability and intention to leave the United States after a temporary stay before admitting the person into the country as a visitor.

So, much like the processes described above in choosing categories through which to apply for permanent residency, it is important to seek competent legal counsel to become fully apprised of not only the application options but also the potential pitfalls, consequences, and "side effects" of each one before embarking on a particular application process.

CANADIAN CITIZENSHIP

For many Americans, the prospect of becoming a Canadian citizen is terrifying, even the ultimate act of treason, while for others it is a coveted opportunity. As you can see, it is a very personal decision. Millions of people around the world would welcome the opportunity to become a Canadian or U.S. citizen and be able to work and live anywhere in Canada or the U.S. Each year approximately 160,000 people become Canadian citizens. Canada recognizes dual citizenship, which means that you can become a Canadian citizen without giving up your U.S. citizenship. Many folks hold valid passports from both the United States and Canada at the same time (I am a living example). Once again there are many rules and regulations surrounding citizenship with which you must contend. Canadian citizenship is obtained in one of the following three ways.

1. BIRTH IN CANADA

Under current law, with few exceptions, anyone born in Canada to parents legally permitted to reside there is automatically a Canadian citizen. Furthermore, that child can remain a Canadian citizen regardless of residence or citizenship unless he or she chooses to renounce that citizenship at some point. A good example is Senator Ted Cruz, a Texas Republican, who was born in Calgary to a U.S. citizen mother, giving him U.S. citizenship. However, there have been questions about his political campaign seeing that he is a Canadian citizen who was born on Canadian soil. This would not prohibit him from running for president (naturalized citizens are barred), but he has decided to renounce his Canadian citizenship because, "as a U.S. senator, I believe I should be only an American."

2. BIRTH ABROAD

Under laws passed on April 17, 2009, amending the Citizenship Act, if you are in the first generation born outside Canada after 1947, to at least one parent who is a Canadian citizen, then you are automatically a Canadian citizen without having to become a permanent resident in Canada. You don't need to apply for citizenship, but you may need to apply for a certificate to prove your citizenship. To apply for a certificate, you need to fill out Form CIT 0001 — Application for a Citizenship Certificate (and supplemental forms) and file it along with your C$100 application fee.

If your parent is also a Canadian citizen born outside Canada to a Canadian parent (second generation born outside Canada), then you have no automatic right to Canadian citizenship. To become a Canadian citizen in this scenario, your Canadian citizen parent must sponsor you under the family category for permanent residence, and once approved you must move to Canada. Immediately upon your arrival, your Canadian parent can apply on your behalf to be granted citizenship. To apply as an adult, you need to fill out Form CIT 0002 — Application for Canadian Citizenship — Adults (and supplemental forms) and submit it with your C$100 processing fee. To apply for your minor child, you need to fill out Form CIT 0003 — Application for Canadian Citizenship — Minors (and supplemental forms) and submit it with a C$100 processing fee.

For the adopted children of Canadian citizens living abroad, retaining Canadian citizenship wasn't an option until December 22, 2007, when Bill C-14 amended the Citizenship Act to make it permissible. With the amendment in 2009, children adopted abroad by a Canadian citizen automatically get Canadian citizenship as long as they are a first generation adoption. To get your adopted child Canadian citizenship, you are required to fill out Form CIT 0003 — Application for Canadian Citizenship — Minors (and supplemental forms) and submit it with a C$100 processing fee. I did this with both of my adopted daughters so they now hold dual Canada-U.S. citizenship.

Losing Citizenship

In 1977, Prime Minister Pierre Trudeau declared his "once a Canadian, always a Canadian" policy. It basically means that, if you were born in Canada after February 14, 1977, you can't lose your Canadian citizenship unless you specifically renounce it. Between 1947 and 1977, if you were born outside Canada to a Canadian citizen parent, or acquired the nationality or citizenship of another country by "any voluntary and formal act other than marriage," you lost your Canadian citizenship. This caused a lot of confusion, so to simplify things a new amendment to the Citizenship Act came into effect on April 17, 2009. This amendment allows CIC to automatically recognize Canadian citizenship for those born abroad after 1947 retroactive to their date of loss (because of some expatriating act) or date of birth.

Resuming Citizenship

If you were a Canadian citizen in the past but gave up, or renounced, your citizenship to take the citizenship of another country, you may be able to resume your Canadian citizenship. To be eligible to do so, you must first apply to become a permanent resident of Canada after your loss of citizenship and live in Canada at least one year to be eligible to apply for citizenship. To resume your citizenship, you need to file CIC Form CIT 0301 — Application to Resume Canadian Citizenship along with the C$100 filing fee and supporting documentation (photos, two pieces of identification, birth certificate, etc.). If you lost your citizenship as a minor (under 21) between 1947 and 1977 because your Canadian parent(s) didn't register your birth abroad and you are part of the first generation born abroad, you are now automatically a Canadian citizen under the new amendment.

Renouncing Citizenship

Formally renouncing your citizenship is a much easier process for Canadians than for Americans, but the motivation is generally not there like it is for Americans. As outlined in Chapter 5, Canadians are generally taxed based on their residency in Canada. If they choose to live abroad, the tax obligation to Canada typically ceases (see our companion book *The Canadian in America*). However, Americans are taxed based on their citizenship no matter where they live. As a result, many Americans have attempted to renounce their U.S. citizenship to avoid the onerous tax filing requirements of the IRS. To renounce your Canadian citizenship, you file CIC Form CIT 0302 — Application to Renounce Canadian Citizenship (and supplemental forms) and the C$100 filing fee along with the supporting documentation. You will then be sent a Certificate of Renunciation by the federal government. If you automatically became a citizen at the passing of the new amendment to the Citizenship Act that came into effect on April 17, 2009, but want to renounce your Canadian citizenship, there is a streamlined process you can take. You need to fill out Form CIT 0496 — Application to Renounce Canadian Citizenship (R7.1) (along with supplemental forms) and submit it to CIC. There is no application fee.

3. NATURALIZATION

The primary method used to obtain Canadian citizenship by American citizens is naturalization. You are eligible to apply for Canadian citizenship after becoming a permanent resident and residing in Canada for at least 1,095 days (three years) in the past four years. The process to obtain citizenship is the same whether you became a permanent resident under an economic or a family category.

You may be able to include some of the time you spent in Canada before becoming a permanent resident, and you can use the citizenship calculator on CIC's website to assist you in determining if you qualify. Applying for citizenship is a relatively easy process that requires you to file CIC Form CIT 0002 — Application for Canadian Citizenship — Adults (for minor children, use CIC Form CIT 0003) along with the C$100 filing fee, two color photographs, and the supplemental supporting documentation. This form is onerous because you have to provide the details of every trip you have taken out of Canada in the past four years, so start tracking them now! Be aware that, if you have a criminal record or are being investigated for a crime, you are not eligible to apply without clearing it up first. You will also have to get clearance from the FBI and your local state police before your application will be approved, and there is a form in the application packet to do so.

Once CIC receives your application, you will be fingerprinted for the purpose of conducting a nation-wide police check through the Royal Canadian Mounted Police (RCMP) system, and you may be requested to attend a personal interview with a CIC officer. He or she will ensure you can both speak and write English or French and have a general understanding of the rights and responsibilities of being a Canadian citizen as well as Canadian history, politics, and geography. Only persons aged 18 to 54 are required to take the citizenship test. Everyone else is exempt. The test is generally written to assess your linguistic abilities and your knowledge of Canada. In some cases, it can be given orally by a judge. To prepare for the test, check the Canadian government website, where you'll find a free booklet entitled *Discover Canada*, which contains the information you'll need for the test. If you pass the test, 1 of 27 citizenship judges stationed across the country (your application will be routed to the closest judge) will review your application to ensure you meet all of the requirements for Canadian citizenship; if you do, you'll be invited to a citizenship ceremony where you'll take the oath of citizenship and receive your certificate of Canadian citizenship. In the unlikely event you do not pass the written test, you'll receive a notice asking you to appear for a short interview with your citizenship judge, where the test questions will be administered orally so you can show you meet the language and knowledge requirements. If the Canadian citizenship ceremony is anything like the U.S. citizenship ceremony I experienced, it will be enjoyable. The most powerful part is generally when people share their testimonies of how they came to Canada and how thankful they are to be Canadian citizens.

PROS AND CONS OF CANADIAN CITIZENSHIP

Table 3.2 presents some of the pros and cons you should consider before becoming a Canadian citizen. As you can see, there is very little downside to taking out Canadian citizenship.

TABLE 3.2
PROS AND CONS OF CANADIAN CITIZENSHIP

Pros	Cons
• If you have both U.S. and Canadian citizenship, you can work and live anywhere in the United States or Canada without restriction. • Canadian citizens can be non-residents for tax purposes. When you leave, your tax filing obligation stops except for certain Canadian-source income.	• Citizenship may create diplomatic and consular difficulties between the two countries if legal or other difficulties arise when you are traveling outside Canada or the United States. • You are required to file Canadian tax returns and be subject to the departure tax if you ever leave Canada.

Pros	Cons
• You need not relinquish your American citizenship.	• As a U.S. citizen, you must continue filing U.S. taxes for the balance of your life no matter where you live in the world (including Canada).
• Citizens can't lose their citizenship for criminality, while permanent residents can.	• You may now be subject to certain Canadian legal proceedings.
• You are eligible to attend Canadian educational institutions and pay citizen tuition rates.	• You can be called for jury duty.
• You can vote in Canada and help to shape the political landscape there.	
• You can carry both a U.S. and a Canadian passport for traveling purposes.	
• You can sponsor parents and children for Canadian citizenship.	
• Your children are eligible for Canadian citizenship if they are born abroad.	
• You can run for prime minister as well as municipal and provincial government positions.	
• You can return to Canada and its universal health-care system anytime in the future.	
• You can have unrestricted ownership of certain Canadian corporate entities.	
• You can hold high-level security jobs.	
• You have someplace to go to escape the U.S. draft!	

Obviously, becoming a Canadian citizen is a very personal decision and needs to be considered seriously in light of the pros and cons above. Our firm has experience assisting people in making this decision.

DUAL CANADIAN-U.S. CITIZENSHIP

I am living proof, and so are most of our clients! We have even worked with people who have moved from the United Kingdom to the United States to Canada and obtained citizenship in all three countries. This is completely legal, and you do not necessarily give up citizenship in one country for that in another. Dual citizenship comes about because the citizenship applications for both countries are separate. You do not apply for dual citizenship. You are simply a U.S. citizen applying for Canadian citizenship.

For Americans, becoming a Canadian citizen used to mean they automatically lost their U.S. citizenship. Before 1986, the U.S. Department of State involuntarily revoked your U.S. citizenship if you performed an "expatriating act" such as becoming a citizen of another country or working for its government. Many U.S. citizens residing in Canada received a Certificate of Loss of Nationality from the Department of State in such circumstances. However, in most cases, your citizenship can be reinstated if you wish. Since 1986, the act of applying for Canadian citizenship does not automatically mean you intend to renounce your American citizenship. You are simply an American citizen who applies for, and is granted, Canadian citizenship. The result is dual Canadian-U.S. citizenship.

Since Trudeau declared his "once a Canadian, always a Canadian" policy in 1977 and the new amendment passed in 2009, Canadians cannot lose their Canadian citizenship even if they have citizenship in another country. This issue came up for debate in 2006 when tens of millions of dollars were spent to bring home from Lebanon non-resident Canadian citizens who were not necessarily paying Canadian taxes. Some people incorrectly believe that taking up U.S. citizenship requires that you renounce your Canadian citizenship because, in the citizenship oath ceremony, there is language to the effect of the individual "renouncing" all former citizenships or loyalties. However, the reality is that you can retain your citizenship with another country as long as that country recognizes you as a citizen, despite having taken up citizenship in another country. The U.S. government has neither the jurisdiction nor the power to dictate whom the Canadian government recognizes as its citizens (and vice versa). As a result, taking up Canadian citizenship will lead to dual citizenship, or even multiple citizenship, as long as each respective country continues to recognize it.

To me, dual citizenship is the ultimate in freedom since I can work and live anywhere in the two greatest nations in the world. In addition, what a heritage to pass on to your children! Canadian citizenship is not for everyone, though, so ensure you understand all that is involved before you make your decision.

AMERICAN DERIVATIVE CITIZENSHIP

Many people living in Canada, though they have never lived in the United States a day in their lives, may be U.S. citizens and not even know it! This is an important issue since, if you are a derivative citizen, you have tax filing requirements in the United States. On the other hand, you can be eligible for U.S. Medicare when you "snowbird" in the United States (see our companion book *The Canadian in America*). The derivative citizenship rules provide that you may be a U.S. citizen depending on where you are in your family tree. You may be able to claim U.S. citizenship if one or both of your parents were U.S. citizens and/or resided in the United States. Determining whether you are a derivative citizen is a bit complex because the rules have changed over the years. The following decision tree (Figure 3.2) should assist you in determining whether you are a derivative citizen of the United States, but you should consult with an experienced immigration attorney to confirm your derivative citizenship.

FIGURE 3.2

DERIVATIVE CITIZENSHIP DECISION TREE

In trying to establish derivative citizenship, it may be difficult to provide enough substantive evidence to the U.S. CIS that your parents were U.S. citizens and/or resided in the United States for the required time periods. Birth certificates and proof of a U.S. address are typically required but often difficult to come by, particularly in small towns or counties. The rules surrounding derivative citizenship are complex, and you'll likely require the services of a good immigration attorney to build your case before exercising your right to derivative citizenship. However, before doing so, you should recognize that you become liable to file U.S. tax returns, subject to U.S. estate and gift taxes, and so on, so ensure you fully understand all of the implications of exercising your right to derivative citizenship and what can be done beforehand to mitigate any negative consequences (see Chapter 5).

APPLYING FOR U.S. CITIZENSHIP

With the current backlog at the U.S. CIS, you can "short-circuit" the derivative citizenship process by applying for a passport at the U.S. Department of State. You fill out Form DS-11 — Application for a U.S. Passport and submit it along with U$165 and two recent photographs of yourself. You'll get an answer sooner this way and be able to determine your next course of action. Alternatively, you can file Form N-600 — Application for Certification of Citizenship with U.S. CIS along with the U$600 fee and two photographs to determine your U.S. citizenship.

RENOUNCING U.S. CITIZENSHIP

Formally renouncing your citizenship has now become a difficult, lengthy (and in some cases costly) process because Congress is trying to stem the flow of people renouncing their citizenship and in turn no longer filing U.S. tax returns (remember, the United States taxes individuals based on citizenship and domicile, not physical presence). For American citizens who have taken up citizenship in Canada and want to rid themselves of the nuisance of filing U.S. taxes, they may be in for a rude awakening. The rules state that, even if you have formally renounced your citizenship, you might still be required to file U.S. income tax returns and pay U.S. taxes for the next 10 years (see Chapter 5 for more details). There is a little known, little used provision in the Immigration Act that bars expatriates from entering the U.S. if they relinquish their citizenship, which could easily be enforced in the future with no additional laws needing to be passed. This is something else to factor into your decision-making. Under certain conditions, you may be able to renounce your citizenship if you are returning to your "home" country (e.g., Canada). Either way, renouncing your U.S. citizenship is a very personal decision and should be considered carefully.

SURRENDERING YOUR GREEN CARD

Since green card holders (permanent residents) are also required to file U.S. tax returns, voluntarily surrendering your green card may subject you to the same expatriation rules as U.S. citizens if you have held your green card for eight years or more. Furthermore, if you have lived in Canada for six months or more with a green card in your back pocket, you have technically relinquished it because a green card is a "use it or lose it" proposition. Since holding a green card is considered permanent lawful residence, you must demonstrate to the U.S. CIS that you are actively using the right granted to you, or the "intent to abandon" rules may apply. The two primary duties are residing in the United States and filing U.S. tax returns annually. If this describes your situation, don't lose hope, because possession is still 9/10ths of the law! Because you haven't formally handed your green card to a U.S. CIS agent, you may still be able to use it, but we recommend you seek competent immigration help. Obviously, surrendering your green card is a very personal decision and needs to be considered carefully. We have talked to many folks who have surrendered their green cards, only to regret it deeply afterward when they wanted to move back to the United States to escape the cold Canadian winters and live out the balance of their lives. In some recent cases with our clients, their green cards were taken away when they crossed the border into the United States.

BECOMING A CANADIAN RESIDENT

Once you have completed the transition to Canadian residency and officially given up American residency (but not citizenship), there is a whole new set of items to consider.

FILE TAX RETURNS

As American citizens (or green card holders), you are required to file U.S. tax returns even though you are tax residents of Canada. This requirement leads to untold complications and complexities because, as Canadian residents, you have to file Canadian returns as well, but it is the obligation you have as an American citizen living in Canada. With proper tax planning and preparation, you should be able to avoid most double taxation (see Chapter 5, "Double Taxes, Double Trouble").

STAY OUT OF THE U.S.

To demonstrate that you have established your ties with Canada, it is best if you postpone any lengthy stays in the United States for at least two years and preferably three. Don't return to the United States for extended periods of time (e.g., six months), and if you do go there be sure it is for short visits to family (it always helps to document your trips).

REVIEW YOUR ESTATE PLAN

As outlined in Chapter 7, "Till Death Do Us Part," now is the time to have your Canadian estate plan put in place by a qualified Canadian estate-planning attorney familiar with American citizenship issues. As an American citizen, not only are you subject to U.S. income taxes, but the estate and gift tax rules apply to you as well. You need to ensure that your children are cared for and that all your financial affairs are managed according to your wishes in the event you become incapacitated. In addition, you need to ensure that your children have guardians and that your estate can be settled quickly (in both the United States and Canada) when you pass away. These are serious issues that need to be addressed immediately.

REGISTER, APPLY FOR, SUBSCRIBE

As outlined in the next chapter, you should register your vehicle in the province in which you are residing (you typically have 90 days) and get a valid driver's license (you typically have 30 days). You should also get the appropriate Canadian homeowner, auto, and liability insurance policies. See Chapter 2 for further details in these areas. A credit card is a must in Canada, and you should apply for one upon your arrival. See Chapter 6 for the difficulties and solutions in building a credit rating in Canada.

CANCEL, CANCEL, CANCEL

This is the time to cancel your American medical insurance (after you receive your provincial health-care card), driver's license, vehicle registration, cell phones, Internet service, and credit cards to clearly establish your ties with Canada. It is usually best to mail them back to the issuing authority along with a letter stating that you are now a Canadian resident.

ESTABLISH A C$ INVESTMENT PORTFOLIO

Depending on your tenure in Canada, you should establish a Canadian-dollar-based investment portfolio at a discount brokerage firm. Provided that it is structured correctly, your portfolio can reduce your Canadian and U.S. tax bill while funding your future C$-based liabilities during retirement, Canadian expenditures, and so on. See Chapter 10 for more details in this area.

4 MOVING YOUR STUFF

Take your flocks and herds, as you
have said, and go.
— EXODUS 12:32

Despite the many tax, immigration, and estate planning issues you may encounter when making the transition to Canada, moving your physical assets there is what garners most people's attention. In light of 9/11, Canada and the United States signed the Smart Border Declaration on December 12, 2001. The intent of this declaration was to outline an action plan to collaborate in identifying and addressing security risks without hampering the transfer of legitimate travelers and goods. The countries agreed to share information and intelligence to strengthen the coordination between the enforcement agencies in addressing common threats. However, there can still be much frustration in this process because, in our experience, when you contact Canada Border Services Agency (CBSA), the answer to your question is typically different every time you call. To that end, we suggest you document the time and date of each call along with the name of the agent. Call three times for any question; then take the best answer and be prepared to defend it with the documentation you have. You may still endure some inconvenience at the border, but you should get some marks with the customs agent for your efforts. Here are a few other things to consider when moving your physical assets to Canada.

AUTOMOBILES

For some reason, most Americans insist on taking their automobiles to Canada when they move there. However, moving your automobile to Canada is a tricky proposition and should be avoided if possible, particularly for long-term or permanent moves. Because of the reasons listed below, you will typically get a higher price in the United States when you sell than you would in Canada, and trust us . . . it is a lot easier to move cash! To start with, you will need to determine if your vehicle is admissible into Canada by the Registrar of Imported Vehicles program by consulting Transport Canada's List of Vehicles Admissible from the United States (www.riv.ca). This comprehensive listing is available online but is generally restricted to most vehicles, motorcycles, off-road vehicles, and RVs less than 15 years old. You will have to pass the federal inspection by the Registrar of Imported Vehicles to be able to register your vehicle in Canada.

Before leaving the United States, you will also have to notify U.S. Customs 72 hours before crossing that you are exporting a vehicle, provide a copy of your vehicle's title, and be subjected to an inspection to ensure that vehicle ownership is properly documented.

There are several other issues in trying to take your automobile to Canada with you that you should consider.

MILES VERSUS KILOMETERS

The primary denominations of both your speedometer and your odometer are in miles, so to have them converted to kilometers when your transition to Canada is complete will cost you some money. To convert your automobile from miles to kilometers in Canada costs approximately C$1,000, provided the requisite parts for your make and model can be found. If you choose not to spend the money, your vehicle will be worth less when you try to sell it in Canada because of this issue. Furthermore, to import your U.S. vehicle into Canada, you will have to pay to have metric speedometer and odometer labels (provided by the inspection center) installed.

SAFETY STANDARDS

Vehicles manufactured to meet U.S. safety standards do not comply with Transport Canada standards. For example, the most common things required are daytime running lights, an infant restraint kit, a child tether anchorage point, eight-kilometer-per-hour bumpers, and a French label for supplementary restraint system airbags that require maintenance. As a result, vehicles that are less than 15 years old can generally be imported because they can usually be modified, at a reasonable cost, to meet Canadian standards. Note that, if you imported your vehicle from another country into the United States and now want to move it to Canada, in all likelihood it will be inadmissible.

EMISSIONS TEST

Your American vehicle has a high likelihood of passing emission standards in Canada because they tend to be lower than in the United States. This is particularly true if your vehicle originated in California, where emission standards are at their highest. While vehicle emission testing isn't standard across all provinces in Canada, British Columbia and Ontario have mandatory testing. As a point of interest, the American Lung Association cites the following 15 cities as having the highest levels of smog in the United States: (1) Los Angeles (plus five other cities in California), (7) Houston, (8) Dallas-Fort Worth, (9) Washington/Baltimore/Northern Virginia, (10) El Centro, CA, (11) San Diego/Carlsbad/San-Marcos, CA (plus two more cities in California, (14) Cincinnati, OH/Middletown, KY/Wilmington, IN, (15) Birmingham/Hoover/Cullman, AL. In Canada, the 15 highest smog levels are (1) Kitchener, ON, (2) Toronto, ON, (3) Windsor, ON, and three other cities in Ontario, (7) Montreal, QC, (8) St. Catharines, ON, (9) Kejimkujik, NS, (10) Oshawa, ON, (11) Halifax, NS, (12) Quebec, QC, (13) St. John, NB, (14) Vancouver, BC, (15) Calgary, AB.

DUTIES AND TAXES

At the border, you will be required to fill out CBSA Form 1 — Vehicle Import Form, which must be kept in the vehicle until it is successfully registered with the province in which you will be residing. There is a non-refundable filing fee of C$195 plus the Goods and Services Tax (GST) due at the border at that time. There will also be duties and taxes owing that you should get assessed beforehand by calling CBSA. How much you will pay depends on the year, make, and model of your automobile and its estimated value based on its condition. These duties and taxes are required at the time of your crossing, or your vehicle will be impounded until you pay them.

INVESTIGATION

Be prepared for a lengthy stay at the border crossing. Officials don't allow automobiles into Canada easily because the government is trying to stem the flow of stolen vehicles and parts from the United States being sold in Canada. You will also be subject to a secondary screening by the RCMP in your province of residence and won't be able to register your vehicle until you get a clearance certificate from them.

REGISTRATION

In most provinces, you must register your vehicle with your province of residence within 90 days of taking up residency since your state plates will be considered expired, and you could face fines for driving an unregistered automobile. However, one pleasant surprise is that the cost of registering your vehicle in Canada is generally far less than in the United States. For example, Alberta charges C$75 for one year of auto registration. In the United States, the state auto registration fees can be punishing (U$400 or more) if they are based on the value of your vehicle (as in Arizona).

DRIVER'S LICENSE

Most provinces require you to obtain a local driver's license within 90 days of taking up residency. You will need to prove you are legally permitted to reside in Canada. Some provinces require extensive measures, such as writing the driver's exam and taking an eye test, a reaction test, and a road test. Others simply issue you a driver's license when you present a valid state driver's license. The rules vary by province, so you should check with your local provincial authorities on what is required from you and the appropriate timelines before you move. In Alberta, for example, the annual fee for your driver's license is C$15.

We have received inquiries about getting an international driving permit for use in Canada. Although Canada recognizes it, a valid U.S. driver's license can get you a driver's license in your province of residence helping to establish your residency for health-care and tax purposes. International driving permits are issued only by the American Automobile Association and the American Automobile Touring Alliance's National Automobile Club, but getting a driver's license from the province will require just as much effort as getting an international driving permit. If you are not moving to Canada but going to reside there for no more than six months at a time, your state driver's license is accepted in your province of residence, and an international driving permit is not needed.

MISCELLANEOUS

Autos from the southern states are not viewed as favorably as local cars in Canada (unless they are antique or collector cars) because they lack the undercoating required to counter the effects of the salt and/or deicing chemicals used in Canada during the winter. After-market undercoating is not as effective and tends to cost about C$350. You will also have to install a block heater to get your vehicle started during the winter months, and be sure to use oil that is thinner to ease starting when it is bitterly cold. You may also need a new thermostat so your vehicle runs warmer in the winter and the heater is more effective in defrosting your windows. Be sure to buy a window scraper/snow sweeper and keep it in your vehicle. Finally, window tinting on the driver's and passenger's doors will be considered illegal in most provinces, so be prepared to pay to have it removed (C$200).

A REAL-LIFE EXAMPLE

Why sell your vehicle before moving to Canada? Maybe my personal experience will convince you to do so. My wife and I decided we would take her 1987 Toyota Tercel hatchback with us after we got married in Arizona and moved to Alberta in 1992. I watched as a customs agent checked every number inside and outside my car and compared it to the information contained in their database. After the inspection, the agent proudly announced that there would be duties and taxes of C$427 payable at that time or the vehicle would be impounded until the amount was paid. For a young couple starting out, it was a lot of money. We were then told we needed to get a clearance certificate from the RCMP before we would be permitted to register the vehicle. We booked an appointment with our local RCMP detachment. At the appointed time, we met the RCMP officer for the inspection. There were countless questions on when the car was purchased, where, for how much, and so on. We had to produce a host of documentation, including the bill of sale and title, to prove ownership. Once we got our clearance certificate, we registered our vehicle.

Since we arrived just before winter in November, we had a block heater installed and changed our thermostat so the car would run hotter. Regardless, all our little Tercel managed in the winter months were two small "peep holes" in our front window and one small "peep hole" on each side window. And our tires were generally flat on one side for most of the winter, making for a rough ride! We lived in Calgary and made frequent commutes up to Edmonton to visit family and friends. Between these two cities is the little city of Red Deer, renowned for its large RCMP training detachment. On one occasion, as we were driving through Red Deer, we were pulled over and given a C$25 citation for having tinting on our driver and passenger side windows. After investigating how much it would cost to remove the tinting and our future prospect of returning to the United States, we decided to leave the tinting on. A few months later the RCMP cited us again in Red Deer. After that, we decided to roll down our front windows, both summer and winter, as we drove through Red Deer, and we were never cited again!

HOUSEHOLD GOODS

This section deals with some of the things to consider in moving your personal goods to Canada. One obvious thing you can do is sell or give away a lot of your personal items so you have less to pack and less to transport. Whatever isn't sold at a garage sale, or given to family or friends, consider giving it to charity in the United States because you will be able to get a receipt and deduct it from your U.S. tax return (no such deduction for donated goods in Canada). Before heading to the border, one thing you can do to speed up the process is prepare two typewritten copies of all the items you plan on taking with you to Canada as part of the "settling of your personal effects." This list should be broken down by items that will accompany you and those to follow later. The list should include a description of the item, approximate value, make, model, and serial number where available. At the border, a CBSA agent will fill out Form B4 — Personal Effects Accounting Document on your behalf based on the list of goods you provide. Alternatively, you can download and fill in the form prior to your arrival to help speed up the process.

DUTIES AND TAXES

Items accompanying you and those to follow are considered part of the settling of your personal effects, and you won't be assessed any duties or taxes on them. There are three criteria to meet to avoid paying duties: ownership, possession, and use. You must own the items, have them in your possession, and actively use them. If you own them and don't use them, then you'll owe duties. There are a few exceptions, though. For example, if you sell or give away any of your settled effects within one year of moving to Canada, or begin using them in a commercial enterprise, duties are owed immediately. Furthermore, if you are returning to Canada after an absence of more than one year, any single item you bring across the border worth more than C$10,000 is subject to duty on the overage. If you have been out of the country for less than five years, all of the items you bring back must have been purchased at least six months before your reentry. That is why it is important to bring receipts and documentation to provide the authorities with the means to accurately assess things. Residents out of the country for more than five years are exempt from the six-month ownership rule. Exactly how the government polices all of this we aren't sure, but you should at least be aware of it before you make the transition. No doubt the burden of proof will be on you, or you could be at the mercy of the government authorities.

WEDDING GIFTS

If you get married in the United States and then make the transition to Canada, you are permitted to bring your wedding gifts with you duty free. The wedding must have taken place no more than three months prior to your entry or your gifts follow you up to three months after your wedding day in order to qualify as "duty free." You must have owned and possessed them prior to your arrival, but you are given an exemption on the "use" requirement if you import them within the required time periods. In my case, I was married in Tucson and went on a honeymoon to Aruba before making the transition to Calgary. A friend who had driven down for our wedding offered to take all of our wedding gifts back to Calgary for us, on the way to his final destination in Edmonton (thanks Barry K.!). Despite our calls beforehand and a letter explaining the situation, CBSA authorities refused entry of our wedding gifts without paying duty. We had violated the possession criterion. Our friend drove back to Great Falls, Montana, and dropped our wedding gifts off at my sister-in-law's house. Once we settled in Calgary, we made the trek down to Montana to pick them up and bring them to Calgary. Needless to say, we ate a lot of macaroni and cheese during that time period until we got all of our cooking utensils.

ALCOHOL AND TOBACCO

If you meet the age requirement of the province you are entering (generally 19 but in some cases 18, as in Alberta, Manitoba, and Quebec), you are permitted to bring in limited amounts of alcohol and tobacco. If you have a wine cellar or cigar collection you want to bring with you, you will pay dearly in duties and taxes since they are personal effects you cannot settle duty free. You can call the provincial authority ahead of time to assess and pay the duties in advance to speed up your entry. Canada is a big believer in the "sin taxes" on alcohol, tobacco, and gasoline and as a result protects this income stream vigorously. You are limited to bringing the following quantities into Canada with you duty free.

ALCOHOL
- 1.5 liters or 53 imperial ounces of wine
- 1.14 liters or 40 ounces of liquor
- a total of 1.14 liters or 40 ounces of both liquor and wine

- 24 x 355 milliliters (12 ounces) for a maximum of 8.5 liters of beer or ale

TOBACCO

- 200 cigarettes
- 50 cigars (including Cuban cigars!)
- 200 grams (7 ounces) of manufactured tobacco
- 200 tobacco sticks

FIREARMS

To keep its citizens safe, Canada has restrictions on bringing firearms into the country. "The right to bear arms" is part of the American Constitution but doesn't apply in Canada. If you plan on bringing firearms into Canada, you must be at least 18 years old and bring a non-restricted weapon with you. You will be required to obtain a Possession and Acquisition License (PAL) issued by the RCMP and to meet the safety-training requirements before your license is granted. To obtain your PAL, you will need to fill out Form RCMP 5592 — Application for Possession and Acquisition License under the Firearms Act and remit it with the C$60 fee. Your application will normally be processed within 45 days and is good for five years, when it has to be renewed. To import your firearms, you will need to fill out Form RCMP 5589 — Non-Resident Firearm Declaration and remit C$25; you then have up to 60 days to get your PAL.

To import ammunition, fireworks, or any type of explosives, you are required to have written authorization from the Explosives Regulatory Division of Natural Resources Canada. You can obtain more details at www.nrcan.gc.ca or call 1-613-948-5200.

I have a friend who imported both a pistol and a rifle into Canada in 1991 from the United States successfully. As long as you call beforehand, fill out the appropriate paperwork correctly, don't possess a restricted weapon, and don't have a criminal record, you should be able to import your firearms with relative ease. You can obtain more information at www.cfc-cafc.gc.ca or call the Canada Firearms Centre (part of the RCMP) at 1-800-731-4000.

PETS

The movement of domesticated pets (dogs, cats, and ferrets) originating in the U.S. up to Canada is relatively easy. All animals are subject to an import inspection but are exempt from the C$30 inspection fee if they originate in the U.S. For dogs, you must have a certificate from your pet's veterinarian that the dog had a rabies shot within the past three years prior to entering Canada.

If the pet is not accompanying you, there will be additional paperwork, permits, and clearances required. It stands to reason that any unusual or exotic pets, animals, or insects might be barred from entry into Canada. As a result, you should call CBSA in advance of your move to determine if there are any additional requirements.

MONETARY INSTRUMENTS

When moving to Canada, don't take any significant amount of cash (greater than C$10,000), traveler's checks, personal checks, money orders, stock or bond certificates, or other negotiable instruments with you when you cross the border. For amounts in excess of C$10,000, you must declare that amount at the American border when you leave, and it just stands to reason that you will be detained and asked to explain the source of it and why you are carrying it with you. If the amount is greater than U$10,000, you will need to fill out U.S. Department of Treasury Financial Crimes Enforcement Network (FinCEN) Form 105 — Report of International Transportation of Currency or Monetary Instruments and file it with U.S. Customs and Border Protection (note: don't file the predecessor form to this one — Customs Form 4790). In addition, you will need to fill out Form E677 — Cross-Border Currency or Monetary Instruments Report — Individual and file it with CBSA, which will forward it to the Financial Transactions and Reports Analysis Centre of Canada (FINTRAC) for assessment and analysis. This is just part of Canadian and American attempts to stop money laundering and control the flow of money to criminal and terrorist organizations.

To avoid these complications, you are well advised to transfer these items electronically through pre-established channels (wire from a bank) since they are traceable transactions and the financial institutions will fill out and file this myriad of paperwork for you. Note that the American financial institution automatically reports any cash transactions (deposits or transfers) in excess of U$10,000 on U.S. Department of Treasury Financial Crimes Enforcement Network Form 105 — Report of International Transportation of Currency or Monetary Instruments and files it with the Bureau of U.S. Customs and Border Protection. Transactions in excess of C$10,000 are automatically reported on Form E667 — Cross-Border Currency or Monetary Instruments Report — General and automatically sent to the FINTRAC. Remember to declare any amount above C$10,000 if it is coming by mail using Form E667, or by courier using Form E668 — Cross-Border Currency or Monetary Instruments Report made by Person in Charge of Conveyance and attach it to Form E667.

Now, we know what you are thinking . . . why not just move $9,900 in a series of transactions to avoid all this reporting? Because it is considered a crime called "structuring," which is arranging to give or receive amounts of less than $10,000 to avoid the reporting rules. You may recall Rush Limbaugh in the United States (a prominent Republican radio talk-show host), whose representative at U.S. Trust suggested he do that; U.S. Trust then paid a $10 million fine. See Chapter 10, "Money Doesn't Grow on Trees," for more details on how to legally move your cash and other financial instruments to Canada.

HIRING A MOVER

When planning to move your physical goods to Canada, it's best not to flip through the Yellow Pages, close your eyes, and let fate decide which mover you are going to hire based on where your finger lands. We recommend you look for a certified mover through an organization such as the American Moving and Storage Association (moving.org). Its website is full of good information and gives you an opportunity for recourse in the event a move goes awry, because companies approved to use the trademark agree to a code of conduct providing complete disclosure, written estimates, etc. We recommend EZ Canada Moving (ezcanadamoving.com) as they specialize in moves from the U.S. to Canada. For full disclosure purposes, we receive no compensation or referral fee of any kind from EZ Canada Moving for our recommendation. We also have working relationships with importers and moving consultants here in the U.S. so contact us if you need help. You can also contact the Better Business Bureau (BBB), but despite its great reputation our experiences have shown it is an unreliable source for finding trustworthy vendors. Our firm has been solicited by the BBB to join, but we have refused because it is willing to admit almost any financial planner who submits a form and a check without undertaking the due diligence required to determine if the planner is held to a suitability standard or a fiduciary standard (see Chapter 13, "Mayday! Mayday!").

Hiring a professional mover is the easiest and most expensive way to get your stuff to Canada. A family of four with 8,000 pounds of stuff moving 1,200 miles will cost approximately $3,000 during the summer months, but you can usually save about 10% by moving during the off season (October to May). Be sure to deal with a reputable firm, or accompany the driver to the weigh station when the truck's weight is recorded when empty, and again when full, to ensure you are getting an accurate weigh-in of your goods. If you want to save some money, consider packing and unpacking all of your goods yourself, and buy your own packing boxes and tape from a discount retailer rather than from the moving company, since it will tend to mark them up 10–20%. If you want to save even more money, rent a truck through U-Haul, Ryder, or some other company. We had the good fortune of getting a new truck that U-Haul wanted to move from Calgary to Phoenix so it could be tested in the hot weather. As a result, we got a greatly discounted rate, and we got to drive a brand-new truck. Many new companies are now offering to do the driving for you. They drop off a crate or trailer at your home that you pack. When you are finished, they come and pick it up and drop it off for you at the address you specify. If you do some comparison shopping, you can see they are slightly cheaper than U-Haul and far cheaper than a full-service mover. Remember to keep track of all your expenses, and keep your receipts because they may be deductible on both your Canadian and your U.S. tax returns in the year you move.

VISITING THE UNITED STATES

Once you have settled in Canada and begin making plans for your first trip back to "the homeland," consider the things listed below to make your trip easier.

PASSPORT

Be sure to take your American passport with you (if you have one) or your Canadian passport, because the Department of Homeland Security requires a valid passport for Americans, Canadians, and Mexicans entering the United States under the Western Hemisphere Travel Initiative. You also want to take your Canadian passport to ensure you have it on record when you left the country and when you returned. Some dual citizens believe it is better to show your American passport when you enter the United States and your Canadian passport when you enter Canada again because, as a citizen of those respective countries, entry is automatic. In some ways, it is really irrelevant because your Canadian passport clearly states your country of origin as America, so the border agents already know you are a dual Canadian-U.S. citizen.

GIFTS

You are permitted to take back to the United States personal use items or those intended as gifts of U$800 per recipient tax and duty free (your personal exemption), or if married you can file a joint application and claim U$1,600. You are limited to 200 cigarettes, 100 cigars (nothing from Cuba!), and one liter (33.8 ounces) of alcohol every 30 days. Note that these items are included in your personal exemption amount, so plan carefully. You will have to fill out U.S. Customs and Border Protection Declaration Form 6059B to declare all of the goods you are bringing into the U.S. This is the blue form we are all familiar with when traveling to the U.S. as it is usually handed out on the plane before landing.

LUGGAGE

Be aware that virtually all airlines now charge a fee of $25–$50 or more if any of your bags exceeds 50 pounds. This is particularly true if you are planning on bringing back a lot of stuff from the United States. To protect yourself from this charge, don't buy the big suitcases on wheels that have expansion panels in them. Keep to the medium-sized suitcases, and pack a collapsible duffel bag in case you are over or want to bring more goods back than expected. Also be aware that most airlines will allow you one carry-on (which fits under the seat or in the overhead bin), one purse or similar item, and two pieces of checked luggage per person. If you exceed these amounts, you will face additional charges as well.

FOOD

A common question our firm fields is "Are there any prohibitions on any foods taken to the United States?" It has been our experience that, as long as the food isn't grown in the United States, border agents will typically allow it in with little or no difficulty. We have successfully brought confectionary goods, pancake mix, sausage, homemade preserves, and various grocery items back with us to the United States. However, you can count on any piece of fresh fruit being confiscated (like our Granny Smith apple recently), so you should eat it before you check in.

BRINGING IT BACK

You are permitted to bring back to Canada C$200 per person duty free for absences of 24 hours or more (no alcohol or tobacco though) and C$800 for absences of 48 hours or more (as declared on CBSA Form E311 — Canada Border Services Agency Declaration Card, the tear-off tab form we are also all familiar with). These amounts apply to goods purchased or received as gifts and brought back with you when you travel. For absences of seven days or more (as declared on CBSA Form E24 — Personal Exemption CBSA Declaration), you must declare items that will follow your entry into Canada via courier, mail, etc. See above for the quantities of alcohol and tobacco you can bring into Canada with you duty free. All items must be for your own use and not for resale.

TRAVEL TO CUBA

It is common for Canadians to travel to Cuba for business and vacation purposes. In fact, there are vacation package deals advertised regularly in Canada for leisure trips to Cuba. As you may be aware, Americans are generally prohibited from traveling to Cuba or engaging in commerce with Cuba (buying Cuban cigars) because of the Cuban Missile Crisis in the 1960s. For personal travel, it is legal to travel to Cuba only on "People-to-People" licensed trips involving cultural or educational exchanges with Cubans. These licenses are granted by the U.S. Treasury Office of Foreign Assets Control, and very few tour operators have been granted a license. Your itinerary must be full of cultural activities that exclude going to the beach, fishing, or sightseeing. To engage in business, you must be appropriately licensed by the Department of Treasury or face civil penalties and criminal prosecution when re-entering the United States. Furthermore, the U.S. government has set up enforcement of these rules at U.S. airports and pre-clearance facilities in third-party countries. Unfortunately, these rules apply based on your citizenship, so, even if you are living in Canada, beware taking advantage of a good deal to Cuba to escape the Canadian winter. We suggest you visit Arizona, Florida, or California instead! It is uncertain whether these rules will change with Fidel Castro facing health problems and his powers passing to his brother, who appears to be more pro-American, so stay tuned.

DOUBLE TAXES, 5
DOUBLE TROUBLE

Is it right for us to pay taxes to Caesar or not?

— LUKE 20:22

Of all the areas to consider in your move, taxes are by far the most complex yet potentially beneficial area. This is particularly true if the planning is done before making the transition to Canada. Some folks make the generalization that you will always pay less tax in the United States than in Canada, and many people use that claim as their sole reason to avoid a move to Canada. In our experience, retired Canadians in the U.S. generally pay less income tax than in Canada. However, if you look at income taxes and payroll taxes combined (and health care), working Canadians may end up paying more income tax in the United States than they would in Canada (see the case studies in Appendices E and F). It depends a lot on your individual tax situation now, how it projects into the future, the province you are moving to, the makeup of your family, your sources and types of income, and what both governments end up doing with their respective tax systems in the years to come. Paying more income tax (along with the colder weather and suspect health care) deters many people when considering a move to Canada. Generally, the evidence is there to confirm that thinking, because in 2014 Tax Freedom Day fell on April 21st for Americans (according to the Tax Foundation) versus June 9th for Canadians (according to the Fraser Institute). It is interesting to note that for Albertans Tax Freedom Day is the earliest, on May 23rd, while Newfoundland is the latest, on June 22nd. In the U.S., Tax Freedom Day is March 30th in Louisiana and May 9th in Connecticut and New Jersey. Income taxes are a large part of most everyone's budget, but with proper tax planning and then competent tax preparation to implement the planning there are some tremendous opportunities to take advantage of before entering Canada. As you will see, U.S. citizens and green card holders have the thorny issue of filing in both countries. This chapter outlines some of the key things you need to know in the area of tax planning when making the transition from the United States to Canada or living in Canada as a U.S. citizen or green card holder.

It is important to note the difference between tax planning and tax preparation. Tax preparation is purely a historical event. You simply take the tax slips recording the transactions from last year, input them into the tax software, and hit the calculate button. Based on the luck of the draw, you either get a refund or have an amount due. Tax planning, on the other hand, takes actions in the current tax year to use legal tax avoidance techniques to reduce your tax bill in advance of your tax preparation. It is also important to differentiate between tax avoidance and tax evasion. Tax avoidance employs techniques permitted by law to reduce your tax bill and ensure you pay the appropriate amount throughout the year. Tax evasion is the intentional defrauding of the tax authorities and what is legally due to them.

Interestingly enough, our firm receives the bulk of its calls and our website gets the most traffic from February to April of each year because that is when newly minted Canadian residents realize they need to file a Canadian tax return for the first time. That also seems to be the time when people, who have moved to Canada, realize they should have done some pre-planning because they are confronted with the harsh realities of filing their tax returns in both countries. We get questions such as "Do I need to file in the United States? What income do I have to declare? On which return?" To answer these complex questions, people typically turn to their reliable American certified public accountant (CPA) or tax preparer to get their U.S. returns filed — if they determine they need to file at all. Then, for the sake of convenience, the chartered accountant (CA) — soon to be CPA as all the designations in Canada are merging — closest to them in their city prepares their Canadian returns. Everything is filed on time, and they take comfort in the fact that they have made it successfully through their first Canadian tax season. Unfortunately, it's a false sense of security because in our experience very few accountants know how to properly prepare these returns unless they are practicing regularly and consistently in this area. Furthermore, American citizens who earn U.S. wages and have U.S. withholding are not entitled to the "automatic" extension to June 15th. Many tax preparers don't know how to coordinate the preparation of the Canadian and U.S. returns, they don't know how to properly apply the Canada-U.S. Tax Treaty, and they can't ensure that all the necessary compliance issues related to foreign assets are fulfilled in both countries. Further, in our experience, if you have two different people preparing your Canadian and U.S. returns, the chance of your tax situation not being optimized, or your returns not being in compliance, goes up exponentially. It is only a matter of time before one of the taxing authorities catches a compliance issue and the "hate mail" starts to fill your mailbox or your tax bill is higher than it should be and no one is the wiser. We have seen situations in which the compliance issue is caught and the client goes back to the original accountant to draft a response to the tax authorities or to explain the penalties and interest. Suddenly, that accountant is no longer an expert in Canadian or U.S. tax, phone calls are no longer returned, but your check has been cashed. One more point before I tackle the complexities of Canada-U.S. taxes: if a lack of planning prior to your departure results in an unexpected large tax bill in Canada and/or the U.S., our firm will not condone or participate in any techniques we believe to violate current income tax laws to reduce your tax bill (yes, we have been asked).

TAX FILING REQUIREMENTS

UNITED STATES

U.S. Citizens and Green Card Holders
Many people move to Canada and just stop filing U.S. tax returns because they believe that, since they no longer live in the United States, they don't have to file tax returns there anymore. Unlike Canada, which generally imposes a tax filing requirement based on physical residency, under U.S. income tax rules American citizens and green card holders are

considered to be residents of the United States for income tax purposes. What many Americans in Canada, CAs, and CPAs don't realize is that U.S. citizens and green card holders are required to file U.S. income tax returns annually on their worldwide income, irrespective of where they live and where that income is earned. This means you have to file a U.S. 1040 tax return annually and declare your worldwide income, including any Canadian employment income, investment income, rental income, business income, capital gains, and so on — adjusted for U.S. dollars. You have to take the view that filing a tax return each year with the IRS is one of the privileges of being an American citizen or holding a green card. The United States is one of the few countries on the planet that imposes income tax based on citizenship or permanent residence, not residency. Other countries with similar rules are the Philippines, Eritrea, and Vietnam.

We also receive additional inquiries at the beginning of June from confused CAs, CPAs, and Americans in Canada about the automatic U.S. tax filing extension to June 15th. U.S. citizens and resident aliens living in Canada are entitled to an automatic tax filing extension until June 15th, but they must pay their taxes by the April 15th deadline. Further, U.S. citizens or resident aliens who earn U.S. wages and have U.S. withholding are not entitled to the "automatic" two-month extension and must file and pay any taxes owing by April 15th. You can request an additional extension to October 15th by filing Form 4868 — Application for Automatic Extension of Time to File U.S. Individual Income Tax Return before June 15th. However, any taxes owing must be paid on April 15th, or outstanding amounts will be subject to interest and penalties. Nonresident aliens living in Canada who earn U.S. wages and have U.S. withholding are not entitled to the "automatic" extension to June 15th and must file and pay their taxes by April 15th or risk penalties and interest. However, if non-resident aliens have no withholding on those wages, they are entitled to the automatic extension to June 15th to file their returns and pay their taxes.

One side note is that U.S. green card holders who return to Canada without obtaining a U.S. immigration reentry permit put their green cards at risk of forfeiture (see Chapter 3 for more details). We have seen pronouncements by some practitioners that, if you are in Canada with a green card and you didn't obtain a reentry permit, just continue filing U.S. tax returns to prove to U.S. immigration authorities — if you are ever asked — of your intention to return to the United States. Despite this tax filing position, being out of the United States longer than a year without a reentry permit brings the "intent to abandon" rules into play, and your green card is subject to forfeiture at the discretion of the border agent doing the screening. Your U.S. tax filing information is now available to the border agent on the screen, so your chances of losing your green card are almost assured if you have not been filing your returns and spending the majority of your time in Canada

Foreign Account Tax Compliance Act

There are hundreds of thousands of Americans in Canada (and millions abroad), many of whom don't file income tax returns with the IRS despite the clear rules requiring it. If you find yourself in this position, you aren't alone, but you can no longer ignore the problem. Commissioner Douglas Shulman was sworn in as the head of the IRS on March 24, 2008, after President George Bush appointed him and the U.S. Senate confirmed the appointment on March 14th. Commissioner Shulman's main focus after taking office was to develop strategies to increase international tax compliance as tax avoidance is estimated to cost the IRS an estimated $100 billion per year . . . and he succeeded. In March 2010, Congress passed sweeping laws known as the Foreign Account Tax Compliance Act (FATCA) specifically to target non-compliant U.S. taxpayers committing tax evasion with foreign accounts. The intent of these laws is to target wealthy U.S. taxpayers living in the U.S. and committing U.S. tax evasion with assets offshore in a tax haven. However, these laws cast a huge net on far more taxpayers than intended, and as a result many innocent U.S. taxpayers living in Canada are getting caught. This has created a lot of media attention that has created a public outcry around the world from U.S. citizens and resident aliens living abroad that are innocent but getting caught up in the large dragnet the IRS has created. Despite the outcry, there seems to be little sympathy from the IRS or concessions made on these ridiculously complex rules, and those who ignore FATCA will get into trouble . . . these laws have teeth!

In addition to the public outcry from individual U.S. taxpayers around the world, there was an international outcry from financial institutions. The reason is that, starting June 30, 2014 (delayed twice to give financial institutions time for implementation), FATCA requires foreign banks, investment firms, insurance companies, and other financial institutions to register with the IRS and, in doing so, agree to report to the IRS financial and account information for accounts with "substantial U.S. owners." Willing participants in the program may be required to withhold 30% on certain payments to their U.S. clients if those clients are not in compliance with FATCA, as outlined below. To encourage these financial institutions to "cooperate," firms choosing not to register will be subject to a 30% withholding tax on certain U.S. source payments made to them! The effects of these actions are far reaching.

For example, by disclosing this information to the IRS, financial institutions are likely in violation of local data protection, confidentiality, and bank secrecy laws in their home country. To get around this, the U.S. government entered bilateral agreements with over 100 foreign governments that allow the foreign financial institutions to report the details of U.S. account holders to their country's tax authority, which in turn will forward these details to the IRS. On February 5, 2014, Canada's Department of Finance announced it had signed an intergovernmental agreement with the U.S. under the existing Canada-U.S. Tax Treaty to share information on U.S. persons with accounts in Canada that total $50,000 or more effective July 1, 2014. (Happy Canada Day!) Incredibly, Canada negotiated with the U.S. that RRSPs, RRIFs, TFSAs, and RDSPs are exempt from reporting under FATCA and will not be disclosed. In addition, Credit Unions with less than $175M in deposits are exempt from reporting. However, U.S. tax filers still need to declare these accounts on their tax return as outlined later with the new foreign account disclosure forms the IRS has.

Under the intergovernmental agreement with Canada, any client with aggregated accounts in excess of $50,000 will have the following information provided to CRA (and subsequently to the IRS) by their financial institution:

1. "The name, address, and U.S. TIN [Tax Identification Number] of each Specified U.S. Person that is an Account Holder of such account;

2. the account number (or functional equivalent in the absence of an account number);

3. the name and identifying number of the Reporting Canadian Financial Institution;

4. the account balance or value (including, in the case of a Cash Value Insurance Contract or Annuity Contract, the Cash Value or surrender value) as of the end of the relevant calendar year or other appropriate reporting period or, if the account was closed during such year, immediately before closure;

5. in the case of any Custodial Account:
   (a) the total gross amount of interest, the total gross amount of dividends, and the total gross amount of other income generated with respect to the assets held in the account, in each case paid or credited to the account (or with respect to the account) during the calendar year or other appropriate reporting period; and
   (b) the total gross proceeds from the sale or redemption of property paid or credited to the account during the calendar year or other appropriate reporting period with respect to which the Reporting Canadian Financial Institution acted as a custodian, broker, nominee, or otherwise as an agent for the Account Holder;

6. in the case of any Depository Account, the total gross amount of interest paid or credited to the account during the calendar year or other appropriate reporting period; and

7. in the case of any account not described in subparagraph 2(a)(5) or 2(a)(6) of this Article, the total gross amount paid or credited to the Account Holder with respect to the account during the calendar year or other appropriate reporting period."

In addition, according to the "Annex I: due diligence obligations," your financial institution is required to look for U.S. "Indicia" by conducting electronic searches for:

1. "Identification of the Account Holders as U.S. citizens or residents

2. Unambiguous identification of a U.S. place of birth

3. Current U.S. mailing or residence address (including U.S. P.O. Box)

4. Current telephone number

5. Standing instructions to transfer funds to an account maintained in the U.S.

6. Currently effective power of attorney or signatory authority granted to a person with a U.S. address; or

7. An 'in-care-of' or 'hold mail' address that is the *sole* address the Reporting Canadian Financial Institution has on file for the Account Holder."

One last point is in addition to the above, any investment manager that has "actual knowledge" their client is a "specified U.S. person," they have an obligation to include that account information so it can be reported to CRA as well. As you can see, this IRS initiative is very pervasive but has proven to be effective. At the time of writing, a lawsuit was filed against the Canadian government by two American citizens living in Ontario to block their information from being passed to the IRS. Their attorney is arguing that any of their personal information given to the IRS violates their rights as Canadians under the Charter of Rights and Freedoms. This will have to be worked out in the courts, so stay tuned.

Likewise, the IRS is now exchanging the same information so that these foreign governments can root out their own tax evaders at the same time. Another imposition of these rules is that foreign financial institutions are now required to ask their existing and prospective clients if they have ties to the U.S. It is yet to be seen if the U.S. person does not disclose this information to the foreign financial institution, or lies, whether he/she may be caught by cross-referencing information from the IRS. Many financial institutions are simply refusing to do business with U.S. owners anymore and are involuntarily closing their accounts. Foreign hedge funds, mutual funds, and private equity funds are liquidating U.S.-based assets to avoid any issues with the IRS. The bottom line is that the U.S. is using its economic muscle to coerce cooperation from financial institutions around the world to successfully root out U.S. tax evaders. It started in Switzerland, with some of the toughest bank secrecy laws in the world, when UBS was permitted by the Swiss government to hand over thousands of names and account details of U.S. owners to the IRS.

From the 2011 tax year forward, FATCA requires virtually all U.S. tax filers to file Form 8938 — Statement of Specified Foreign Financial Assets with their tax returns if the total value of "specified foreign financial assets" is above U$50,000 at year end (U$100,000 for married couples) or exceeds U$75,000 at any time during the tax year (U$150,000 for married couples). If you are living abroad, the threshold for filing Form 8938 is U$200,000 at year end (U$400,000 for married couples) and U$300,000 during the tax year (U$600,000 for married couples). Specified foreign financial assets include foreign accounts at foreign financial institutions (but not the foreign branch of a U.S. institution), foreign partnership interests, foreign securities (mutual funds, stocks, bonds), foreign trusts in which you are the grantor, foreign-issued life insurance and annuities, foreign hedge funds, and private equity funds. However, these items are not included in the definition of specified foreign financial assets: foreign real estate held directly, foreign currency held directly, personal property held directly (art, antiques, precious metals, jewelry, cars, collectibles), or foreign pensions. Failure to report foreign financial assets on Form 8938 may result in an IRS penalty of U$10,000 (up to U$50,000 for continued failure after IRS notification). Are we having fun yet?

In addition to filing Form 8938, there is a host of other onerous tax filing requirements that you need to be aware of. First, you are required to file U.S. Department of Treasury Financial Crimes Enforcement

Network (FinCEN) Form 114 (formerly TD F 90-22.12 — Report of Foreign Bank and Financial Accounts) requiring you to disclose your interest in financial accounts outside the United States, including RRSPs, RRIFs, bank accounts, LIRAs, etc. in Canada. These must be electronically filed through FinCEN's website. "Non-willful" violations because of reasonable cause will not be penalized, but all others are subject to a U$10,000 penalty per violation. "Willfully" failing to file can lead to penalties as high as the greater of U$100,000 or 50% of the balance of the foreign account. Second, if you own Canadian mutual funds, income trusts, and registered plans, or own or have an interest in a foreign trust, you may be required to file Form 3520 — Annual Return to Report Transactions with Foreign Trusts and Receipt of Certain Foreign Gifts. In this case, the failure to file penalty is the greater of U$10,000 or 35% of any distributions from your Canadian investments, trusts, and registered plans! In addition, you may be required to file Form 3520A — Annual Information Return of Foreign Trust with a U.S. Owner. Failure to do so may subject you to penalties of the greater of U$10,000 or 5% of the gross value of the trust assets. If you have an RRSP/RRIF in Canada, you no longer need to file Form 8891 — U.S. Information Return for Beneficiaries of Certain Canadian Registered Retirement Savings Plans. On October 7, 2014, the IRS simplified the tax treatment of these plans by automatically recognizing the tax deferral per the Canada/U.S. Tax Treaty. Third, if you have an interest in a Canadian company, you need to file Form 5471 — Information Return of U.S. Persons with Respect to Foreign Corporations; or another myriad of IRS filing requirements and penalties can be imposed (see Chapter 11). In most cases, applying the for-eign-earned income exclusion and foreign tax credits should result in no additional tax, which begs the question why are U.S. taxpayers living in Canada subject to these ridiculous rules to begin with?

So what if you are one of the thousands of American citizens (including derivative citizens) or green card holders living in Canada but haven't filed U.S. tax returns? Or suspect that your returns have not been filed correctly? You have essentially five options, outlined in detail below.

1. Do Nothing
Many non-compliant taxpayers are taking a "wait and see" approach to what the IRS is going to do under the other programs listed below.

They are also watching the media for stories on others coming forth to see how the IRS treats them and so far that waiting has paid off. We do not recommend waiting anymore as recent changes to the Offshore Voluntary Disclosure Program outlined below simply don't warrant waiting anymore. Further, the IRS continues to put systems in place to catch non-filers, and, as Canadian financial institutions register with the IRS and report your account info, your days are numbered. Consider the following situations, which often lead to a notice from the IRS asking you to file a return:

- simply crossing the border into the United States;
- becoming a beneficiary of a U.S. estate or trust;
- receiving American-source investment income;
- selling U.S. real estate that you own;
- choosing to return temporarily to the United States as a snowbird, to retire there, or to care for an ailing family member there;
- receiving a U.S. employment opportunity requiring a move from Canada;
- becoming eligible for an American-source pension such as Social Security; or
- sponsoring a family member for a green card.

2. Offshore Voluntary Disclosure Program

When the IRS announced FATCA and was in the process of receiving thousands of names from the government of Switzerland, it announced the first Offshore Voluntary Disclosure Program (OVDP) in 2009. This program resulted in 15,000 disclosures and $3.4B in back taxes. With this success, the IRS launched another Offshore Voluntary Disclosure Initiative (OVDI) in 2011 which resulted in another 15,000 disclosures and $1.6B in back taxes. Starting in January 2012, the IRS began an open-ended Offshore Voluntary Disclosure Program (OVDP) that allowed folks with foreign accounts to come forward and disclose them, pay any taxes, interest and penalties owing, and get right with the world rather than risk detection by the IRS through FATCA, under which criminal prosecution is possible. Through OVDP, the IRS has reduced (but still substantive) standardized penalties that give non-compliant taxpayers the opportunity to calculate, with some certainty, the total cost of getting into compliance with the IRS. So far, 45,000 taxpayers have taken advantage of the program with $6.5B in taxes, penalties and interest collected. However, for those living in Canada, there has been much controversy surrounding voluntary disclosure because the intent is not to evade taxes as Canada is not considered a tax haven. Moreover, if taxes have been paid to Canada, there would be a foreign tax credit against most, or all, of any U.S. taxes owing, but this does not erase the hefty penalties owing through OVDP (as outlined previously).

On June 18, 2014, IRS Commissioner John Koskinen announced new "streamlined offshore procedures" for U.S. tax filers living both outside and inside the U.S. who have not been properly reporting their foreign accounts and the income from them. We believe these are very positive changes that will give many "U.S. persons" a better way to come into compliance because of the substantial reduction in penalties. This comes after many "U.S. persons" living in Canada have illustrated to the IRS that they weren't trying to evade taxes (especially in Canada) and they shouldn't be penalized so harshly for failing to simply report these accounts. Here is how to get into compliance with the IRS and begin sleeping at night.

Non-Filers Living Outside the U.S.
(*The American in Canada*)

For those living outside the U.S., if your non-filing was due to "non-willful conduct" and you meet the "non-residency" requirement, no "failure-to-file," "failure-to-pay," "accuracy-related," "information return" or "FBAR" penalties will apply. This is indeed good news, but it is important to define terms:

Non-Willful Conduct — "conduct that is due to negligence, inadvertence, or mistake or conduct that is the result of a good faith misunderstanding of the requirements of the law."

Non-Residency Requirement — "in any one or more of the most recent three years for which the U.S. tax return due date (or extension) has passed, the individual did not have a U.S.

abode AND the individual was physically outside the United States for at least 330 full days."

Abode — "The location of your abode often will depend on where you maintain your economic, family, and personal ties." See IRS Publication 54 for more details and examples.

If you meet the definitions above, you are eligible to file under the new streamlined OVDP procedures which require:

1. **File Returns/Amendments** — For each of the three most recent tax years that have passed (with extensions), file delinquent Form 1040 or amended Form 1040X tax returns along with all required disclosures (Forms 3520, 3520A, 5471, 8938). At the top of each return you file (paper filing only, no e-filing) write in red ink "Streamlined Foreign Offshore" to ensure they are processed through the new procedures. In addition, you must remit all taxes due and all applicable statutory interest for each return at the time you file your returns!

2. **File FBARs** — You will need to file the most recent six years delinquent FBARs (FinCEN Form 114 — previously Form TD F 90-22.1) electronically at FinCEN (www.fincen.gov/forms/bsa_forms/) and follow the instructions there. If you have trouble, you can call the FinCEN helpline at 1-703-905-3975.

3. **Certification** — Complete and sign "Certification by U.S. Person Residing Outside of the United States for Streamlined Foreign Offshore Procedures" which is a new form the IRS is providing in draft form at the time of this writing (see exhibit 5.1 below). This document is the taxpayer certifying they are: 1) eligible for the streamlined procedures; 2) all FBARs have been filed; 3) attesting to "non-willful" conduct.

4. **Failure to Make a Timely Treaty Election** — For example, if you have made a contribution to a Canadian charity and declared it on your U.S. return without taking a treaty election, you are required to submit: 1) a statement requesting an extension of time to make the election along with the applicable treaty provision; 2) sign a statement under penalties of perjury describing what led to the failure to make the election, how you discovered the failure and, if you relied on a professional advisor, the engagement with the advisor and his/her responsibilities; 3) a completed Form 8833 — Treaty-Based REturn Position Disclosure Under Section 6114 or 7701(b) for each return where applicable in the past three years.

If you don't have a Social Security Number or an Individual Taxpayer Identification Number, you can submit an application along with your tax returns to get one issued. Mail everything to:

Internal Revenue Service
3651 South I-H 35, Stop 6063 AUSC
Attn: Streamlined Foreign Offshore, Austin, TX 78741

Non-Filers Living Inside the U.S.

For those living inside the U.S., you have likely been filing U.S. returns but you are out of compliance because you have not filed any FBARs, Treaty elections or other disclosure forms as outlined above. Again, if your non-filing was due to "non-willful conduct" as described above, no "failure-to-file," "failure-to-pay," "accuracy-related," "information return" or "FBAR" penalties will apply! However," the Title 26 miscellaneous offshore penalty is applied in your situation and is equal to 5% of the highest aggregate balance/value of the taxpayer's foreign financial assets that are subject to the miscellaneous offshore penalty during the years in the covered tax return period and the covered FBAR period."

If you meet the definitions above, you are eligible to file under the new streamlined OVDP procedures which require:

1. **File Amended Returns** — For each of the three most recent tax years that have passed (with extensions), file amended Form 1040X tax returns along with all required disclosures (Forms 3520, 3520A, 5471, 8938). At the top of each return you file (paper filing only, no e-filing) write in red ink "Streamlined Foreign Offshore" to ensure they are processed through the new procedures. In addition, you must remit all taxes due, all applicable statutory interest and all Title 26 miscellaneous offshore penalty amounts for each return at the time you file your returns!

2. **File FBARs** — You will need to file the most recent six years delinquent FBARs (FinCEN Form 114 — previously Form TD F 90-22.1) electronically at FinCEN (www. fincen.gov/forms/bsa_forms/) and follow the instructions there. If you have trouble, you can call the FinCEN help-line at 1-703-905-3975.

3. **Certification** — Complete and sign "Certification by U.S. Person Residing Inside of the United States for Streamlined Foreign Offshore Procedures" which is a new form the IRS is providing in draft form at the time of this writing (see exhibit 5.1 below). This document is the taxpayer certifying they are: 1) eligible for the streamlined procedures; 2) all FBARs have been filed; 3) attesting to "non-willful" conduct.

4. **Failure to Make a Timely Treaty Election** — For example, if you have made a contribution to a Canadian charity and declared it on your U.S. return without taking a treaty election, you are required to submit: 1) a statement requesting an extension of time to make the election along with the applicable treaty provision; 2) sign a statement under

FIGURE 5.1

CERTIFICATION OF U.S. PERSON RESIDING IN THE U.S.

Certification by U.S. Person Residing in the United States
for Streamlined Domestic Offshore Procedures

Name(s) of taxpayer(s): _____

TIN(s) of taxpayer(s): _____

Note: Spouses should submit a joint certification if they are submitting joint income tax returns under the Streamlined Foreign Offshore Procedures. If this certification is a joint certification, the statements will be considered made on behalf of both spouses, even though the pronoun "I" is used. If spouses submitting a joint certification have different reasons for their failure to report all income, pay all tax, and submit all required information returns, including FBARs, they must state their individual reasons separately in the required statement of facts.

Certification:

I am providing amended income tax returns, including all required information returns, for each of the most recent 3 years for which the U.S. tax return due date (or properly applied for extended due date) has passed. I previously filed original tax returns for these years. The tax and interest I owe for each year are as follows:

Year List years in order	Amount of Tax I Owe (Form 1040X, line 19)	Interest	Total
Example			
2010			
2011			
2012			
Total			

I failed to report income from one or more foreign financial assets during the above period.

I meet all the eligibility requirements for the Streamlined Domestic Offshore procedures.

If I failed to timely file correct and complete FBARs for any of the last 6 years, I have now filed those FBARs.

During each year in either my 3-year covered tax return period or my 6-year covered FBAR period, my foreign financial assets subject to the 5% miscellaneous offshore penalty were as follows:

[List Year]

Name, City, and Country of Financial Institution/Description of Asset	Account Number	Year Account Was Opened or Asset Was Acquired	Year-End Balance/ Asset Value (state in U.S. Dollars)

CERTIFICATION OF U.S. PERSON RESIDING IN THE U.S.

Page 2

Total			

[If you held no assets subject to the 5% miscellaneous offshore penalty during this year enter "N/A" next to "Total" in the above table. Attach a continuation sheet if necessary. If you attach a continuation sheet, it must be signed with taxpayer name(s) and TIN(s) printed.]

[List Year]

Name, City, and Country of Financial Institution/Description of Asset	Account Number	Year Account Was Opened or Asset Was Acquired	Year-End Balance/ Asset Value (state in U.S. Dollars)
Total			

[If you held no assets subject to the 5% miscellaneous offshore penalty during this year, enter "N/A" next to "Total" in the above table. Attach a continuation sheet if necessary. If you attach a continuation sheet, it must be signed with taxpayer name(s) and TIN(s) printed.]

[List Year]

Name, City, and Country of Financial Institution/Description of Asset	Account Number	Year Account Was Opened or Asset Was Acquired	Year-End Balance/ Asset Value (state in U.S. Dollars)
Total			

[If you held no assets subject to the 5% miscellaneous offshore penalty during this year, enter "N/A" next to "Total" in the above table. Attach a continuation sheet if necessary. If you attach a continuation sheet, it must be signed with taxpayer name(s) and TIN(s) printed.]

[List Year]

Name, City, and Country of Financial Institution/Description of Asset	Account Number	Year Account Was Opened or Asset Was Acquired	Year-End Balance/ Asset Value (state in U.S. Dollars)

Total			

[If you held no assets subject to the 5% miscellaneous offshore penalty during this year, enter "N/A" next to "Total" in the above table. Attach a continuation sheet if necessary. If you attach a continuation sheet, it must be signed with taxpayer name(s) and TIN(s) printed.]

[List Year]

Name, City, and Country of Financial Institution/Description of Asset	Account Number	Year Account Was Opened or Asset Was Acquired	Year-End Balance/ Asset Value (state in U.S. Dollars)
Total			

[If you held no assets subject to the 5% miscellaneous offshore penalty during this year, enter "N/A" next to "Total" in the above table. Attach a continuation sheet if necessary. If you attach a continuation sheet, it must be signed with taxpayer name(s) and TIN(s) printed.]

[List Year]

Name, City, and Country of Financial Institution/Description of Asset	Account Number	Year Account Was Opened or Asset Was Acquired	Year-End Balance/ Asset Value (state in U.S. Dollars)
Total			

[If you held no assets subject to the 5% miscellaneous offshore penalty during this year, enter "N/A" next to "Total" in the above table. Attach a continuation sheet if necessary. If you attach a continuation sheet, it must be signed with taxpayer name(s) and TIN(s) printed.]

[List Year]   Note: Use this seventh year only if your 3-year covered tax return period does not completely overlap with your 6-year covered FBAR period (for example, if your 3-year covered tax return period is 2011 through 2013 because the due date for your 2013 tax return is passed, but your covered FBAR period is 2007 through 2012 because the due date for the 2013 FBAR has not passed).

Name, City, and Country of Financial Institution/Description of Asset	Account Number	Year Account Was Opened or Asset Was Acquired	Year-End Balance/ Asset Value (state in U.S. Dollars)

CERTIFICATION OF U.S. PERSON RESIDING IN THE U.S.

Total			

[If you held no assets subject to the 5% miscellaneous offshore penalty during this year, enter "N/A" next to "Total" in the above table. Attach a continuation sheet if necessary. If you attach a continuation sheet, it must be signed with taxpayer name(s) and TIN(s) printed.]

The assets listed in this certification are my only foreign financial assets subject to the 5% miscellaneous offshore penalty.

My penalty computation is as follows:

Highest Account Balance/Asset Value (enter the highest total balance/asset value among the years listed above)	$
Miscellaneous Offshore Penalty (Highest Account Balance/Asset Value from above multiplied by 5%)	$

My payment information is as follows:

Total Tax and Interest Due	$
Miscellaneous Offshore Penalty	$
Total Payment	$

Note: Your payment should equal the total tax and interest due for all three years, plus the miscellaneous offshore penalty. You may receive a balance due notice or a refund if the tax, interest, or penalty is not calculated correctly.

In consideration of the Internal Revenue Service's agreement not to assert other penalties with respect to my failure to report foreign financial assets as required on FBARs or Forms 8938 or my failure to report income from foreign financial assets, I consent to the immediate assessment and collection of a Title 26 miscellaneous offshore penalty for the most recent of the three tax years for which I am providing amended income tax returns. I waive all defenses against and restrictions on the assessment and collection of the miscellaneous offshore penalty, including any defense based on the expiration of the period of limitations on assessment or collection. I waive the right to seek a refund or abatement of the miscellaneous offshore penalty.

I agree to retain all records (including, but not limited to, account statements) related to my assets subject to the 5% miscellaneous offshore penalty until six years from the date of this certification. I also agree to retain all records related to my income and assets during the period covered by my amended income tax returns until three years from the date of this certification. Upon request, I agree to provide all such records to the Internal Revenue Service.

CERTIFICATION OF U.S. PERSON RESIDING IN THE U.S.

Page 5

My failure to report all income, pay all tax, and submit all required information returns, including FBARs, was due to non-willful conduct. I understand that non-willful conduct is conduct that is due to negligence, inadvertence, or mistake or conduct that is the result of a good faith misunderstanding of the requirements of the law.

I recognize that if the Internal Revenue Service receives or discovers evidence of willfulness, fraud, or criminal conduct, it may open an examination or investigation that could lead to civil fraud penalties, FBAR penalties, information return penalties, or even referral to Criminal Investigation.

In the space below (or on an attached page), provide specific reasons for your failure to report all income, pay all tax, and submit all required information returns, including FBARs. If you relied on a professional advisor, provide the name, address, and telephone number of the advisor and a summary of the advice. If married taxpayers submitting a joint certification have different reasons, provide the individual reasons for each spouse separately in the statement of facts.

CERTIFICATION OF U.S. PERSON RESIDING IN THE U.S.

Page 6

Under penalties of perjury, I declare that I have examined this certification and all accompanying schedules and statements, and to the best of my knowledge and belief, they are true, correct, and complete.

_____   _____
Signature of Taxpayer   Date

_____
Printed Name

_____   _____
Signature of Taxpayer [if joint certification]   Date

_____
Printed Name

FOR ESTATES ONLY:

_____   _____
Signature of Fiduciary   Date

_____
Title of Fiduciary (e.g., executor or administrator)

_____
Printed Name

penalties of perjury describing what led to the failure to make the election, how you discovered the failure, and if you relied on a professional advisor, the engagement with the advisor and his/her responsibilities; 3) a completed Form 8833 — Treaty-Based Return Position Disclosure Under Section 6114 or 7701(b) for each return where applicable in the past three years.

Mail everything to the same address provided earlier. As you can see, you don't escape all penalties like a non-resident, but they have been drastically reduced from the original OVDP.

3. "Quiet Disclosure"

Another alternative is called "quiet disclosure," which means you simply amend your previously filed U.S. tax returns and/or add the requisite disclosure forms for the previous six to eight years. Another approach some have used is filing late returns or simply ignoring past filing requirements and just filing tax returns along with the required disclosures in the current tax year to get into compliance prospectively. Quiet disclosure allows you to avoid the penalties if you did not underreport any income and there is no change to taxable income or tax liability in the prior years. However, most do not qualify for quiet disclosure because either they are non-filers or their taxable income changes (even though their tax liability doesn't change). A far better alternative is to enter the formal program as outlined above and pay the tax, interest, and penalties (for U.S. residents) to get into compliance. The problem with "quiet disclosure" is that you are now on the IRS radar screen, and the likelihood of an IRS examination has increased significantly. The U.S. Government Accountability Office (http://www.gao.gov/products/GAO-13-318) has encouraged the IRS, and it has agreed, to actively seek out those avoiding OVDP through quiet disclosure because it undermines the overall integrity of the OVDP, is not fair to those who have come forward through the correct channels, and provides incentives to other delinquent taxpayers to do the same. Further, quiet disclosure results in lost revenues for the U.S. Department of Treasury! The IRS has publicly stated it will keep an eye out for quiet disclosure returns and pursue those filers under the OVDP. If you already filed "quietly" and were caught and assessed penalties under the old OVDP, unfortunately, there is no relief and any assessed penalties still stand.

4. "Normal" Voluntary Disclosure

Besides OVDP and quiet disclosure, the regular voluntary disclosure practice of the IRS can be used. Set forth in IRS manual 9.5.11.9, Section 4.01 of the Criminal Tax Manual for the U.S. Department of Justice, procedures have been in place for a long time providing direction for any taxpayer who wants to get into compliance with the IRS. They don't have the "discounted" penalties and forgiveness like OVDP, but they may be worth investigating.

Now, we know what you are thinking: "Why don't I just renounce my U.S. citizenship and avoid all of this?"

5. Renounce Your U.S. Citizenship

When confronted with the administrative, financial, tax, and estate planning challenges of being a dual tax resident or dual citizen, many U.S. citizens and green card holders ask us for a way out. One answer we find many advisors and others quick to suggest is to simply renounce your U.S. citizenship or relinquish your green card — and the problem goes away. According to the list of ex-citizens published in the U.S. Federal Register, 1,958 people renounced their citizenship in the second quarter of 2013 alone, and the FBI reported that 4,650 people renounced their citizenship in 2012. As these numbers indicate, renouncing your citizenship can be done, but unfortunately it is not as easy now because of the U.S. Expatriation Tax. Congress got tired of American citizens building their net worth in the United States, renouncing their citizenship, and then retiring to a tax haven to live a tax-free lifestyle for the rest of their lives. In 1996, new laws were passed, amended again in June 2004, and again in June 2008, that impose serious consequences on American citizens who renounce their U.S. citizenship or green card holders who relinquish their permanent resident status. These rule changes conveniently came before the announcement of the first OVDI program in 2009. So before deciding to renounce your U.S. citizenship, or relinquish your green card, consider the consequences of the dreaded U.S. "alternative tax regime" affectionately known as the "expatriation tax."

In past years, if you performed an "expatriating act" (took up citizenship in another country, went to work for a foreign government, enrolled in a foreign military, etc.), you automatically lost your U.S. citizenship. Before 1986, the U.S. Department of State involuntarily renounced your citizenship and mailed you a Certificate of Loss of Nationality. Today that isn't the case, and you shouldn't assume that by becoming a Canadian citizen you have automatically lost your U.S. citizenship. Although there are various ways to renounce your U.S. citizenship, it is generally done by making a formal renunciation in person before a U.S. diplomatic or consular officer in a foreign country, filing the original statement with the embassy/consulate and a copy with the IRS. If you do not renounce correctly, the renunciation has no legal effect. In other words, you now need to make an effort to lose your U.S. citizenship. It's not as easy as it was in the old days!

Prior to the amendments of June 2004, the American government assumed that individuals renouncing their citizenship were doing so for tax-motivated reasons. In certain circumstances, individuals were given the opportunity to dispute this assumption by filing for a ruling by the IRS and not being subject to the rather onerous implications of the U.S. expatriation rules. However, with the amendments of June 2004, the tax-motivated assumption was replaced with the alternative tax regime that applies to a U.S. citizen or green card holder (a long-term resident who has held a green card for 8 of the past 15 years) who satisfies any one of three criteria:

1.   your net worth is U$2 million or more on the date of your expatriation;

2.   your average annual net income tax liability over the previous five years before expatriating was U$160,000 or more (after foreign tax credits) in 2015 (adjusted for inflation); or

3.   you fail to certify, under the penalty of perjury on Form 8854 — Initial and Annual Expatriation Information Statement, that you have complied with all U.S. tax filing obligations for each of the previous five years before expatriation.

If any of these rules apply, you are considered a "covered expatriate" because you are renouncing citizenship to avoid taxes and therefore fall under the alternative tax regime. As a result, you are required to file Form 8854 on an annual basis (U$10,000 penalty for failure to file) along with Form 1040NR — U.S. Nonresident Alien Income Tax Return for a period of 10 years after expatriation, no matter where you live in the world. Form 8854 requires the disclosure of the following information:

- your U.S. Individual Taxpayer Identification Number or Social Security Number;
- your country of residence and address after expatriating;
- your U.S. federal income tax liability for the five taxable years ending before the date of expatriation;
- your net worth on the date of expatriation;
- a statement under the penalty of perjury that all U.S. federal tax obligations have been complied with; and,
- if subject to the alternative tax regime based on net worth and income, the number of days present in the United States during the year of expatriation, a balance sheet of worldwide assets and liabilities, and a detailed statement of worldwide income.

(Even if you renounce citizenship or abandon your green card, it has no effect for tax purposes until Form 8854 is filed.)

Form 1040NR requires you to pay tax on a broader range of American-source income than normally required, including American-source interest, dividends, rent, and other "fixed or determinable annual or periodical gains, profits, and income." This is similar to the taxation of U.S. non-resident aliens except that any capital gains realized on the sale or exchange of property located in the United States and gains realized on the sale or exchange of the stock of a U.S. corporation are included for the expatriate. This means that, if you expatriated holding an investment account in Canada with a Canadian investment manager and realize gains on the sale of Microsoft or Disney stocks, for example, you need to declare those gains on Form 1040NR. (There are also some U.S. gift and estate tax issues to consider, and they are addressed in Chapter 7.)

As a reminder, if you expatriated between June 4, 2004, and June 15, 2008, you are not permitted to spend more than 30 days in the U.S. (60 days if working for an unrelated employer) for the 10 years following your expatriation . . . it is like you never left. This means if you want to attend a funeral, help an ailing friend, accompany your children or grandchildren to Disney World, or just stay in your second home in Florida and end up spending more than 30 days in the U.S. in any calendar year for the 10 years following your expatriation, you have to file 1040 tax returns here in the U.S. and declare your worldwide income. Congress sent a rather clear message that if you want to expatriate, don't come back! We are unsure if they will bring a similar provision back into the expatriation rules in the future but it is possible. Currently, there is a little known, little used provision in the Immigration Act that bars expatriates from entering the U.S. This could easily be enforced in the future with no additional laws needing to be passed, so it is something to factor into your decision-making. In addition, the U.S. government is producing a public list of names of everyone who renounces citizenship (a "shame" list) and once made, it is an irrevocable decision.

The expatriation tax (similar to the "departure tax" when leaving Canada; see our companion book *The Canadian in America*) is assessed in the year of expatriation. All unrealized gains in your assets exceeding U$680,000 (for 2014 and adjusted for inflation) are taxed as income, whether those gains are realized or not. All tax deferred accounts such as IRAs etc. are treated as if they were distributed the day before expatriation. Another "gotcha" is that you are required to irrevocably waive any rights to claim any withholding reduction under another country's income tax treaty with the U.S. related to eligible deferred compensation items that include 401(k), profit sharing plans, and phantom stock arrangements.

In our personal and professional experiences, once people understand the onerous administrative challenges of these laws coupled with the U.S. resident time restrictions, they realize they are trapped, and the decision to renounce their U.S. citizenship fades into the distance. If you decide you still want to proceed with renouncing your citizenship or relinquishing your green card, have your situation reviewed carefully beforehand by someone experienced in these matters; otherwise, the consequences can be drastic. You should note that the alternative tax regime doesn't apply to someone born in the United States to non-U.S.-citizen parents if that individual wasn't present in the United States for more than 30 days during any of the 10 calendar years prior to expatriation and expatriated before reaching 18½. Furthermore, the alternative tax regime doesn't apply to any individual who becomes a U.S. citizen and a citizen of another country at birth if that individual was never a resident of the United States for income tax purposes, never held a U.S. passport, and did not reside or was not physically present in the United States for more than 30 days during any of the 10 calendar years prior to expatriation. In this case, good luck! We have yet to meet anyone who has spent less than 30 days in the United States over the past 10 years!

Our advice is to seek the counsel of a good Canada-U.S. tax person to determine your options and best course of action. If your situation is "precarious," consider consulting with an experienced Canada-U.S. tax attorney (contact us for a referral) with whom you can discuss your tax situation openly and with whom attorney-client privilege applies and the government cannot obtain any information. Have the attorney run the numbers under the different scenarios, understand the risks, and help you make this very personal decision. We just encourage you to take some action as ignoring the problem is not an option anymore . . . you will be ousted somewhere along the way!

NON-U.S. CITIZENS AND NON-RESIDENT ALIENS

So what happens with the expatriation regime if you are returning to Canada after being on a temporary visa in the United States? Fortunately, a different set of rules applies. If you held a U.S. visa and didn't take steps to secure a green card or subsequently citizenship, you will generally be treated as a non-resident alien for U.S. income tax purposes when returning to Canada. You simply hand in your temporary visa to the U.S. authorities at the border, and your tax filing obligation generally ceases. This means you are taxed only on any American-source income, with some exceptions. Income derived from what is referred to as "effectively connected" sources, including income from a U.S. trade, rental property, or business, continues to be subject to U.S. tax even if you return to Canada. The other type of income that non-residents are subject to is referred to as "Fixed, Determinable, Annual, or Periodical (FDAP) income." This income includes American-source interest, dividends, pensions, annuity distributions, alimony, and personal employment consulting income (absent treaty protection). In most cases, any U.S. tax imposed on FDAP income is generally paid through withholding per the Canada-U.S. Tax Treaty (see below). If your U.S. immigration status has been severed and you have returned to Canada, you are required to file IRS Form 1040NR by June 15th of the year following your departure from the United States. On this return, you will report and pay tax on your American-source income (see our companion book *The Canadian in America* for more details).

To properly sever your U.S. tax ties, you are required to file a statement with your final U.S. tax return specifying the date you became a non-resident and that you have a closer connection to Canada. In addition, you are required to file IRS Form 1040C — U.S. Departing Alien Income Tax Return or Form 2063 — U.S. Departing Alien Income Tax Statement depending on your circumstances. These forms are often referred to as "sailing permits" and are supposed to be submitted 30 days prior to the date you depart from the United States. In fact, you are supposed to appear in person in front of the local IRS district director with a whole pile of personal, financial, and other documents to substantiate this departure. Despite these requirements, in our many years of practice and discussion with other U.S. tax practitioners, we have yet to see or hear of the IRS enforcing the filing of these forms or tax practitioners routinely filing them.

REAL-LIFE EXAMPLE

One example of why you want to tie up your loose ends before you leave occurred with a client who moved from the United States to Canada. After arriving in Canada, he just stopped filing returns with the IRS, figuring that since he didn't work or live there anymore his only tax obligation was on his income, which he was now earning in Canada even though he was still trading in a U.S. investment account (see Chapter 10 for more information on keeping accounts in the U.S.) His U.S. custodian kept sending him (with duplicate copies to the IRS) Form 1099 for interest, dividends, and the gross proceeds of his stock sales each year. Although he reported this income on his Canadian income tax return each year, he didn't file a U.S. return. Eventually, he closed his U.S. investment account and moved the remaining funds to Canada (he lost mightily in the tech bubble that popped in 2000). A couple of years later the IRS caught up with him, and he received a letter saying he owed over U$300,000 in taxes (excluding penalties and interest) for that tax year. Of course, we were his first phone call, and after we researched things we determined that the IRS effectively prepared a tax return for him based on the information it had. In particular, it included the gross proceeds from his trading activities, but since the IRS didn't have the adjusted cost basis it had no idea he had actually lost money on his account that year. We filed the required tax return to show the IRS his true net capital loss, and despite the significant amount of time required to gather all the supporting documents a nil return was filed to bring him back into compliance.

In the year of transition to Canada, there are different ways of filing your U.S. returns to minimize your tax liability, and depending on your individual situation several tax and compliance elections may need to be taken as well. These are complex tax returns to complete. Unfortunately, most U.S. CPAs have no idea how to handle Canadian issues on your U.S. return, and usually you end up being out of compliance with the IRS and your local state government from the first U.S. tax return you file after arriving in Canada. It is in your best interest to get the assistance of a professional who works regularly and consistently in the Canada-U.S. tax preparation arena to ensure that you remain in compliance with the IRS, file the necessary start-up return with CRA, and coordinate the preparation of both your U.S. and your Canadian returns to minimize your tax liability in both countries. There is a lot to be said for doing your initial filing correctly to have peace of mind and avoid having the IRS, your local state, or CRA turn on the "hate mail" machines because something hasn't been filed correctly. Your U.S. tax return (and applicable state return) are generally due by June 15th of the year after you take up tax residency in Canada because those filing from abroad are given an automatic two-month extension. However, if you had U.S. wages subject to withholding, your tax return and any taxes owing are due by April 15th. You'll also have to file a part-year and/or non-resident state tax return (and applicable county or city tax return) in the year you leave that state depending on whether that state has an income tax or not. There are nine states with no personal income tax.

- Alaska
- Florida
- Nevada
- New Hampshire (interest and dividends only)
- South Dakota
- Tennessee (interest and dividends only)
- Texas
- Washington
- Wyoming

In contrast, all 10 provinces and 3 territories in Canada have an income tax.

CEASING TAX RESIDENCY IN THE UNITED STATES

Nothing can be more confusing than knowing when you have left the United States as a tax resident and whether or not you need to keep filing U.S. tax returns. Knowing this requires a thorough understanding of the U.S. tax residency rules and how the Canada-U.S. Tax Treaty overrides them in certain circumstances. Again, properly planning your American exit date with your Canadian entry date can provide many benefits, save taxes, and greatly simplify your tax filing situation.

U.S. tax laws define U.S. tax filing requirements based on citizenship, whether you hold a green card, or whether you meet the "substantial presence test." As outlined earlier, U.S. citizens and green card holders are required to file U.S. tax returns . . . period. Under the substantial presence test, a formula is used to calculate the number of days you are in the United States over a three-year period (see our companion book *The Canadian in America* for more details). However, if you were in the United States working on an immigrant visa that expired or wasn't renewed (you left the country, right?), your U.S. tax residency considerations could be tricky in the year you left. If you cease being a U.S. resident during the year, you are considered to have a dual status tax year in the United States and generally file a "dual status" return: that is, a tax resident of the United States for that part of the year you lived there (Form 1040) and a non-resident from the point you departed (Form 1040NR). In this case, you are required to file your U.S. returns "married filing separately" versus "married filing jointly," as you most likely did when living in the United States. The tax rates under married filing separately are much higher than those of married filing jointly because you don't get as many deductions, and each spouse is forced to itemize individual deductions in the year of exit versus taking the standard deduction or combining itemized deductions on a joint return. This generally results in paying a higher level of U.S. tax when you return to Canada than you might have expected. Some good planning here can really bear fruit, so it's important to have someone competent review your U.S. tax filing options and run some numbers before you leave the country; otherwise, you might be in for an unexpected tax surprise! One good thing about leaving the United States is that, unlike in Canada, you aren't subject to a departure tax or exit tax on your assets unless you are subject to the U.S. expatriation tax, as outlined above.

CANADA

Canada bases its income tax system on residency in Canada, not citizenship. When you make the transition to Canada, you are generally taxable on your worldwide income as of the date you move there (take up tax residency). If you move to Canada in the middle of the year, your Canadian tax return, Form T-1 — General Income Tax and Benefit Return, includes your worldwide income (including any American-source income) from the time you establish residency in Canada. Also, any personal tax credits (similar to personal exemptions in the United States) are pro-rated based on the number of days you are in Canada. For most folks, their Canadian tax returns need to be filed by April 30th of the year after they moved to Canada. One thing to note: you can't get an "extension" to file your tax return in Canada, as you can in the United States.

Unlike in the U.S., couples in Canada file separate returns, with each spouse being taxable on their respective income or share of income based on ownership. For this reason, good pre-entry planning will show you how to hold, own, and title your assets to mitigate your tax liability before becoming resident in Canada. After filing your first tax return in Canada, you'll receive a Notice of Assessment from CRA. This notice is sent to all Canadian tax filers after their tax returns are processed and summarizes your income, taxes paid, and any refund or additional tax due. It also shows any corrections CRA made to your original return and may in fact be a reassessment of taxes or refunds owing. Additional information on the notice provides you with a summary of your "RRSP contribution room" (see Chapter 8 for more details) and your RRSP and capital loss carryover amounts (if any). As an American in Canada, it may be prudent to contribute to an RRSP as a means of reducing your Canadian income tax. However, such contributions won't reduce your U.S. tax and may in fact increase it if not handled properly, as outlined above.

We have often been asked for our opinion on which tax authority is worse, CRA or the IRS. In our professional opinion, CRA is far more efficient and tougher to deal with than the IRS. One reason is that CRA requires you to attach all supporting documentation to your return when filed, including tax slips, receipts, etc. For example, when taking foreign tax credits in Canada for U.S. taxes paid, you have to document the actual tax paid and include copies of your U.S. tax slips and the U.S. return itself. CRA has even asked us for copies of canceled checks from our clients to show that they actually paid the additional U.S. tax taken as a foreign tax credit on the Canadian return. Even with electronic filing becoming the norm, CRA often follows up with requests to fax in the supporting documentation.

In the U.S., however, you don't include any slips (except those that show withholding if you paper file), and with electronic filing it is rare that you include a copy of your Canadian return or anything else, for that matter to substantiate the foreign tax credits taken. In certain circumstances, when our clients' returns have been pulled for examination, the IRS will ask for documentation. In all our years of practice, we have never had the IRS ask for supporting documentation for Canadian foreign tax credits taken on a U.S. return! That being said, if you hire the right folks to plan and prepare your returns properly, your "arm's length" dealings with either tax authority should stay that way.

ESTABLISHING TAX RESIDENCY IN CANADA

It can be confusing knowing when you have established tax residency in Canada, and there are some important implications to doing so. CRA considers a number of factors when determining Canadian tax residency. Although Canadian tax law doesn't define the term "resident," the

Canadian tax courts have developed certain guidelines and criteria in determining "factual" tax residency, and the Income Tax Act has defined "deemed" tax residency. These factors include:

- the amount of time you spend in Canada;
- whether or not you maintain a home in Canada, particularly if you have family members living with you in Canada; and
- your "community of interest" in Canada, including holding a provincial driver's license, health-care coverage, bank and investment accounts, location of personal property, and primary place of employment.

CRA Form NR74 — Determination of Residency Status (Entering Canada) can help you to determine if CRA may consider you a resident for tax purposes. It will give you insights into the fact pattern CRA looks at in determining tax residency in Canada. It is important to understand that it isn't any one factor CRA looks at in determining residency (e.g., owning a home in Canada) but a pattern of facts painting a picture that your intention is to stay and live in Canada. The NR74 form is rather tricky and invasive, so we encourage you to avoid preparing or filing it because, legally, you aren't required to do so. It is important to note that CRA provides direction on your residency in Canada but does not specify when you become a resident. Here is where some good planning can bear much fruit!

U.S. citizens who enter Canada as new income-tax residents face potential obstacles and opportunities in connection with the assets they own on the day they establish Canadian tax residency. One huge planning opportunity you have is that, on the date you enter Canada, you are deemed to acquire all property you presently own (except Canadian real estate, certain Canadian private corporations, and pensions) at its fair market value on the date of entry. This is referred to as the "deemed acquisition date" or getting a "step-up" in cost basis. Canadian tax rules deem an individual who establishes Canadian residence to have disposed of and immediately reacquired each investment property owned at proceeds equal to its fair market value immediately before establishing Canadian residency. So, for Canadian tax purposes, any unrealized capital gains you might have in your investment portfolio or real estate in the United States prior to moving to Canada are "erased" for Canadian tax purposes. This is also true if you own property that is in a loss position prior to coming to Canada. Therefore, you should consider carefully what you do with such property before moving to Canada, because you get a "step-down" in cost basis as well. For this reason, we recommend you maintain financial statements for your investment portfolio the day you enter Canada and consider getting a formal appraisal done on your non-Canadian domiciled property(ies) to document the fair market values (adjusted for both U.S. and Canadian dollars) on the date you move to Canada, as they will provide solid documentation to CRA should it ask. This information will also prove extremely helpful for future tax planning and filing.

REAL-LIFE EXAMPLE

We worked with a tech executive originally from Canada who moved to the U.S. to work for a number of years before being asked to relocate back again. He initially entered the U.S. on a temporary visa to work and accumulated a significant net worth through an investment portfolio and highly appreciated company stock acquired while in the U.S. (and a non-resident of Canada). His U.S.-citizen spouse relocated with him, but he wanted flexibility in his plan in case he wanted to return to the U.S. We analyzed his situation and recommended he give up his temporary work visa in the U.S. to end his tax filing obligation with the U.S. Because he held the bulk of the wealth, his U.S.-born spouse would not have to declare any of his income on her continued U.S. tax filings. After taking up tax residency in Canada and ceasing U.S. tax residency in a coordinated fashion, he was able to wipe out hundreds of thousands of dollars of embedded gains in both his investment portfolio and his company shares and pay no tax in either country! He took the step-up in basis opportunity to liquidate the bulk of his company shares and shore up that wealth through a diversified portfolio. His U.S.-born spouse secured an easy immigration path back to the U.S. should he wish in the future because she can sponsor him for a green card.

THE IMMIGRATION TRUST

As a means of encouraging wealthy immigrants to move to Canada versus other countries, CRA permitted a "five-year tax holiday" for those who have never lived in Canada previously. The new immigrant simply put assets into an "immigration trust" before taking up tax residency in Canada and those assets were not taxed for five years. This was an effective strategy until Finance Minister Flaherty tabled his budget on February 11, 2014, and completely did away with this tax planning strategy. Those immigration trusts currently in place are "grandfathered" but no new trusts will get the same treatment.

THE CANADA-U.S. TAX TREATY

To resolve some of the complications that arise when moving between Canada and the U.S., the two countries have negotiated the Income Tax Convention between the United States of America and Canada. Put simply as the Canada-U.S. Tax Treaty (or the treaty), it was first negotiated and signed on September 26, 1980. Since then, the treaty has been revised only five times: June 14, 1983; March 28, 1984; March 17, 1995; July 29, 1997; and December 15, 2008 (known as the Fifth Protocol). Compared with the U.S. Internal Revenue Code or the Canadian Income Tax Act, it is evident that treaty changes occur very infrequently. The purpose of the treaty is to prevent the double taxation of Canadian and U.S. residents on the same income, to provide mutual assistance between the authorities in the collection of taxes, and to authorize the sharing of information to improve compliance.

The Canada-U.S. Tax Treaty "overrides" certain areas of the Canadian Income Tax Act and the U.S. Internal Revenue Code to afford protection from, among other things, double taxation in both countries. An example may help you understand this treaty. If you are a non-resident alien residing in Canada and you generate U$100 in dividends from a U.S. stock, the IRS retains the right to tax this income as American-source income. However, as a Canadian resident, you are required to declare your worldwide income on your Canadian tax return, including the U$100. Without the Canada-U.S. Tax Treaty, the IRS would take a 30% withholding tax on the dividends (U$30), while Canada taxes the dividend at your ordinary income tax rate (assume 19.29% or C$19.29). If there was no treaty or foreign tax credits, you'd pay U$30 plus C$19.29 for a total of approximately $49.29 (assuming exchange rate parity); almost half of your U$100 dividend would be gone (see the "Foreign Tax Credit Planning" section of this chapter). With the treaty, the IRS withholds the treaty rate of only 15%, and Canada permits a foreign tax credit of that amount against Canadian taxes. As a result, C$19.29 – U$15 = $4.29 has to come out of your pocket for a total tax of $19.29 on $100 of dividend. This is one of the issues that the Canada-U.S. Tax Treaty attempts to resolve. As you can see, tax preparation of this nature requires a thorough understanding of the treaty coupled with the knowledge of how to apply it optimally to your unique situation. The key provisions of the treaty are outlined below.

DETERMINING TAX RESIDENCY

If you and the government authorities determine that you meet each of their respective residency laws and are deemed a tax resident of both the United States and Canada, the treaty "tie-breaker" rules can be used to sort out which country has the privilege of taxing you. However, given that U.S. citizens and green card holders are always deemed to be U.S. tax filers for income, gift, and estate tax purposes, the tie-breaker rules are of no help. That being said, if you aren't a U.S. citizen or green card holder, the tie-breaker rules can be applied in the order they are listed in the treaty:

1. the location of your permanent home (principal residence);

2. your center of vital interests — where your personal and economic relations exist;

3. where you "habitually" reside;

4. where you are a citizen; and,

5. if none of the above can determine your residence, Canadian and U.S. tax authorities will agree between themselves who gets to tax you (competent authority).

SHARING INFORMATION

To catch those who might evade taxation on income from one country while residing in the other, both countries have agreed to share tax information on you. In fact, the treaty allows either tax authority to ask for your complete tax file (electronic, paper, or otherwise) from the other country's tax authority. This means that, if you have a U.S. source of income that is not taxed in the United States (e.g., Social Security) and you don't report it on your Canadian return, the chances of the tax authorities catching it have increased significantly. Based on our experience, it appears that real estate transactions, dividends, interest, the sale of securities, and in particular government pension payments are exchanged electronically on a regular basis. Furthermore, the two countries have agreed to collect each other's taxes in certain circumstances. This means that the IRS can use CRA's "long arm of the law" to collect American taxes from Americans in Canada, although we have yet to see this be done. This will become even more evident as the IRS implements FATCA and as Canadian financial institutions begin registering with the IRS and providing information on their U.S. owner accounts. Interestingly enough, CRA will not enforce IRS tax claims if you are a Canadian citizen and resident. However, don't ever plan on taking your grandkids to Disneyland or visiting that ailing relative in the U.S. As noted earlier, your chances of getting caught evading income tax or tripping up on a compliance issue are more pronounced than ever before. To stem the tax evasion occurring in foreign accounts, CRA has modified the T1 tax return to require disclosure of accounts outside Canada on Form T1135 — Foreign Income Verification Statement and is signing tax treaties with countries around the world to allow them to exchange tax information to ferret out those not declaring income.

EXEMPTING CERTAIN INCOME

The treaty sorts out what income is taxed in which country as well as exempts certain income altogether. For example, it provides direction on where capital gains are taxed and exempts up to $10,000 in employment income earned in one country from being taxed in both countries. It also contains specific provisions to eliminate double taxation between the two countries should it occur. Although capital gains on the sale of investments — excluding real estate and business interests, which are always taxable in the country where the real estate or business is located — are generally taxed in the country where the taxpayer is resident, U.S. citizens and green card holders in Canada are always required to report capital gains or losses from their investment accounts on their U.S. income tax returns. We are aware of one CA in Canada who reported capital gains and losses on a dual citizen couple's Canadian returns and did not report them on their U.S. returns. He was taking a treaty election, claiming that they were non-residents of the U.S. Again, the U.S. is unique from a tax filing position and in this case, the Treaty does exclude the gains from the U.S. return. Simply put, U.S. citizen/green card holder = U.S. tax filing requirement.

WITHHOLDING TAXES

For non-U.S. citizens, the treaty specifies the withholding rates for different types of income sourced out of the country. In the previous example, the withholding on dividend income is reduced to 15% rather than the default 30% rate for non-treaty countries as outlined in the Internal Revenue Code. For U.S. sources of income accruing to those in Canada, the current treaty withholding rates are as follows.

- arm's length or government interest — 0%
- dividends — 15%
- Social Security — 0%
- company pension — 15%
- qualified plan distributions (IRAs, 401(k), etc.) — 15% (with the filing of Form W-8BEN)
- rental income — 30% (absent filing a U.S. tax return)

Although treaty withholding tax rates are provided above, U.S. citizens in Canada shouldn't have withholding tax imposed on any American-source income because this income is fully taxable on a U.S. 1040 tax return. Still, we do find Americans in Canada with Canadian investment accounts where U.S. withholding is taken on American-source interest and dividends that the portfolio generates. If that is the case, then proper tax preparation will ensure you recover some, or all, of that tax. We've seen a few Canadian investment firms (TD Waterhouse, RBC) that create two sets of tax slips for Americans in Canada, one for Canadian tax filing purposes and the other for U.S. tax filing purposes. Although it can be a lot of extra paper, trust us, it sure helps on the Canada-U.S. tax preparation side of things! To ensure you get both statements issued and save yourself some tax prep fees, ensure your account is labeled as a "U.S. account," and your custodian will issue both a T5 Canadian slip and a 1099 U.S. slip in their respective currencies (as well as report the account to the IRS under FACTA).

TAXATION OF IRAS AND QUALIFIED PLANS

One of the most popular questions our firm fields from Americans in Canada, Canadian CAs, and financial planners is "How are IRAs, Roth IRAs, 401(k) plans, and the like taxed in Canada?" These complex plans are so misunderstood in Canada that a competent Canada-U.S. transition planner should be sought before doing anything with them. We often get a number of inquiries each month from Canadian financial planners and investment advisors who have stumbled across an American citizen or former U.S. resident who has assets in a U.S. retirement plan. Many of them want to move the money to Canada so they can manage it but are completely unaware of the adverse Canadian and U.S. income tax consequences of transferring these assets to Canada. For a review of the issues in moving these accounts to Canada, see Chapter 10.

Under the Canada-U.S. Tax Treaty, income that accrues within a traditional IRA, 401(k), or other U.S. qualified plan is not taxable in Canada. These plans maintain their tax-deferred status, and no tax or treaty election is required on the Canadian return (unlike RRSPs on the U.S. return). Furthermore, contributions to U.S. employer 401(k) plans are now deductible in Canada under the new Fifth Protocol of the treaty. Your 401(k) contribution is limited to your RRSP contribution room less any other deductions made to an RRSP. Likewise, contributions to an employer's group RRSP are deductible on your U.S. return. However, a deductible contribution to a private IRA is not deductible on your Canadian return, and a deductible contribution to a private RRSP is not deductible on your U.S. return.

REAL-LIFE EXAMPLE

We worked with an American citizen who lived in Canada with his Canadian-citizen spouse. By virtue of his U.S. citizenship and the fact that he lived in Canada for many years, he was required to file tax returns in both countries on his worldwide income. This gentleman made the daily commute from Canada to work in the U.S. before returning to Canada to his wife and family at the end of the day. He was paid by his U.S. employer and issued a W-2 slip annually. Like any good American planning for his future, he took the advice of his U.S. accountant, who told him that, because he wasn't covered by an employer's 401(k) plan, he should make deductible contributions to an IRA for both his wife and himself. He called his U.S. investment manager, who confirmed this good news and made deposits of U$6,000 respectively. His gross income (U$150,000) was reduced by the amount that he contributed to his IRA plans (U$12,000 for that tax year), reflected on his U.S. 1040 tax return (U$138,000 = $150,000 – $12,000). Because his U.S. tax return said his employment income was U$150,000 less the IRA deductions of U$12,000 on page 1, his Canadian CA reported just U$138,000, adjusted for Canadian dollars, on his Canadian tax return. Since this client was able to take a foreign tax credit for U.S. taxes paid on his Canadian return, CRA asked for a copy of his W-2 slip to support the foreign tax credits taken. It didn't take long for CRA to inform this poor soul that he had failed to report his gross income of U$150,000 on the return because CRA doesn't allow a deduction for contributions to individual U.S. qualified plans. This client ultimately received a letter from CRA requesting additional tax and interest on U$12,000 of employment income that should have been declared in the first place. So how much of the tax prep fee did his CA return for not preparing the returns correctly? Nada, and the client had to pay us to adjust the return. This is a great example of a lack of coordination between Canadian and U.S. tax preparers and investment managers.

TAXATION OF ROTH IRAS AND ROTH 401(K) PLANS

Thanks to the Fifth Protocol of the Canada-U.S. Tax Treaty and an ensuing Income Tax Technical News from CRA, the tax treatment of Roth IRAs and Roth 401(k) plans in Canada is finally clarified. Per the treaty, these plans maintain their tax-free status in Canada because they continue to be considered a "pension" for purposes of Article XVIII of the treaty. You need to file a one-time election with your first tax return to CRA to continue to defer the income accrued in the plan so far. However, if you make a "Canadian contribution" to your Roth IRA as a tax resident of Canada, the Roth is no longer considered a "pension" per the treaty, and some of the tax-free status of your Roth has been lost. If you make a Canadian contribution to a Roth IRA, all income (interest, dividends, etc.) accrued up to that contribution remains tax deferred. However, all income generated in your Roth IRA, after the Canadian contribution, must be declared on your Canadian tax return annually. The reason is that the Canadian contribution nullifies the treatment as a "pension" under the treaty, and all income in the Roth after that needs to be declared on your Canadian return. There is no prescribed form to make the CRA election to defer the income; you simply write a letter with the pertinent personal and Roth account information on it and mail it to the Competent Authority in Ottawa (not CRA!). Be sure to keep a copy for your files, and understand that you are not required to make another election for subsequent years.

TAXATION OF TAX-FREE SAVINGS ACCOUNTS

Similar to the Roth IRA in the U.S., TFSAs are the Canadian equivalent of a tax-free savings vehicle (see Chapter 8 for more details). These accounts allow annual contributions (C$5,500 in 2015) that are not deductible on either your Canadian or your U.S. tax return. The earnings grow tax-free from a Canadian perspective, but unfortunately there is no treaty protection like Roth IRAs in Canada. TFSAs were in the early stages of formulation by the Canadian government when the Fifth Protocol of the Canada-U.S. Tax Treaty was being negotiated and, as a result, did not make it into the treaty. Since Roth IRAs were well established in the U.S., the tax-free status of these accounts made it into the treaty. As a result, TFSAs are taxed like regular brokerage accounts on your U.S. return, so you may want to "run the numbers" before starting one.

MEDICARE SURTAX ON NET INVESTMENT INCOME

With the passing of Obamacare came additional taxes on high income earners to pay for it all. In addition to the 0.9% Medicare payroll tax on those exceeding the thresholds below (see payroll taxes later in this chapter), a 3.8% Net Investment Income Tax (NIIT) is added on top of the regular income tax of those in the following modified adjusted gross income thresholds.

TABLE 5.1

INDIVIDUALS SUBJECT TO NET INVESTMENT INCOME TAX

Filing Status	Threshold (U$)
Married, Filing Jointly	250,000
Married, Filing Separately	125,000
Single, Head of Household	200,000

The 3.8% surtax is due on the lesser of your net investment income for the year or the amount your modified adjusted gross income (MAGI) exceeds these income thresholds. As we begin the discussion on various types of investment income, you have to remember the 3.8% net investment income tax (NIIT) is added for higher-income U.S. tax filers. To further complicate things, the IRS has issued new regulations (Treas. Reg. § 1.1411-1(e)) stating that a foreign tax credit is *not* available against the NIIT. This means high-income taxpayers living in Canada will likely owe some tax to the IRS on top of what they owe to CRA. However, this additional tax should be used as a foreign tax credit on your Canadian

return. Throughout this chapter we have provided simplified examples of a taxpayer in Alberta (which has the lowest tax rates in Canada, but the top marginal rate is reached at approximately C$140,000 in taxable income) versus Texas (no state tax, but the top marginal rate is reached at U$465,000 in taxable income filing jointly and U$416,000 filing singly) for the highest income earners in each jurisdiction for comparison.

TAXATION OF INTEREST AND DIVIDENDS

INTEREST

Both Canada and the U.S. tax interest as ordinary income at your respective marginal tax rates, which is the most unfavorable way to be taxed. This makes interest income one of the worst forms of income to receive. However, in the U.S., interest income can be more favorable through the use of municipal bonds (munis) and federal bonds. Muni bonds (bonds issued by cities, counties, states, school districts, airports, etc. for public service projects) are exempt from federal and state taxation (if the taxpayer files tax returns in the same state that issues the muni bond). Federal bonds (Treasury bills, bonds, notes, TIPS) are issued by the federal government to finance federal projects and activities and are exempt from taxation in states with an income tax (see later). These opportunities to tax-optimize your interest income in Canada simply do not exist.

TABLE 5.2

TAXATION OF INTEREST EXAMPLE

Texas		Alberta	
Federal	39.6	Federal	29
State	0	Provincial	10
NIIT	3.8		
Total	43.4%	Total	39%

As this example shows, you can actually pay more on interest income in the U.S. than Canada, but this does not take into account the use of muni bonds or federal obligations that would be applicable here. Interest from American and/or Canadian sources is included on Schedule 4 of your Canadian T1 as well as Schedule B of your U.S. Form 1040. Interest paid from Canadian sources is generally reported on T-3 or T-5 slips versus a 1099-INT in the U.S., but many Canadian institutions are now issuing both statements for the same account to ease the tax preparation of U.S. tax filers. As discussed earlier, if you receive U.S.-source income as an American in Canada, ensure no U.S. withholding is taken when the interest is paid, and ensure you use the offsetting foreign tax credits available to you. One "gotcha" we often see is U.S. investment managers, with no understanding of Canada-U.S. taxes, using municipal bonds or federal debt obligations in the American in Canada's portfolio. What they don't realize is that muni bond and federal bond interest is still fully taxable in Canada. Since muni bonds and federal bonds generally have lower yields than taxable bonds in the U.S., you are giving up yield and not deriving any tax benefit at all! This is a perfect example of the bene-fits of coordinating all aspects of your financial situation under one roof with one advisor overseeing everything (investment management inte-grated with tax planning integrated with estate planning integrated with your retirement objectives). See Chapter 10 for more details on investing in Canada and the U.S.

DIVIDENDS

The taxation of dividends in both countries is a bit tricky because the income distributed by corporations has already been taxed at the cor-porate level. When the dividend ends up in your hands, it is taxed at the personal level, so the federal governments in both countries have put accommodations in place to alleviate the double taxation. In Canada, eligible dividends are grossed up by 138% (to reflect what the company earned pre-tax), and then your marginal tax rate is applied at 39% for an Alberta taxpayer. You then have to subtract the dividend tax credit of 19.29% in Alberta (but it varies by province) to reflect the tax the com-pany has already paid on that dividend.

In the U.S., qualified dividends are taxed differently than non-quali-fied dividends. Qualified dividends are dividends from U.S. corporations and corporations that reside in a country that has a treaty with the U.S. (like Canada). Non-qualified dividends include those from real estate investment trusts, commodity mutual funds, money market or bond funds, and corporations in countries where the U.S. does not have a tax treaty.

TABLE 5.3

DIVIDEND TAXATION IN THE U.S.

Marginal Tax Bracket (%)	Ordinary Dividend	Qualified Dividend
10	10	0
15	15	0
25	25	15
28	28	15
33	33	15
35	35	15
39.6	39.6	20

Dividends from American and/or Canadian sources are included on Schedule 4 of your T1 and on Schedule B of your Form 1040. Dividends paid from Canadian sources are generally reported on a T-3 or T-5 slip versus a 1099-DIV in the U.S. Again, no U.S. withholding tax should be taken if U.S. dividends are paid to you from American sources. Tax paid to CRA on your worldwide dividends is eligible as a foreign tax credit for U.S. tax purposes.

TABLE 5.4

TAXATION OF QUALIFIED AND ELIGIBLE DIVIDENDS EXAMPLE

Texas		Alberta	$100 Dividend
Federal	20	Gross Up	$138
State	0	Federal	29%
NIIT	3.8	Provincial	10%
Total	23.8%	Tax	$53.82
		Fed Div Tax Credit	-20.73
		AB Div Tax Credit	-13.80
		Total	19.29%

TAXATION OF CAPITAL GAINS AND LOSSES

In comparing the taxation of capital gains between Canada and the U.S., Canada includes 50% of the total gain in taxable income and then taxes it at progressive marginal rates. This means that, if your marginal rate is 39% in your province of residence (assume Alberta), your net capital gains rate is essentially 19.5%. The U.S. capital gains rate depends on how long you have held the investment and what marginal tax bracket you are in. For investments held one year or less, the capital gains are taxed as ordinary income, just like interest, at marginal rates. For investments held longer than one year, the following rates apply.

TABLE 5.5

CAPITAL GAINS TAXATION IN THE U.S.

Marginal Tax Bracket (%)	Short-Term Capital Gain	Long-Term Capital Gain
10	10	0
15	15	0
25	25	15
28	28	15
33	33	15
35	35	15
39.6	39.6	20

Realized capital gains are reported on Schedule 3 of your T1 and Schedule D of your Form 1040. In Canada, capital gains are reported on CRA Form T5008 while in the U.S., they are reported on Form 1099B — Proceeds From Broker and Barter Exchange Transactions. You should note that all financial institutions in the U.S. are required to track the cost basis on all taxable accounts and report all taxable transactions to the IRS annually. As a result, the capital gains and losses on your tax return must match the tax information the IRS has from the financial institution. If not, the financial institution's reporting overrides your return!

The treatment of capital losses is fairly different in Canada than in the United States. In Canada, capital losses can be applied against taxable capital gains in that year, with any excess losses carried back three years (through an adjusted return) or carried forward indefinitely. In the United States, capital losses can be applied against capital gains in the current year, plus an additional U$3,000 (U$1,500 if married filing separately) can be applied against other income. Any unused losses can be carried forward indefinitely and netted against future gains or deducted up to the U$3,000 annual limit on any other type of income until fully used up. Unlike in Canada, capital losses can't be carried back in the United States against gains in prior years.

TABLE 5.6

LONG-TERM CAPITAL GAINS TAXATION EXAMPLE

Texas		Alberta	
Federal	20	Federal	29
State	0	Provincial	10
NIIT	3.8	50% is taxable	-19.5
Total	23.8%	Total	19.5%

If you sell appreciated investments owned prior to coming to Canada, there will be different capital gains calculations for Canadian and U.S. tax purposes. As outlined above, you get a step-up or step-down in basis on property owned on the date you entered Canada. When you sell that property, the realized capital gain will be subject to Canadian tax, with a foreign tax credit allowed on your U.S. tax return (if required). However, the reported gain calculation on the Canadian tax return (Form T1) and the U.S. return (Form 1040) could be different. Any assets acquired after entering Canada, including the acquisition of additional U.S. investments, should have the same cost basis for both American and Canadian tax purposes, but the cost basis needs to be adjusted for foreign exchange purposes.

PASSIVE FOREIGN INCOME CORPORATIONS (PFIC)

As a U.S. Form 1040 tax filer living in Canada, you need to be aware of some ridiculously complex rules if the source of the interest, dividends, or capital gain distributions we just wrote about are coming from any Canadian investment vehicles as this may change the taxation of these income items significantly in the U.S. These regulations came about as part of the 1986 Tax Reform Act. The purpose of the regulations was to eliminate the beneficial tax treatment for certain foreign investments. Under prior law, U.S. taxpayers could accumulate tax-deferred income from foreign investments and then, upon sale of the investment, recognize the gain at the long-term capital gains tax rate. The prior law put U.S. mutual funds at a disadvantage as they are required to pass through all income to the shareholder in the year earned. The new PFIC regulations were designed to create a more level playing field for U.S. funds but add an incredible level of complexity to even the simplest of situations.

Then in 2010, after a policy review, the IRS determined that all foreign (non-U.S.) mutual funds and Exchange Traded Funds (ETFs) are to be classified as corporations (rather than trusts) for U.S. tax purposes, and they are now subject to the extremely complex and onerous tax consequences of the PFIC tax regime. Consequently, all U.S. citizens, green card holders, or others required to file a U.S. 1040 tax return (including those residing in Canada or anywhere else in the world) are subject to the ridiculously complex set of PFIC rules if they had more than U$25,000 filing singly (U$50,000 filing jointly and both spouses own the PFIC) invested in any Canadian mutual funds or ETFs.

WHAT IS A PFIC?

Before going any further, it may be helpful to understand the precise definition of a PFIC. A PFIC is essentially a non-U.S. corporation that generates most of its income from passive investment sources such as dividends, interest, rents, royalties, and capital gains. Specifically, if 75% or more of the foreign company's income is passive income, or 50% or more of the foreign company's holdings are held to generate passive income, the company is considered a PFIC. As a result of this definition, all Canadian (foreign) mutual funds, ETFs, labor-sponsored funds, money market funds, real estate funds, and pension funds fall squarely into this definition.

PFIC SHAREHOLDER FILING REQUIREMENTS

Beginning in 2011, the IRS required any U.S. citizens, green card holders, or U.S. 1040 tax filer who owns shares of PFICs above the limits to disclose certain information to the IRS on Form 8621 on an annual basis. In previous years, there was a reporting obligation with respect to PFICs only if there was a transaction related to that investment. Now reporting must be made even if there is no activity, but the IRS provided some relief by forgoing the requirement to file in 2011 and 2012 but making Form 8621 mandatory for tax years 2013 forward if above the limits of investment listed above. Disclosure of a PFIC is required in a "non-registered" account (regular taxable brokerage account); however, there was much debate about PFICs held in a "registered" account (e.g., RRSP, RRIF, or LIRA) until the IRS issued guidance saying PFICs inside these accounts do not have to be disclosed. Further, the Canada-U.S. Tax Treaty provides protection from the taxation of PFICs in a registered account. However, to further complicate things, the IRS revised Form 8621 in December 2012 and included a new Part I — Summary of Annual Information that may apply to all PFICs no matter where they are held; however, Part I is currently "reserved for future use" until the underlying regulations under Section 1298(f) are published, which are undetermined at this time.

In the meantime, if you are subject to the PFIC requirements, you must file IRS Form 8621 for *each* PFIC you own with your tax return, and you have the option of taking one of two tax treatment elections for each one. The first election is to treat the PFIC as a qualified electing fund (QEF), probably the most advantageous of the three methods. The second method is the mark-to-market method, which requires the shareholder to report the annual increase in market value of the PFIC as ordinary income. If neither of these options is selected, the "default" method is employed, and the investment is treated like a Section 1291 fund (excess distributions) which only has a $5,000 de minimis exemption.

TAX TREATMENT OF A PFIC

1. The QEF Election

If the QEF election is taken, a U.S. taxpayer's investment in a PFIC is generally subject to the same tax rules and rates as a domestic investment, except dividends are not considered qualified dividends and subject to ordinary income. The taxpayer includes a pro rata share of the PFIC's ordinary earnings and net capital gains on his or her U.S. tax return each year. Let's look at an example.

An investor owns five shares of ABC mutual fund, a Canadian mutual fund that qualifies as a PFIC. At the end of the year, the mutual fund as a whole earns $50,000 in investment income and $75,000 in capital appreciation. To figure out the tax due according to the QEF method, the investor needs to know her proportionate ownership of the mutual fund so she can calculate the income and gains attributed to her. If there are 500 shares outstanding, we can calculate that the investor holding five shares owns 1% of the fund. Therefore, she is taxed on $500 of investment income and $750 of capital gains on her U.S. return.

This method seems straightforward, but there is one huge obstacle. In order to take the QEF election, the mutual fund (PFIC) must comply with substantial IRS reporting requirements. The PFIC must provide an annual information statement to the shareholder that must include the shareholder's pro rata share of the PFIC's ordinary earnings and net capital gains for that tax year. Because most Canadian mutual fund managers are unaware of these requirements, or may not be willing to comply with them because of the costs involved (that is changing quickly as people pull their money from these mutual funds), the QEF election is not frequently available to U.S. 1040 tax filers invested in Canadian mutual funds.

2. The Mark-to-Market Election

The shareholder can elect to treat the PFIC using the mark-to-market method if the PFIC is considered a "marketable" stock or fund. To be considered marketable, the PFIC must be regularly traded on a national securities exchange registered with the SEC, the national market system established by the Securities Exchange Act of 1934, or a foreign exchange regulated by a governmental authority of the country in which the market is located (e.g., the Toronto Stock Exchange). If the mark-to-market election is taken, the PFIC holder recognizes the gain or loss on the shares of the fund as if he had sold all shares at fair market value at the end of the tax year. The gain or loss is treated as ordinary income on the U.S. return, an unfavorable tax treatment for most individuals. Unrealized losses are reportable only to the extent that they offset previously reported gains.

Upon sale of the PFIC shares, all gains are reported as ordinary income, whereas losses are reported as capital losses on Schedule D. Let's look at some examples to illustrate the potential adverse tax consequences of the mark-to-market method.

First, let's look at the issue of taxation on unrealized capital gains from mutual funds. Let's assume you purchase $50,000 of XYZ fund, a Canadian mutual fund that qualifies as a PFIC but does not provide the necessary information to select the QEF option. Therefore, you elect the mark-to-market tax treatment. At the end of the year, your position in the fund is worth $60,000, a 20% gain. Let's also assume that the fund is managed in a tax-efficient manner, so no capital gain distributions occurred during the year. On your Canadian tax return, no tax is due from this investment since no distributions were made from the fund. However, for U.S. tax purposes, you would be taxed on the $10,000 gain in value according to the mark-to-market tax method. Further, this gain would be characterized as ordinary income for U.S. tax purposes . . . an unfavorable tax outcome. The same tax disadvantages hold true for Canadian-listed Exchange Traded Funds and all other funds that qualify as PFICs.

Let's turn to an example involving the sale or disposition of an asset using the mark-to-market method. To start the illustration, let's assume you buy $50,000 of QRS fund that is *not* a PFIC. The investment does very well, and you sell it later the same year for $75,000. In Canada, half of the gain is taxable. Let's use the highest tax rate for this illustration. If the investor is a resident of Nova Scotia, the top tax rate is 50%. Therefore, the tax rate on the capital gain would be 25%. For U.S. purposes, the gain would be taxed at 20%, the top long-term capital gains tax rate (we assume the 3.8% NIIT does not apply). Since the Canadian tax exceeds the U.S. tax, no tax is due in the U.S. because of the foreign tax credits permitted by the Canada-U.S. Tax Treaty.

Let's look at the scenario again, but this time the investment qualifies as a PFIC. For U.S. tax purposes, you pay the top ordinary income tax rate on the gain, which is currently 39.6% (once again we assume the NIIT of 3.8% does not apply). The tax rate in Nova Scotia remains at 25%. Since the U.S. tax exceeds the Canadian tax, you could owe the IRS 14.6% of the $25,000 gain, an additional $3,650 in tax if no other foreign tax credits are available.

3. Excess Distributions (Section 1291)

If neither election is made, the PFIC will be considered a Section 1291, and the shareholder will be subject to even more complex and generally less favorable treatment. The general penalty for investing in a PFIC is that "excess distributions," including gains from the sale of the PFIC, are thrown back over the shareholder's holding period and subject to tax at the shareholder's highest ordinary income tax rate in each throwback year. The definition of an "excess distribution" is twofold:

1. The part of the distribution received from a Section 1291 fund in the current tax year that is greater than 125% of the average distributions received in respect to such stock by the shareholder during the three preceding tax years (or, if shorter, the portion of the shareholder's holding period before the current tax year).

2. Any capital gains that result from the sale of PFIC shares.

Let's look at an illustration of the "excess distribution" rules at work. A Canadian resident buys 100 shares of REM fund (a PFIC) on January 1, 2013, valued at $1,000 per share for a total investment of $100,000. The fund distributes $80 per share in dividends every year. On December 31, 2012, the shares were sold for $250,000. Since the dividends each year never exceeded the prior year's amount, there are no excess distributions relating to dividends. However, since the sale resulted in a capital gain of $150,000, the gain is an excess distribution and will be allocated over the life of the investment. In particular, the excess distribution would be allocated $50,000 for 2013, $50,000 for 2014, and $50,000 for 2015. The taxable amounts in 2013 and 2014 are taxed at the highest marginal tax rate for those tax years (35%). Further, the resulting additional tax for 2013 and 2014 draws an interest charge as if it were an underpayment of taxes for the year in question. Fortunately, amended returns don't need to be filed; the underpayment of taxes is simply included on line 16c of Form 8621. The allocation of the final $50,000 of gains is added to ordinary income on line 21 on the 2015 1040 and subject to the taxpayer's marginal tax bracket for that year.

Moreover, the taxable amounts allocated to the prior year PFIC period are not included in the investor's income. Rather, the tax and interest are added to the investor's tax liability without regard to other tax characteristics. This means that tax and interest are payable even if the investor otherwise had a current loss or net operating carryovers.

As you can see, the complexity and punitive nature of the PFIC rules render most individual U.S. 1040 tax filers incapable of filing their own returns without qualified, professional assistance. The American Institute of CPAs (AICPA) wrote a letter to the IRS in May 2013 asking the IRS to provide an exemption for certain shareholders in PFICs, including shareholders with ownership of less than 2% in a PFIC, shareholders who don't know they own a PFIC, or a PFIC that did not notify its shareholders of its status as a PFIC. This would eliminate many innocent taxpayers from having to comply with these complex, draconian tax rules. Congress is currently considering changes to the PFIC rules but we don't expect much to be done, given how polarized Congress is at the moment.

TAXATION OF PENSIONS

COMPANY PENSION PLANS

In Canada, your employer's pension is taxable as ordinary income but is offset with a C$2,000 non-refundable tax credit. Your U.S. pension is taxed as ordinary income as well. Any Canadian tax paid on your U.S. pension can be taken as a foreign tax credit on your U.S. return, if you are required to file one. If you are no longer a tax resident of the U.S. but have a company pension from the U.S., it will be subject to a 15% U.S. withholding by the IRS per the treaty. Any withholding by the IRS can be used as a foreign tax credit on your Canadian return.

U.S. SOCIAL SECURITY

The Canadian tax treatment of U.S. Social Security benefits paid to an American in Canada is not as favorable if you were a U.S. tax resident only. There, Social Security benefits are partially taxed on the U.S. return. The first 15% of your benefits are tax free no matter how much money you make. If your income is between U$32,000 and $44,000 (U$25,000 and $34,000 if filing singly), 50% of your benefit is taxable. Income in excess of U$44,000 ($34,000 if filing singly) means the maximum 85% of your benefit is taxable. In Canada, you get a 15% deduction from your Social Security benefits on your Canadian tax return to arrive at the net 85% taxable amount. However, even if your income is low enough to qualify for the 50% inclusion amount in the United States, CRA still taxes 85% of your benefit amount. Per the treaty, government pensions (Social Security, Canada Pension Plan, and Old Age Security) are taxed exclusively in the country where the taxpayer is physically resident. If you are an American in Canada, your U.S. Social Security benefits are taxed only in Canada. See Chapter 8 for more details on qualifying for U.S. Social Security benefits.

REAL-LIFE EXAMPLE

For lower-income retirees, the difference in taxation of Social Security benefits between Canada and the U.S. can have some far-reaching implications. An elderly couple visited us hoping we could save them some tax in Canada, given the Canada-U.S. issues they had. They were U.S. citizens who had recently moved to Canada to be closer to their children. The couple's only sources of income were U.S. Social Security and a small state-employee pension. In the U.S., their income was low enough to qualify for only 50% of their Social Security being taxable. After applying their personal exemptions, over age 65 exemptions, and the standard deduction, their net tax liability in the United States was minuscule to their gross income, leaving more income available to sustain them. As tax residents of Canada, 85% of their Social Security benefits were now taxable at the higher Canadian rates. Further, they had to file separate returns and had fewer deductions and credits to reduce their tax any further. To complicate things further, the U.S. dollar was $1.5484 against the Canadian dollar at that time, increasing the amount of C$ income taxable on their Canadian returns, pushing them further up the marginal tax bracket. Needless to say, they left our office in tears as the increased tax in Canada on their fixed income amounted to a significant cut in their standard of living. There was virtually nothing that could be done for this couple, and they were considering moving in with one of their children. This is a situation in which some good pre-planning and understanding your financial situation prior to a move to Canada are critical in any comprehensive transition plan.

OLD AGE SECURITY

Just like Social Security, Americans in Canada collecting OAS do not report this on their U.S. returns, per the treaty. OAS is taxable only in Canada and subject to ordinary income tax rates. One caution: you could lose all of your OAS benefits as they are subject to a "clawback" if your worldwide income is more than C$71,592 in 2015. If your income exceeds C$116,103 (adjusted quarterly), all of your OAS is clawed back, essentially resulting in a 100% tax on your OAS benefits. Conversely, if you become a non-resident of Canada living in the U.S., your OAS is not subject to the clawback at all and is taxed the same as Social Security, with at least 15% of your benefits tax-free, as outlined earlier. This is one major reason why our analyses have revealed that, in general, retirees are better off living in the U.S. for income tax purposes. Not only can you begin collecting up to an additional C$6,764.88 annually (adjusted quarterly for the CPI) per person in 2015 because the clawback no longer applies to you, but also there is no withholding by CRA. See Chapter 8 on how to qualify for OAS.

CANADA PENSION PLAN/QUEBEC PENSION PLAN

CPP/QPP is taxed as ordinary income in Canada subject to your marginal tax rates. Fortunately, there is no "clawback" for CPP or QPP because these are benefits earned during your working years (see Chapter 8 on how to qualify for CPP/QPP). Just like OAS, CPP and QPP are more favorably taxed in the U.S. because they are taxed just like Social Security. If you are entitled to receive CPP and U.S. Social Security as an American in Canada, be aware that your CPP can affect your Social Security benefits through the Windfall Elimination Provision (WEP), discussed further in Chapter 8.

TAXATION OF RENTAL PROPERTIES

U.S. TAX FILERS

Rental Income

For some valid reasons (e.g., a temporary relocation to Canada for employment), many Americans in Canada decide to keep their homes in the U.S. and rent them out or acquire a rental property in Canada for rental income purposes. As U.S. tax filers, they are required to include the income and expenses on Schedule E with their Form 1040 (no matter where the property is located). Schedule E is used to report your net income or loss on rental property to the IRS. You are required to report your gross rental income less any reasonable and ordinary expenses (insurance, property/rental taxes, mortgage interest, management fees, cleaning, utilities, repairs, etc.) on this form to arrive at a net rental income or loss (in the appropriate currency, of course). Interestingly enough, you must depreciate the rental property on your U.S. return, while "capital cost allowance" is optional on the Canadian return.

As a resident of Canada for tax purposes, you are also required to include the gross rental income and expenses on Form T776 of your T-1 tax return adjusted for Canadian dollars. However, unlike in the United States, you aren't required to take capital cost allowance on the property, though you may want to consider it to reduce the amount of rental income you have to declare. If the property generates a net profit after expenses, foreign tax credits from the U.S. 1040 return may be available to reduce some or even most of the double taxation.

Sale of Rental Property

If you own a rental property when you move to Canada, we recommend you get an appraisal of the U.S. property to establish the cost basis for both U.S. and Canadian tax purposes. The reason is that, when you sell a rental property after moving to Canada, you have to declare the gain on both your U.S. and Canadian returns in their respective currencies. Since you must depreciate the property on your U.S. return, you are subject to the nasty depreciation "recapture" when selling your second home. This means all of the depreciation you have taken on the property over the years is added back in the year of sale and subject to a 25% tax rate. This can lead to some unexpected tax consequences on the U.S. return, particularly when you did not take any capital cost allowance in Canada and factoring in any currency gains and losses. Foreign tax credits may not be enough to offset all of the U.S. tax liability in this situation. Realized capital gains are reported on Schedule 3 of your T1 and Schedule D of your Form 1040 (for details on how capital gains are taxed, see the previous section).

NON-U.S. RESIDENTS

Rental Income: Tax Filing Requirements
U.S.

With the devastated real estate market in the U.S. and a Canadian dollar at parity with the U.S. dollar, many Canadians (non-residents of the U.S.) have purchased a second home or condo in the United States (see our companion book *The Canadian in America* for a comprehensive review of this topic). In some cases, you may rent it out to friends, family members, or others, but you should be aware of both the U.S. and Canadian tax implications of renting out a U.S. property. Under U.S. tax rules, American-source rental income is taxed in one of two ways: (1) remit withholding tax on gross rents; (2) file a U.S. Form 1040NR income tax return.

Generally, if you apply a 30% withholding tax on any "gross" rents you receive, your tax obligation has been fulfilled with the IRS. Gross rents refer to all rents received without any deductions for ordinary and usual expenses against the property. However, rental properties have expenses to take against the rent, which means the 30% withholding on gross rents is an overpayment of your tax obligation. To remedy this overpayment, you need to file Form 1040NR, as outlined below.

The second way the IRS taxes rent is through the filing of a U.S. Form 1040NR income tax return on a "net" rental income basis. Net rental income is "gross" rents less any ordinary and usual expenses, such as property/rental taxes, mortgage interest, insurance, management fees, utilities, etc. It is also important to note that a deduction for depreciation — capital cost allowance for Canadian tax purposes — is mandatory for U.S. income tax filing purposes. Generally, the majority of Canadians who rent U.S. real estate are better off filing a U.S. tax return on a "net" basis. The net rental income amount is subject to the ordinary marginal tax rate but will likely be substantially lower than remitting the 30% withholding tax.

You must file your 1040NR tax return, along with Schedule E, by June 15th of the following year. If you do not meet this date, you can no longer take any deductions, and the 30% withholding tax on gross rental income applies, along with penalties and interest for that tax year. As you can see, it's important to address this issue correctly from the beginning, or you could end up overpaying your taxes.

In addition to the federal tax filing requirements outlined above, there may be state taxes owing depending on the state in which your property is located. Below are the tax forms required for the most common sunny states.

- **Florida** — no state income tax filing requirement
- **Texas** — no state income tax filing requirement
- **Arizona** — file Form 140NR
- **California** — file Form 540NR
- **Hawaii** — file Form N-15

If the property doesn't generate net rental income (gross income less expenses and mandatory depreciation), a state income tax return isn't required unless the property is sold.

CANADA

As a resident of Canada for tax purposes, you are required to include the gross rental income and expenses on Form T776 of your tax return adjusted for Canadian dollars. However, unlike in the United States, you aren't required to take capital cost allowance on the property. If the property generates a net profit after expenses, foreign tax credits from the U.S. 1040NR return may be available to reduce most double taxation.

Sale of U.S. Rental Property
We have had countless Canadians (who are not U.S. citizens or green card holders) contact us (often too late) about the tax implications of selling their U.S. rental properties. Many are confused about the U.S. tax withholding requirements and whether they have to file a tax return or

not. When you sell U.S. real estate, the IRS reserves the right to tax you on any gains. The profit is generally measured as the difference between the net proceeds from the sale (after commissions, closing costs, etc.) and your "adjusted cost basis" in U.S. dollars. Your adjusted cost basis is the purchase price of the property plus the cost of permanent improvements, less the depreciation taken.

For Canadian purposes, the sale of a U.S. rental property as a Canadian resident is a taxable event and needs to be declared on your Canadian tax return(s) and taxed as a capital gain. Since the sale is included on your U.S. return, it can lead to double taxation. This is where competent Canada-U.S. tax preparation will ensure that tax paid in the United States is taken as a foreign tax credit on your Canadian return to mitigate the double taxation. It's important to take into account currency gains and losses as well. As a result of currency fluctuations, the net gain or loss is generally different on the Canadian and American income tax returns. If you were a resident of Canada prior to September 27, 1980, you can take advantage of the Canada-U.S. treaty, so that only the gains accruing since January 1, 1985, will be taxed (see our companion book *The Canadian in America* for a comprehensive review of this topic).

TAXATION OF PRINCIPAL RESIDENCE

U.S.

If you move to Canada and retain your principal residence in the U.S. for personal use, it converts to a "second home," and added complications can result. Since both the Canadian and U.S. tax authorities recognize only one principal residence, your principal residence in the U.S. now becomes a vacation home, and your new home in Canada becomes your principal residence for U.S. purposes. Gains that accrued while you lived in the home are exempt from taxation up to U$500,000 per married couple, U$250,000 per single person. However, to claim this capital gains exemption when you sell, you must have lived in the home for two of the past five years. If you don't sell your U.S. home within five years of moving to Canada, all of the gains will be taxable on your U.S. return when you sell.

CANADA

In Canada, there is an unlimited capital gains exemption for your principal residence. Your U.S. property gets a step-up in basis when you take up tax residency in Canada, which means all embedded gains in your property are wiped out for Canadian purposes. Any gains accrued from the time you entered Canada to the time of sale have to be converted into Canadian dollars and put on your Canadian return. However, you have a principal residence for living purposes, but for tax purposes you can "designate" a principal residence to CRA using Form T2091 — Designation of a Property as a Principal Residence by an Individual even if you don't habitually live there (investment properties excluded). This opens up some planning opportunities to potentially select the home that has the highest embedded gains as your principal residence and pay no tax in Canada.

SOCIAL INSURANCE NUMBER

Similar to the Social Security Number (SSN) issued in the U.S., a Social Insurance Number is issued in Canada, but note that they are two completely different numbers for two different countries! Your SSN is of no use in Canada except to get a U.S. credit rating that may be of assistance in obtaining credit in Canada (see Chapter 6 for details). Don't attempt to give your SSN to a Canadian bank or use it on a Canadian tax return; you'll cause yourself no end of grief because CRA will not recognize your SSN and kick out your tax return. Besides, it can be considered fraud if you try to pass off your SSN as a SIN!

Once you have taken up residence in Canada and are permitted to work via a valid visa or permanent residence (see Chapter 3), you are required to apply for a Social Insurance Number using Form NAS-2120 — Social Insurance Number Application. Once you complete it, gather the supporting documentation, visit your local office, or mail all of this to Service Canada — Social Insurance Registration Office, not to CRA. In about three weeks, you'll receive your Social Insurance Card in the mail. You need a SIN because income paid to you from an employer, interest from a bank account, or dividends from a mutual fund at a brokerage firm need to be tracked to a SIN for income tax purposes. As a result, you won't be able to work, or open a bank or brokerage account, unless you provide your SIN. Likewise, any wages and payroll taxes need to be tracked to your SIN to ensure you establish the necessary coverage to qualify for Canada Pension Plan. Unlike the U.S., which issues an Individual Taxpayer Identification Number to non-working spouses or dependents for tax purposes, Canada issues everyone a Social Insurance Number. Remember to keep this number safe since identity theft is alive and well in both the U.S. and Canada.

FOREIGN TAX CREDIT PLANNING

By far the most complex, least understood, yet potentially beneficial area in your move is that of foreign tax credit planning. Foreign tax credits are a dollar-for-dollar credit allowed by CRA and/or the IRS and the treaty to eliminate the double taxation of the same income by both the United States and Canada. The aim is to alleviate the U.S. taxpayer of taxes owed in the United States when taxes are required on the same income in Canada (or any other country). Despite its good intentions, the IRS makes it difficult to completely avoid being double taxed on the same income, for the following reasons.

- The IRS limits the amount of foreign tax credits you can use in any one year by a ratio of your U.S. income to your total world income.
- Foreign tax credits are thrown into two different "buckets" depending on the type of income they are derived from: passive or general limitation.
- Foreign tax credits are given a "life" of the current year when generated, one year back, and 10 years to carry forward. If they aren't used up in the specified time frame, they expire.
- States with an income tax may not permit a foreign tax credit, which results in double taxation at the state level.

In addition, Canada makes it difficult to use foreign tax credits on your Canadian return because, as outlined earlier, it requires a thorough documentation of the foreign tax credits paid to the IRS. The key to good foreign tax credit planning is having a well-designed tax strategy for your assets in Canada and the U.S. Any income generated by your investment portfolio goes on your U.S. tax return, but the tax liability associated with that income is paid by the taxes paid in Canada (which is much better than having to pay them out of pocket). This is where an experienced Canada-U.S. investment manager should be brought onto your transition team. In either case, the key is not to let the "tax tail wag the investment dog."

A SIMPLIFIED EXAMPLE

Assumptions
- You have C$10,000 in a Canadian bank GIC.
- The Canadian GIC pays 4% interest annually (C$400).
- The prevailing Canada-U.S. exchange rate is C$1 = U90¢.
- You are a resident of Alberta and a U.S. citizen.

Canadian tax
- You are in the highest marginal rate for ordinary income, which is 39%.
- Therefore, C$400 x 0.39 = C$156, the amount of tax on your Canadian interest.

U.S. tax
- Declare C$400 x 90¢ = U$360 as ordinary interest income on your U.S. return.
- Take C$156 x 90¢ = U$140.40 in passive foreign tax credits on your U.S. tax return.
- Assuming you are in the U.S. 25% tax bracket, U$360 x 0.25 = U$90 tax liability.
- Use U$140.40 in foreign tax credits to offset U$90 in tax, giving you no additional U.S. tax due on the interest income.
- The excess foreign tax credit of U$50.40 (U$140.40 − U$90) can be carried back one year or forward for 10 years.
- If not for the foreign tax credits, you would pay 39% + 25% =

64% tax on your Canadian interest (C$256) versus 39% alone in Canada (C$156).

As you can see from this simple example, without proper understanding and accounting of the foreign tax credits, double taxation is inevitable. Many people have gone to their local CPA or CA (unfamiliar with foreign tax credits) and ended up paying far more taxes than they were legally obligated to pay.

KEY TAX DIFFERENCES

Following are some of the key differences in the tax systems between Canada and the United States.

- For married couples in the United States, you can choose married filing jointly or married filing separately when filing your tax return.
- In Canada, each person files his or her own tax return, while in the United States you have several filing statuses, including single, head of household, or qualifying widow.
- In Canada, common-law and same-sex marriages are accepted as a federal filing status, but for the U.S. federal return you must be legally married. Individuals living common-law can file jointly at the federal level and jointly in the states where common-law marriages are recognized, as listed below.
  - Alabama
  - Colorado
  - District of Columbia
  - Georgia (if created before January 1, 1997)
  - Idaho (if created before January 1, 1996)
  - Iowa
  - Kansas
  - Montana
  - New Hampshire (for inheritance purposes only)

- Ohio (if created before October 10, 1991)
- Oklahoma
- Pennsylvania
- Rhode Island
- South Carolina
- Texas (no state income tax)
- Utah
- In Canada, your deductions are calculated as a credit against your tax liability.
- In the United States, you deduct the higher of the basic standard deduction the government gives to you or your "itemized" deductions (add up your mortgage interest, state income or sales taxes, property taxes, auto registration, charitable giving, etc.) from your income before arriving at your taxable income.
- In the United States, separate tax returns are filed with the IRS and the applicable state, while in Canada you file these tax returns together and send them to the federal government (except in Quebec).
- Canada doesn't tax any gains on the sale of your principal residence. The United States provides only a U$250,000 ($500,000 for married couples) exemption, after you meet certain tests, on any gains attributed to the sale of your principal residence.

TABLE 5.7

2015 FEDERAL TAX BRACKETS

Canadian Taxable Income ($)	Per Return	U.S. Taxable Income ($)	Filing Single
0–44,701	15%	0–9,225	10%
44,702–89,401	22%	9,226–37,450	15%
89,402–138,586	26%	37,451–90,750	25%
138,587 +	29%	90,751–189,300	28%
		189,301–411,500	33%
		411,501–413,200	35%
		413,201+	39.6%

TABLE 5.8

2015 DEDUCTIONS

2015 Deductions	Canada ($)	U.S. ($)
Personal amount/spousal amount/ standard deduction/personal exemption	11,327/11,327	4,000/6,300
Mortgage interest	x	✓
Property taxes	x	✓
Auto registration	x	✓
Provincial/state or sales taxes	x	✓
Medical expenses	3% threshold	10% threshold
Charitable contributions	75% of income	50% of income
Contributions to political parties	✓	x
Safe deposit box	✓	✓
Tuition and education	✓	✓

TABLE 5.9

CREDITS

2014 Credits	Canada ($)	U.S. ($)
Child tax credit	x	1,000 per child
Foreign tax credit	✓	✓

U.S. PHASE-OUTS

With Congress finally settling on some new tax laws, it also brought back the phase-out of itemized deductions and personal exemptions for high-income taxpayers. For married couples with adjusted gross income (AGI) in excess of $309,900 ($258,250 for single), they will lose 2% of their personal exemption(s) for every $2,500 of AGI above the threshold. This means married couples will lose all of their personal exemptions when their income reaches $432,400.

Itemized deductions (mortgage interest, state taxes, property taxes, charitable contributions) are reduced by 3% of the amount exceeding the same thresholds. Thankfully, there is a limit on the phase-out, and you will still be able to deduct at least 20% of your itemized deductions. These policies are part of the mindset in Congress to have the wealthiest taxpayers pay more — I thought we already had a progressive tax system for that (higher tax brackets for higher incomes?).

Now let's compare one of the most expensive states in the union (California) with the cheapest province in Canada (Alberta), using the latest data available.

TABLE 5.10

2015 PROVINCE/STATE TAX INFORMATION

Alberta Taxable Income ($)	Per Return	California Taxable Income ($)	Filing Single
0 +	10%	0–7,749 (est.)	1%
		7,750–18,371	2%
		18,372–28,995	4%
		28,996–40,250	6%
		40,251–50,869	8%
		50,870–259,844	9.3%
		259,845–311,812	10.3%
		311,813–519,687	11.3%
		519,688+	12.3%

2015 Deductions	Alberta	California
Standard deduction/personal exemption	18,214	3,906/212
Mortgage interest	x	✓
Property taxes	x	✓
Auto registration	x	✓
Provincial/state taxes	x	✓
Medical expenses	3% threshold	10% threshold
Charitable contributions	75% of income	50% of income
Contributions to political parties	✓	x
Safe deposit box	✓	✓

When you move to Canada, you should familiarize yourself with the tax slips and forms in Table 5.11 so that you are better prepared when it comes time to file your first tax return.

TABLE 5.11
TAX SLIPS AND FORMS

Tax Slip	Canada	U.S.
Wages/bonuses/commissions	T-4	W-2
Self-employment	T4(A)	1099-MISC
Interest	T3, T5	1099-INT
Dividends	T3, T5	1099-DIV
U.S. Social Security	T4A(P)	SSA-1099
Canada Pension Plan	T4A(P)	NR4
Old Age Security	T4A(OAS)	NR4(OAS)
Company pension	T4A	1099-R
RRIF	T4RIF	NR4
RRSP	T4RSP	NR4

Tax Form	Canada	U.S.
Personal tax return	T-1	1040
Changed personal return	T1-ADJ	1040X
Capital gains/losses	Schedule 3	Schedule D
Dividends/interest	Schedule 4	Schedule B
Charitable donations	Schedule 9	Schedule A
Corporate tax return	T-2	1120
Partnership tax return	T5013	1065 or K-1
Trust tax return	T-3	1041

To see how these tax systems work compared with each other, see the comprehensive case studies in Appendices E and F of this book.

ALTERNATIVE MINIMUM TAX

Both the United States and Canada have an alternative minimum tax (AMT) system. AMT is a means of preventing high-income taxpayers, with lots of deductions, from paying no tax (hence the minimum tax). The tax policy behind the AMT is to force these people to pay some tax into the system, and the intention is similar in Canada. In Canada, your AMT calculation is done on CRA Form T691 — Alternative Minimum Tax. AMT occurs rarely in Canada because Parliament has kept the regular income tax rates and the AMT coordinated.

For higher-income taxpayers moving to Canada who have to keep filing U.S. returns, there is a looming tax nemesis to be aware of as tax planning brings your ordinary income down. In the United States, when your taxes are prepared, your tax situation is run through the normal 1040 tax return, and your "regular" income tax liability is calculated based on your itemized deductions, personal exemptions, and so on. This amount is compared with the amount you had withheld during the year, and a refund or balance owing is calculated. What most folks don't realize is that their tax situation is also run through Form 6251 — Alternative Minimum Tax — Individuals at the same time, and they have to pay the higher of their regular income tax or the disaffectionately known "stealth tax." The problems with the AMT system are listed below.

- You don't get all of the deductions under the regular income tax system (namely, state income taxes and property taxes only).
- With higher-income taxpayers, the basic AMT exemption for 2015 of U$83,400 (for married couples)/$53,600 (for singles) is phased out.
- AMT rates are 26% on the first U$185,400 of AMT income for married couples and singles, and 28% thereafter (essentially a flat tax).

If you are a high-income taxpayer, with lots of deductions, moving to Canada with a continued U.S. tax filing obligation, you should be aware of the impact the AMT may have on you.

PAYROLL TAXES

If you will work in Canada, be aware that payroll taxes there are much lower than in the U.S. In Canada, payroll taxes consist of Canada Pension Plan and Employment Insurance. For 2015, the Canada Pension Plan contribution is 4.95% on a maximum amount of C$53,600 in "pensionable earnings" less the basic yearly exemption of C$3,500. As a result, the maximum Canada Pension Plan contribution is C$2,479.95. The Employment Insurance contribution rate is 1.88%, with maximum insurable earnings of C$49,500, leading to a maximum contribution of C$930.60. Combined, there is a maximum payroll tax of C$3,410.55 for 2015.

In the United States, the first U$118,500 of your wages in 2015 are subject to the Social Security (known as FICA) contribution of 6.2%. That equals a payroll tax of U$7,347 annually. You are also subject to the Medicare contribution of 1.45% with no limits. With the introduction of new taxes to pay for Obamacare, there is an additional 0.9% Medicare tax (for a total of 2.35%) on all wages exceeding U$250,000 for married couples ($125,000 married filing separately) and U$200,000 filing singly (or head of household). If you earn U$118,500 in income in 2015, you will pay a total of U$7,347 + $1,718.25 = $9,065.25 compared with a maximum of C$3,410.55 in Canada. However, the benefits differ between the systems, as outlined in Chapter 8. In summary, Canadians are eligible for a maximum CPP benefit of approximately C$12,459.96 annually in 2014 plus a maximum OAS benefit of approximately C$6,764.88 annually for a total benefit of C$19,224.84 per person. Adding the OAS for a non-working spouse, the maximum CPP and OAS benefits could be as high as C$25,989.83 for a married couple. In the United States, the maximum Social Security benefit you can receive is U$31,956 in 2015, and your spouse automatically qualifies for half of your amount even though nothing was paid into the system. This means that the maximum Social Security benefit for a married couple in the United States could be as high as U$47,934. As you can see, you pay more — but you may get more!

In the United States, it is more common to control the amount of income tax you want withheld from your paychecks. Through Form W-4 — Employee's Withholding Allowance Certificate, you are able to increase or reduce the amount of income tax withheld. The idea is to allow you to pay in the amount you are required without being forced to overpay, essentially giving the IRS an interest-free loan. In Canada, Form TD1 — Personal Tax Credits Return is used to accomplish the same thing as a W-4, but its use is generally reserved for when you change employers, get divorced, or face some other circumstances.

As explained earlier, the level of Social Security taxes payable in the United States is significantly higher than the social insurance taxes payable in Canada on the same level of income.

SALES TAXES

Another factor to consider in your move is federal and provincial sales taxes. In Canada, there is the Goods and Services Tax (GST) of 5%. There is also a provincial sales tax (PST, except for Alberta), which can easily add another 8%. This is a total of 13% in additional sales taxes on most items purchased. In Ontario, New Brunswick, Newfoundland and Labrador, Nova Scotia, and PEI, there is the Harmonized Sales Tax (HST), which essentially combines the GST and PST. The problem with the HST (and why it was repealed in BC) is that it adds a provincial sales tax to items that are subject to GST but were not under PST. Examples include gasoline/diesel and services (haircuts, advisory services . . . yikes!). Believe it or not, most folks residing in Canada and the U.S. end up paying more taxes to their local governments than they do to their federal governments. When you take into account property taxes (generally lower in the U.S.), sales taxes (gas, alcohol, tobacco), license fees (motor vehicle, hunting/fishing), and income/estate taxes, you typically end up paying over half of your tax bill to your local state and province. In the U.S., there is no federal sales tax like the GST, but most states have a sales tax that ranges from 4% to 6%, similar to the sales tax of most provinces. In addition, most municipal governments have a sales tax that typically ranges from 0% to 7%.

SHOW ME 6
THE MONEY

He took his purse filled with money
and will not be home.
— PROVERBS 7:20

This chapter aims to clear up some of the misconceptions about exchanging money and to provide some insights into overcoming a seemingly difficult issue for some folks. When making the transition to Canada, you will have to convert your American dollars to Canadian loonies at some point. The technical term, cash management, deals specifically with matters related to your net worth (assets less your debts), currency exchange, and cash inflows/outflows. In our experience, assets on both sides of the border lead to a lot of complexity and inconvenience, so we generally recommend that you try to consolidate all of your assets on the Canadian side of the border where prudent. There can be some other hidden landmines in keeping assets in the U.S., particularly if they remain in American dollars. Here are some points to consider in the area of cash management when making the transition to Canada.

CURRENCY EXCHANGE FACTS AND MYTHS

Ask most Canadians, and they can tell you within a penny or two what the Canadian-American exchange rate is. In our opinion, some of Canada's national pride rises and falls in relation to the exchange rate of the Canadian dollar versus the U.S. dollar. However, ask most Americans the same question, and they generally don't know what the rate is. Nowhere have we dealt with more confusion or deliberation of decisions than in the area of currency exchange. This section aims to clear up some misconceptions and confusion so you can begin to move forward with confidence in this area. With the meteoric rise of the Canadian loonie against the U.S. dollar over the past few years, it has garnered the attention of many people, and there are calls to peg the Canadian loonie to the U.S. dollar or to create a common currency in North America similar to the Euro. As of this writing, it appears that the record-high closing rate for one American dollar in relation to the Canadian loonie occurred on January 18, 2002, at $1.6132, with the record-low closing set on November 7, 2007, at $0.9170.

MYTH: YOU MAKE (OR LOSE) MONEY WHEN YOU CONVERT

One of the biggest misconceptions is that you lose (or make) money when you exchange U.S. dollars for Canadian loonies. Nothing could be further from the truth. The thinking goes, if you lose money during currency exchange, there must be ways of making money too! On one day, the following exchange rates were observed.

$1 American
= $0.6819 Euro
= $0.9391 Canadian
= $7.7819 Hong Kong
= $71.1979 Jamaican

The first thing to note is that most of these countries use the "dollar" as the name for their currency, and therein lies the problem. Because the currency has the same name, people assume it should have the same value. It does not. This is because they are different currencies, from different countries, with a different value associated with each one. A European Euro is different from a U.S. dollar, which is different from an Italian lira, which is different from a Canadian loonie. Different currencies from different countries (even if they have the same name) have different values ascribed to them by the supply and demand of a particular country's currency in the world. If you stop thinking about Canadian dollars and start calling them Canadian loonies, then you'll be better able to deal with the currency exchange issue.

To further illustrate the point, suppose you exchange one American dollar for one Canadian loonie. According to the example above, you'll receive C$0.9391 for your American dollar. People believe that, since they are getting 6.09¢ less, they have "lost" money. If that argument holds true, if you take your American dollar and exchange it into Jamaican dollars, you'll "make" $70.1979! If you exchange just over 14,000 American dollars, you could become a millionaire in Jamaica! But we all know a Jamaican millionaire is a lot different from a Canadian millionaire, who is different from an American millionaire. Consider as well, if you were to convert your C$0.9391 right back into American dollars the next day, how much would you receive? You're right, pretty much one American dollar (less any transaction fee and any overnight movements in the currency exchange), so where did you lose money in the currency exchange? And where did you gain money?

The real issue is the difference in living expenses you will incur in Canada versus the United States. If the expenses (food, shelter, taxes, gas, autos, health care, etc.) are higher in Canada and your currency conversion leaves you with more loonies in your pocket, then the currency exchange may be inconsequential because you have higher living expenses in Canada for the same lifestyle. We all know it is cheaper to live in Jamaica, but you have to look at the other aspects of the lifestyle to get some insight into whether becoming a millionaire in Jamaica is worthwhile.

The other factor that comes into play is the fluctuation in exchange rates over time. For example, if you have a fixed American pension and lived in Canada over the past few years, you faced a loss of purchasing power in Canada because the Canadian loonie has increased 52% in relation to the American dollar from January 18, 2002 (61.99¢ all time low), to December 31, 2013 (94.02¢). This is particularly true if your American pension is your primary source of income.

MYTH: SOMEONE KNOWS WHERE THE EXCHANGE RATE IS GOING

We don't know how many times people have asked for our opinion on where the Canada-U.S. exchange rate is going. The resounding answer is that we have no idea, but in our view "a bird in the hand is better than 1.01 birds in the bush." First, as seen in Figure 6.1, waiting for a better exchange rate has been the wrong thing to do for most of the past five years. Second, in 2002, who knew that this would be the case? Research has shown that even the most prudent currency traders, economists, and investment managers can't make successful predictions over any extended period of time. If they could, they wouldn't tell you, and they would no longer need to make predictions — they would have more money than they had ever dreamed of getting.

FIGURE 6.1

CANADIAN-U.S. EXCHANGE RATES, 1973–2013

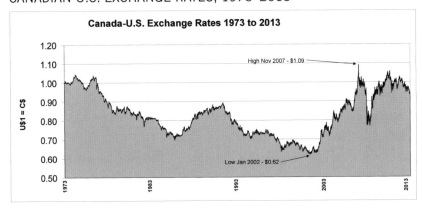

A number of factors influence the Canadian-American exchange rate and make it impossible to predict with any consistency where the rate is going over the long term. The causes of currency exchange fluctuations are what economists love to talk about at parties. We have limited knowledge in this area and offer you the following key factors that the experts agree influence the exchange rate:

- the difference in inflation rates between Canada and the United States;
- the difference in productivity performance;
- the tax system and the tax burden imposed on the citizens of each country;
- the difference in interest rates;

- the difference in non-energy commodity prices;
- the difference in trade and current account balances;
- the difference in fiscal balances;
- the economic growth prospects of each country;
- the political issues and political stability in each country; and
- the need to borrow money by each government.

Despite all of this economic jargon, the bottom line is, whichever currency is more desired by the world, that currency will enjoy a higher exchange rate. It is simple supply and demand, and the world wants Canadian loonies more than it wants American dollars over the past few years. Canadian economists have often theorized about how to fix the problem, including abandoning the floating currency and adopting the U.S. currency wholesale, "pegging" the Canadian dollar to the U.S. dollar, or forming a North American "dollar" with the United States and Mexico. We will leave all of this to the economists, but the question to ask is "What do we do now?"

If you will need Canadian loonies in the future, be sure you have Canadian loonies available, and put the "currency speculating" aside. Likewise, if you will need U.S. dollars in the future, be sure to keep some U.S. dollars to meet that need. We have seen folks devastate their Canadian retirement plans because they decided to currency speculate and leave their money in American dollars when they had an ongoing permanent need for Canadian loonies. They watched their retirement nest eggs decline significantly and kept hoping for the American dollar to bounce back. This unintended overconsumption of their American-dollar retirement assets could have long-term effects on their financial security.

Even though we don't know where the currency rate is going, we do know that the Canadian-American exchange rate fluctuates about 100 basis points every day. If you need to exchange currency at some point in the future, be aware that there are some currency exchange tools available that you might want to consider using to take advantage of the normal fluctuations in the exchange rate. For example, if you need to make a purchase in the short term but want to buy at the lower end of the daily fluctuation, you might want to make a "currency bid" with your currency broker. A currency bid is an agreement to purchase a certain amount of foreign currency at a fixed price sometime in the future. This scheme will allow you to avoid the current spot rate and make a bid to purchase the currency at the lower end of the daily fluctuation. The problem is if the currency exchange is in an upward pattern, your bid may never get filled. A currency bid can be put out for a maximum of 30 days and canceled or amended at any time with no penalty. Another tool available is a forward contract, an agreement to purchase a certain amount of foreign currency at some point in the future at a rate set today. This is for those who know they will need foreign currency in the future to fund a purchase and want to lock in the exchange rate now. The saying "a bird in the hand is better than two in the bush" is reflected by a forward contract because it can be set for up to a year in advance. The drawback is an expense in the currency rate you receive the farther out you want the contract to go.

Nobody can predict the future, and it is really our emotions that are driving our decisions . . . and this spells trouble. For example, when we ask "What rate does the exchange have to achieve for you to convert?" we typically get an off-the-cuff answer. Sure enough, when that exchange rate arrives, the decision to wait for an even better rate is made, and the tendency is to ride the exchange rate back down again. Soon your life revolves around the currency exchange section of the newspaper, and your mood for the day is dictated by what happened in currency exchange markets overnight. Is this any way to live? What a way to spend your golden years . . . glued to the newspaper watching the exchange rates (or the stock market, for that matter).

MYTH: WAIT TO CONVERT

Often people struggle with deciding when to convert their American dollars into Canadian loonies, and "waiting for a better exchange rate" is the game they decide to play. The typical thinking is you can do better if you wait. What many don't realize is they have just made a prediction — that the exchange rate will improve by the time they need to exchange dollars into loonies. They have entered the realm of currency speculation, and frankly there are better ways of speculating on the currency exchange direction, such as buying currency futures contracts. Besides, there are currency traders with millions of dollars and all kinds of equipment monitoring global currency markets in the hope of conducting currency transactions to pay their bills. If there is money to be made in currency speculation, many others will make it ahead of you. So how do you determine when to convert?

The decision to convert should be determined by what you are trying to achieve (your personal goals and objectives). If you are moving to Canada permanently to retire, never to return to the United States, you will have an ongoing need for Canadian loonies, and it may make sense to convert your money now because you know with certainty what the exchange rate is today and how much you'll end up with. If the current exchange rate is sufficient now and the long-term projections of your financial situation in Canada show a high probability of your assets lasting your lifetime, why not exchange dollars now, avoid any currency speculation, and get on with your life? Why not just do it now and avoid the other issues that come with leaving assets in the United States — such as the potential for double probate, double estate and income taxes, etc. — as outlined in the other chapters of this book? At a minimum, understand the sensitivity of your financial situation to currency exchange fluctuations and make an informed decision. A prudent, deliberate, ongoing strategy of currency exchanges over a period of time may make the most sense in your situation. Your financial plan provides the guidepost for your decision making because, without it, important decisions such as exchanging your U.S. dollars are driven by emotions, not by sound financial reasons. The time to exchange your assets is when you can achieve your desired lifestyle per your financial plan. This approach allows you to remove the currency fluctuations from your retirement projections.

Your U.S.-Canada transition planner can assist you in making this important decision. Exchanging your U.S. dollars for Canadian loonies can be an emotional experience, but our firm can help you to make the decision that is right for you. You want to avoid currency exchange whenever possible because you have to pay the currency exchange broker or bank (see below). Therefore, it may make sense to leave some funds in a U.S. bank account if you plan on making regular trips to the United States for the winter months, to visit friends and family, and so on (see our companion book *The Canadian in America*).

FACT: HOW TO CALCULATE EXCHANGE RATES

Another misconception we often encounter involves the calculation of exchange rates. Typically, when U$1 = C$0.90, folks think that U$1.10 = C$1, which is simply not the case. Here is how currency exchange calculations work:

- If U$1 = C$0.90, you have to take 1 divided by 0.90 to find the reverse currency. Specifically, 1/0.90 = $1.111, which means that, when U$1 = C$0.90, C$1 = U$1.111.

To make it easier on yourself, take the price of an item and divide it by the appropriate exchange rate to determine how much it will cost in your desired currency. For example,

- a toque at West Edmonton Mall, Alberta, costs C$11: 11/0.90 = U$12.22;
- a sombrero at the premium outlet mall in Chandler, Arizona, costs U$11: 11/1.11 = C$9.91.

FACT: THERE IS AN EXPENSE TO CONVERTING

Although, as we previously discussed, you don't lose money when you convert American dollars into Canadian loonies, there is a transaction expense to consider. Financial institutions "shade" the "spot" rate of the Canadian-American exchange rate and use it as another source of profit for shareholders. You can tell by comparing the exchange rates online or in the newspaper (the spot rates in the market) with those posted at your local bank or the "currency exchange carts" at the airport. The difference can be significant. Understand this service is unregulated and a huge source of profits for the banks. In some cases, using your American credit card in Canada for purchases in Canadian dollars may be better or worse. By shading the exchange rate on your purchases in Canada or applying additional fees, the credit card companies make a small fortune, and you may have no idea. The next time you get your credit card statement look for any additional fees or the rate the company exchanged your purchase at, and then locate the historical rate — you may grimace. We encourage you to be informed beforehand.

Here are some things you can do to reduce the expense of converting your American dollars into Canadian loonies.

- Ask your currency exchange provider to give you a rate as close to the current spot rate as possible (don't prevent the provider from making a living, but make sure you aren't getting gouged). The spot rate is what the market is paying at that moment, when the currency exchange isn't shaded at all.
- Accumulate your dollars and convert them in one lump sum rather than make several smaller transactions, because bigger transactions generally get a better exchange rate.
- Determine the expenses associated with using your American-dollar credit card for Canadian-dollar purchases, and if prohibitive avoid using your American-dollar credit card at all; find a credit card company that issues Canadian-dollar cards instead so you can control the exchange rate better rather than take the prevailing rate the credit card company decides for that day.
- Avoid using your bank unless you have a good relationship with it; then ask your banker to give you the spot rate or something as close to it as possible.
- Avoid the currency exchange carts in airports or be sure to compare their rates to a discount currency broker or the spot rate in the newspaper or online whenever possible.
- Avoid converting cash since doing so is more expensive. Consider traveler's checks, bank drafts, money orders, or personal checks instead.
- Make sure you do comparative shopping, particularly if you are exchanging large sums.
- If you have an account at a Canadian brokerage firm, it may offer you competitive exchange rates as part of its customer service to you, particularly if you already have a U.S.-dollar account.
- Canadian casinos typically provide excellent exchange rates in the hope you'll leave some of your money in their machines or at their tables.

- Be aware that most U.S. banks won't convert your American dollars to Canadian loonies. However, banks in the United States owned by a Canadian bank are more inclined to offer this service to their clients.
- Leave sufficient U.S. dollars in the United States to meet your currency needs each year or, as mentioned previously, enough Canadian dollars in Canada to meet your needs there.

MORTGAGES

There are huge differences in mortgages between Canada and the U.S., and they clearly favor the latter, so be prepared for this change in Canada. Since buying a home is typically the single largest purchase you'll make in your lifetime, getting the right mortgage should be of primary consideration as well. Make sure you get the right mortgage with the right terms from the right (read honest) mortgage broker.

AMORTIZATION

In the United States, the typical mortgage is amortized over 15 or 30 years, while it is 25 years in Canada. A 25-year amortization will obviously increase your monthly payments from a 30-year mortgage, but which mortgage you select in Canada will depend on your individual circumstances. There are a number of other loan options (e.g., anniversary payments) to consider besides these conventional loans that may better suit your goals and objectives.

FIXED INTEREST RATES

In Canada, the typical mortgage fixes your interest rate for up to 10 years (at an increasingly higher interest rate), and then it is adjusted to the prevailing rate when it matures. You are required to bear the risk of any interest rate changes, which is why you see most Canadians vigorously paying off their mortgages. This is where a U.S. mortgage has a big advantage over those in Canada, because you can fix your interest rate for the full 15- or 30-year amortization — the bank bears the interest rate risk. This can make a huge difference in stabilizing one of your largest debts over the long term. The other nice thing with mortgages in the United States is that they use simple interest calculations, while in Canada interest is compounded semi-annually. This means you'll pay more interest in the United States if you make the minimum payment for the entire term of the mortgage, but you'll pay less if you ever get in arrears, because there is no interest on the interest, as there is in Canada. Likewise, U.S. lenders will typically charge a late fee for payments made in arrears, while these fees are typically prohibited in Canada.

One thing we have noticed many times with Americans moving to Canada is the loss of their mortgage interest deduction. You can't deduct your mortgage interest or property taxes anywhere on your Canadian return (see Chapter 5 for more details). However, your Canadian mortgage interest may be deductible on your U.S. return if your individual tax situation permits it, but be sure you understand exactly what is going on. If you have a 7% mortgage and you are in the 25% marginal tax bracket, it means that for every $1 you give to the Canadian bank in interest the IRS gives you 25¢ back. Notice that you are still out of pocket 75¢. We have an even better deal: you give us $1, and we'll give you 99¢ back. We'll do that all day long, but who will end up with all of your money? Your mortgage is still an out-of-pocket expense to you.

We also see the strategy of investing the mortgage amount, rather than paying off the mortgage, to get a better return. Your after-tax mortgage rate can be calculated as $7 \times (1 - 0.25) = 5.25\%$. The argument goes "I should be able to do better than 5.25% in the markets, so I'll get a bigger mortgage, make the minimum payments, and maximize my investments." The flaw in this argument is "Are you guaranteed to do better than 5.25% in the markets?" If your money goes into a tax-deferred vehicle, the benchmark is 5.25%. But what if your money is in a taxable brokerage account and you get a return of 7%? You'll have to pay taxes on the income earned, so guess what — you are no further ahead. If you invest the money for capital gains, which can be taxed more favorably (only half the gain is taxed in Canada), you have to remember that markets don't go straight up. If you take a bigger mortgage so you can watch your portfolio go up, your business case falls apart if the markets go down (we saw this with the popping of the tech bubble in 2000 and more recently with the real estate bubble).

PREPAYMENTS

Here is another area that makes U.S. mortgages far superior to Canadian mortgages. Most U.S. mortgages have no prepayment penalties, while Canadian financial institutions typically impose penalties for prepayments, restrict them to the loan anniversary, or simply don't allow any prepayments at all. In the United States, you can send in as much additional money above your monthly mortgage payment as you wish, and it all gets applied to the principal. This means you can pay off your mortgage whenever you have the funds to do so (if you have a conventional mortgage). Many Canadian institutions set up biweekly payment schedules at little or no charge to you because it is a very effective strategy to pay off your mortgage sooner. American financial institutions are often happy to oblige with a similar plan because there are many hidden costs and fees, of which you need to be aware. That is why this approach typically doesn't make sense; you can accomplish the same thing by making an extra payment on your mortgage per year.

DOWN PAYMENTS

To purchase a home in Canada, you are required to put 25% or more down to avoid paying for mortgage insurance from the Canada Mortgage and Housing Corporation (CMHC). In the United States, the requirement is only 20% to avoid paying for mortgage insurance from the Federal Housing Authority (FHA) or a private insurer such as Fannie Mae. Depending on your situation, you may be able to work with your lender to find ways of structuring your mortgage to avoid the mortgage insurance while putting less than 25% down. Under recent changes to slow down the meteoric rise in debt being carried by Canadians, the finance minister announced that mortgage insurance will be limited to homes under $1M. If you purchase a home for $1M+, you must put down 20% or more, and you will not qualify for any mortgage insurance through CMHC. In addition, home equity lines of credit are now reduced to 80% of the home's value versus 85%.

CLOSING COSTS

It has been our experience that closing costs in Canada are typically higher than those in the United States. In particular, lender fees in the

United States are around U$400 versus C$1,000 in Canada. In addition, legal fees and land title fees are seen in the closing costs in Canada but not in the United States. However, you typically don't need a termite inspection in Canada! The other difference when closing on a house in Canada is that you typically use an attorney to handle the transaction. In the United States, you use a title company almost exclusively to complete the transaction, and title insurance is a good thing. Note that realtor commissions are generally higher in the United States. In Canada, the typical commission is 6% on the first $100,000 and then 3% on the balance. In the United States it is typically a flat 6%.

MISCELLANEOUS

There are a couple of other things you won't see in Canada that are common in the United States. For example, points (discount points, loan original points, and seller paid points) are seen only in the United States. You also won't see "impound" or "escrow accounts" in Canada. This is where the U.S. mortgage lender will automatically roll your homeowner insurance and property taxes into your monthly payment (without consulting you) so they can be "pre-collected." The insurance company or local government sends the bill directly to the mortgage company, which pays the money out of your escrow/impound account. In Canada, you receive those bills directly.

APPLYING FOR A MORTGAGE

In qualifying for a mortgage, things can get a little tricky (see "Establishing a Credit Rating" below). Be sure to provide copies of your IRA statements and other investment accounts you have in the United States (or Canada) to your mortgage broker, who should take them into account in the underwriting process. It helps to have a letter of introduction from your banker in the United States that outlines your mortgage and line of credit history with the bank and your history of repaying borrowed amounts. You should also have a letter typed up by your mortgage broker stating your Social Insurance Number in Canada and your Social Security Number in the United States so he or she can match up the two records. In the letter, request the broker to contact the American credit agencies to get a full credit report from the United States. It should satisfy the Canadian mortgage underwriter and result in a favorable interest rate and mortgage terms for you. Thankfully, some Canadian banks have bought banks in the United States, and they better understand your needs and how to get a mortgage using a U.S. credit rating (see Canadian-friendly companies later in this chapter).

ESTABLISHING A CREDIT RATING

Many Americans with excellent credit ratings in the United States move to Canada and are shocked when a cell phone company wants payment in advance before starting service, they can't get a Canadian credit card, or they don't qualify for a mortgage. Don't take it personally; this is common because you don't have any kind of credit rating tied to your Social Insurance Number with the Canadian credit agencies. To resolve this problem, there are some things you can do in anticipation of your move.

FICO SCORE

FICO stands for Fair Isaac & Co., the Minnesota-based firm that created this scoring system in the early 1950s and updated to the FICO®8 Score in 2009 that is used in Canada today. These scores range from 300 to 850 and gauge the level of your credit risk (the higher the score, the less risky you are to extend credit to, and the lower the interest rate offered). A score under 620 is considered high risk or "subprime," and it's likely you won't be extended any credit, particularly a mortgage. The score is created by giving different weights to the various criteria in your financial situation and is comprised of the following:

- 35% — your payment history (paying your bills on time);
- 30% — amounts owed (your total debt outstanding);
- 15% — length of credit history (yours will be short);
- 10% — new credit (recently applied for or issued debt);
- 10% — the type of credit used (mortgage versus auto loan versus credit card).

In the 1990s, mortgage lenders started using the score to rate prospective customers, and then in 1999 California passed a law requiring the lenders and the three national credit bureaus (Experian, TransUnion, and Equifax) to disclose your credit score to you. Today your credit score is used by most Canadian and American lenders to make instant decisions on extending credit to you, but this has led to increased credit-reporting errors that have negatively impacted innocent people's credit scores. As a result, the two credit-reporting agencies in Canada, Equifax and TransUnion, have to provide your credit report to you once you request it, and you are entitled to ask for it in writing as often as you wish at no charge, but you still have to pay a fee to see your actual score. We recommend you review and monitor your credit rating annually. You can get a host of information on your credit at the Government of Canada Financial Consumer Agency at www.ic.gc.ca/eic/site/oca-bc.nsf/eng/h_ca02146.html.

BEFORE YOU APPLY

Before you start the process of establishing a credit rating in Canada, you need to have a Social Insurance Number, which you'll need for every credit application you complete (see Chapter 5 on how to obtain one). In desperation, some folks start applying for credit cards at every bank, department store, or gas station, anywhere to get some form of credit. They don't realize that they may actually be damaging their credit rating. Each credit application you make is reported to the credit-reporting agencies in Canada and reduces your credit rating (new credit component). They think you are getting desperate for money and are applying wherever you can to keep yourself afloat. If your applications are subsequently rejected, your credit rating will sink even lower. This means that, when you are approved for a mortgage, for example, you'll have to pay a higher interest rate because you are perceived as being a higher credit risk (i.e., your FICO score is low).

TRANSFER YOUR CREDIT RATING

We have seen some success in transferring a credit rating to Canada by using your current American credit card to apply for and secure a new credit card with the Canadian subsidiary of the same company. My wife did this with American Express in 1992 when she moved to Canada from the United States. However, prepare yourself because this tactic will typically take many phone calls to both the Canadian and the American sides of your credit card company before you are successful in moving your credit rating and membership rewards points (exchanged at the prevailing exchange rate) to Canada. The beauty of this strategy is that it allows you to get an instant credit rating with your desired credit card in Canada based on your credit rating in the United States, and you don't lose any of your membership points. Another alternative is to call the U.S. credit reporting agencies that have branches in Canada (Equifax and TransUnion) and ask them to transfer your U.S. credit rating to the Canadian subsidiary to establish a credit rating (see more below).

APPLYING FOR A CREDIT CARD

When you apply for a credit card, it's best to do so in person with an officer at the bank of your choice. The bank may tell you it isn't necessary since this is a routine process, but tell the bank you are new in the country and have an established credit rating in the United States it will need to obtain. You'll be surprised at how familiar most Canadian banks are with this process, so it should go smoothly, particularly if you make a substantive deposit at that time. Regardless, to prepare for this meeting, gather the following.

- **Letter of reference:** get a letter of reference signed by your bank manager in the United States that lists all of your credit transactions with that bank (mortgages, lines of credit, etc.) and your history in paying on time, never defaulting, etc. This letter carries a lot of weight in the process, especially since the Canadian institution can call the bank manager in the United States and verify everything.
- **SSN/SIN:** have original Social Security and Social Insurance cards available. Instruct the loan officer to use your Social Security Number to contact the American credit-reporting agencies to obtain an American credit report. Equifax and TransUnion (see below) are credit-reporting agencies located in both Canada and the United States, but their systems are

separate, and it has been our experience that they rarely, if ever, talk to each other. Experian is located just in the United States.

- **Identification:** be sure to provide an original passport or birth certificate to verify who you are.
- **Credit card:** take your current American credit card with you so the institution can make copies and verify your existing credit history.
- **Pay stubs:** if applicable, take both your American pay stubs and your current Canadian pay stub if you have one. You should also take your letter of offer, stating your starting salary in Canada.
- **Deposit:** it helps a lot if you have a U.S. bank draft for some amount you are ready to deposit into your bank account when opened. You'll typically get a higher level of service because the loan application officer is more motivated if you have money deposited with the institution. You'll most likely be able to secure a bank credit card at the time of your deposit as well.
- **Credit union:** besides the major banks in Canada, you could consider one of the provincial credit unions or smaller financial institutions. You may find better customer service and lower fees.

You will need to fill out the standard credit card application with the bank to start the process. Be sure a copy of all the information above is attached to the application along with a letter signed by the loan application officer requesting an American credit bureau check be done as well. This letter should clearly outline your Social Security Number and Social Insurance Number so that the appropriate match is made when your credit reports come in. Also ensure that your previous American address(es) are on the application form and in the letter. All of this information should allow the bank to issue a credit card to you with a healthy limit and low interest rates. As you begin using it, be sure to pay off your balances in a timely fashion to start establishing your credit rating in Canada. You should obtain a copy of your Canadian credit report at least annually from the two primary credit-reporting agencies for the first few years to confirm that your credit rating is getting established in Canada.

AMERICAN-FRIENDLY COMPANIES

It has been our experience that there is more success with American Express (call New Accounts — Special Handling at 1-800-453-2639) than with Visa and MasterCard when transferring your credit card to the Canadian subsidiary. Many of the Canadian banks, such as Toronto Dominion (owns Bank North Group in the United States), Bank of Montreal (owns Harris Bank), and Royal Bank of Canada (owns RBC Centura), are good starting places for Americans to obtain a credit card or secure a mortgage. We have heard that TD Canada Trust understands the plight of those moving to Canada from the United States and has successfully met their unique mortgage and banking needs. If you are already a customer of the U.S. subsidiary, it stands to reason that it should be easier to move your credit rating up to the Canadian bank that owns it. Also, because these companies have locations on both sides of the border, they tend to have a better idea of how to get an American credit report and give it its due weight in the underwriting process. There are three American credit-reporting agencies they will need to contact: Equifax (1-800-685-1111 or www.equifax.com), TransUnion (1-877-322-8228 or www.transunion.com), and Experian (1-888-397-3742 or www.experian.com). If you have an American-friendly company you have dealt with, please let us know (book@transitionfinancial.com), and we will be sure to include it in the next edition of this book or on our website at www.transitionfinancial.com.

TILL DEATH 7
DO US PART

*Man is destined to die once
and then the judgment.*
— HEBREWS 9:27

By far the most neglected area we see with folks making the transition to Canada is will and estate planning. Unfortunately, the judgment of your estate plan won't come to light until after you can no longer do anything about it. Just like U.S. income taxes, American citizens are subject to U.S. gift and estate taxes even when living in Canada. That is, you can move to Canada with all of your assets and, at your passing, pay U.S. estate taxes even though you don't have a single penny physically located in the United States! The use of more sophisticated estate planning techniques such as trusts is more common in the United States because of the complex estate and gift tax rules and the fact trusts are a "flow-through" entity for tax purposes. In Canada, a simple will can accomplish many things when you become an angel. In fact, many Americans mistakenly believe they should get their U.S. estate plan updated before moving to Canada. However, when moving to another country, estate planning becomes much more complex, particularly when property spans both countries and U.S. citizenship issues are added. In our opinion, estate planning is the most important area of planning you can do for yourself and your family. Consider the following questions.

- Is your American will or revocable living trust valid in Canada?
- What will happen to your spouse and dependents if you die suddenly in Canada?
- Will your spouse be able to get access to any funds to meet family obligations?
- What taxes will you pay in the United States and/or Canada in the event of your death?
- What will happen to your assets in Canada? Those in the United States?
- Can your heirs in the United States receive any of your assets?
- Who will care for your children if you and your spouse die simultaneously?
- Who will file your taxes, pay your bills, or care for your children in the event of your incapacity?
- In the event you end up in a coma, will you want the "plug pulled"? How will that decision be communicated?
- Will you want your body buried or cremated? In Canada or the United States?
- If you inherit assets from America, are they taxed? Where?

Estate planning is all about how much control you want in a variety of circumstances, including death and incapacity. A secondary consideration is saving every court cost, attorney fee, and tax possible. Sometimes we hear "If I'm dead, I'm dead. What do I care?" If you don't want to determine the course of events in the situations listed above (don't want to spend the money to get an estate plan), your province of residence (or state where the asset is located) has default laws called intestate laws (intestate literally means to "die without a will") that will decide for you, and your estate will incur the attendant costs and delays that come with having no control. However, most people, when presented with the options, aren't content to let anybody but them decide what to do with what has taken a lifetime to accumulate, their health-care decisions, or their bodies. A Canadian estate plan is needed. You just need to consider the cost of a Canadian estate plan as part of the overall expense of moving to Canada.

Estate planning for Americans relocating to, or living in Canada can be extremely complex. It deserves much more attention than this book can provide because some areas have been tested in American and Canadian courts, there are some gray areas, and some scenarios have yet to be played out. We recommend you use a qualified Canada-U.S. estate planning attorney accepted by the Bar in Canada (one familiar with U.S. citizenship issues) to get the appropriate counseling to determine which estate planning documents you need to achieve the level of control you want. How much counseling will you get with a downloaded do-it-yourself will or trust kit? In our experience, most Canadian estate planning attorneys have no idea of the complexity involved when planning for Americans living in Canada. The estate planning attorney drafts the documents; once they are completed and executed, most folks sit back, let out a sigh, and take comfort that their estate plans are done. Unfortunately, it's a false sense of security because there is much to do in implementing your estate plan. Assets may need to be re-titled, documents need to be filed where they can be retrieved easily, and those having a role in your estate plan need to be briefed on your intentions. In our biased opinion, a team approach with an experienced Canada-U.S. transition planner as the quarterback is generally your best option.

TAXES AT DEATH

CANADA

Many people wrongfully assume there is no estate or death tax in Canada. They simply aren't aware of the "deemed disposition tax" in Canada that occurs at one's death. Similar to the departure tax when you leave Canada, this tax kicks in when you die in Canada and applies to your worldwide assets. At the first spouse's death, things such as RRSPs/RRIFs and IRAs can be rolled over to the surviving spouse to continue their tax deferral (provided the surviving spouse is named as the beneficiary on the RRSP/ RRIF or IRA account). However, at the second spouse's passing, you must report on your final Canadian T1 tax return the full value of your RRSPs, the capital gains on all investment real estate (including those properties in the U.S.), stocks or bonds, shares of your small business, plus any other income realized in the year of death. Needless to say, with some provinces in Canada reaching income tax rates of 48% or more, this can be a significant tax burden, particularly if you have illiquid assets (a small business or farm). In addition to the federal tax burden, the provinces get their share of the proceeds plus a variety of additional probate fees that they levy individually, as outlined in Table 7.1 (although they are fairly nominal and are coming under some legal scrutiny as of late). Probate fees alone aren't that expensive, but when an attorney is brought in to sort out the complexities, the expense can go up significantly, particularly since the probate process can last a year or more in certain provinces.

TABLE 7.1

PROVINCIAL PROBATE FEES

Province	Probate Fee Schedule	
Alberta	$25 for estates under $10,000	
	$100 for estates between $10,000 and $25,000	
	$200 for estates between $25,001 and $125,000	
	$300 for estates between $125,001 and $250,000	
	$400 for estates of $250,001 +	
British Columbia	$0 for estates under $25,001	
	$208 administration filing fee for estates exceeding $25,000	
	$6 per $1,000 or part of $1,000 by which the value of the estate exceeds $25,000 but is not more than $50,000	
	Plus $14 per $1,000 or part of $1,000 by which the value of the estate exceeds $50,000	
Manitoba	$70 for the first $10,000, plus $7 for every $1,000 or portion thereafter	
New Brunswick	up to $5,000	$25
	$5,001 to $10,000	$50
	$10,001 to $15,000	$75
	$15,001 to $20,000	$100
	Over $20,000	$5 per $1,000 or portion
Newfoundland and Labrador	$60 for the first $1,000 and $0.50 per $100 thereafter plus $60 for the order	

Northwest Territories and Nunavut	Value of all property, real and personal, within the Northwest Territories, after deducting all debts and liabilities against that property $25 for estates $10,000 or less $100 for estates of more than $10,000 up to $25,000 $200 for estates of more than $25,000 up to $125,000 $300 for estates of more than $125,000 up to $250,000 $400 for estates over $250,000
Nova Scotia	$78.54 for estates not exceeding $10,000 $197.48 for estates exceeding $10,000 up to $25,000 $328.65 for estates exceeding $25,000 up to $50,000 $920.07 for estates exceeding $50,000 up to $100,000 $920.07 for estates exceeding $100,000 plus $15.53 per $1,000 (or portion thereof) in excess of $100,000
Ontario	$5 per $1,000 for estates of $1,000 up to $50,000 and $15 per $1,000 thereafter
PEI	$25 for estates $10,000 or less $100 for estates of more than $10,000 up to $25,000 $200 for estates of more than $25,000 up to $50,000 $400 for estates of more than $50,000 up to $100,000 $400 for estates over $100,000 plus $4 for each $1,000 or portion thereafter
Quebec	$99 to probate the will for natural person $111 to probate the will for a legal person
Saskatchewan	$7 per $1,000 (real estate is subject just to the equity in the property — fair market value less mortgage)

Yukon	There may be a fee to obtain a grant of probate letter for an estate not exceeding $25,000 in value. For an estate exceeding $25,000 in value, there is a fee of $140.

UNITED STATES

For American citizens or green card holders moving to or living in Canada, the myriad of taxes at your passing needs to be considered carefully because, as outlined above, you are still subject to U.S. estate and gift taxes on your worldwide estate. This means there can be up to five different taxes at your death, including estate taxes, gift taxes, generation-skipping transfer taxes, state death taxes, and federal/state income taxes. Most of these are cumulative taxes and, without the proper forethought and estate plan in place, could result in the loss of the bulk of your estate. As you can see in Table 7.2, with no or improper estate planning, these taxes can be more punitive than the deemed disposition tax at death in Canada because they are based on the value of your entire estate, not just on the capital gains on certain assets.

TABLE 7.2

ESTATE DEPLETION OF THE RICH AND FAMOUS

	Gross Estate	Settlement Costs	Shrinkage
Walt Disney	$23,004,851	$6,811,943	30%
Alwin C. Ernst, CPA	$12,642,431	$7,124,112	56%
J.P. Morgan	$17,121,482	$11,893,691	69%
Elvis Presley	$10,165,434	$7,374,635	73%
John D. Rockefeller, Jr.	$160,598,584	$24,965,954	16%

Settlement costs include the estate taxes, court fees, legal and accounting fees, probate fees, and so on that go into settling these estates after death. Even though Rockefeller's estate was the largest, he was able to keep more of his estate through proper estate planning and by including charitable gifting as part of his plan. A brief discussion of each of these five potential taxes at death is outlined below.

Estate Taxes

The estate tax regime has endured a number of changes over the past number of years, making will and trust planning very difficult. However, on January 2, 2013, President Obama signed the American Taxpayer Relief Act, which provided some very favorable changes and likely some permanence to the rules (would that be asking too much?). This will allow much better planning and a more fair and reasonable approach to U.S. estate planning in the years to come.

The IRS manages the estate tax system, and you have to understand that your worldwide estate (including all of your assets in Canada) is included in the estate tax calculation. This includes items such as:

- the value of any life insurance proceeds payable to the estate, or from policies on the deceased's life owned or controlled by the deceased, including policies where the deceased transferred ownership and all control within three years prior to death;
- any gifted assets (exceeding any applicable gift tax exemptions) transferred during your life;
- the transfer of any assets where you retain an interest for your life or the right to change or terminate the transfer;
- the commuted value of a monthly corporate pension that continues to your beneficiary at your death;
- assets that are held in joint tenancy with your spouse or any other person;
- your house(s), automobiles, RVs, boats, household and personal goods, furniture, fixtures, appliances in the United States, Canada, and anywhere else in the world; and
- annuities, RRSPs/RRIFs, IRAs, and company-defined contribution plans like 401(k) plans, profit-sharing plans, and money purchase plans.

To report all of this at your passing, the IRS kindly provides Form 706 — United States Estate (and Generation-Skipping Transfer) Tax Return. This form needs to be filed by your estate within nine months of the date of your death. For those who prepare these forms (it should be a good estate planning attorney with a tax designation or an accountant who prepares them on a regular basis), it is clearly understood that you don't mail them to the IRS in an envelope — they are in a box. The documentation (including copies of your wills and trusts), schedules, evaluations, appraisals, and so on required by the IRS make this tax return a major undertaking.

Estate tax rates start at 18% and rise to 40% at just U$1 million in taxable net worth above the exemption (see discussion below). Subject to the exemptions discussed below, everything above $1 million in taxable net worth is taxed at the flat rate of 40%. Specifically, the estate tax is calculated in Table 7.3.

TABLE 7.3

CURRENT U.S. ESTATE TAX RATES

Taxable Estate (U$)	Tax Rate	Cumulative Tax Owing (U$)
0–10,000	18%	1,800
10,001–20,000	20%	3,800
20,001–40,000	22%	8,200
40,001–60,000	24%	13,000
60,001–80,000	26%	18,200
80,001–100,000	28%	23,800
100,001–150,000	30%	38,800
150,001–250,000	32%	70,800
250,001–500,000	34%	155,800
500,001–750,000	37%	248,300
750,001–1,000,000	39%	345,800
1,000,001+	40%	345,800+

To protect some (or potentially all) of your estate, Congress gives you a "unified" gift and estate tax exemption (a "coupon" or the "unified credit") that can be used during your lifetime, at your passing, or partly at each. For 2015, the gift and estate tax exemptions for U.S. Citizens and U.S. domiciled residents are $5.43 million per person over your lifetime, or at your passing, and now adjusted annually for inflation (unified credit of $2,117,800). This is a welcome relief to many farmers, investment property owners, and small-business owners who, in the past, found themselves in a cash crunch to pay the estate taxes owing on the value of the estate when it consists of just illiquid assets! This has made the U.S. estate tax much less of an issue except for the largest of estates. Previously, to take full advantage of the unified credit for a married couple ($5.43 million for each) required complex trust and estate planning. This has been greatly simplified with the "portability of the estate tax exemption." In order for a married couple to take full advantage of the estate tax exemption, spousal "A" and bypass "B" trusts were needed. Now portability means the unused portion of the decedent spouse's exemption automatically gets added to the surviving spouse's exemption without the need for a trust. The only requirement is to file an estate tax return using Form 706 with the IRS, even if there is no taxable estate, to port the remaining exemption to the surviving spouse. An example may help.

TABLE 7.4

OWNERSHIP AND VALUE OF ASSETS

Asset Titling	Fair Market Value (U$)
Solely owned — husband	5,000,000
Life insurance — husband	1,000,000
Solely owned — wife	1,000,000
Jointly owned — husband and wife	3,000,000
Total	10,000,000

FIGURE 7.1

OLD "AB" TRUST PLANNING

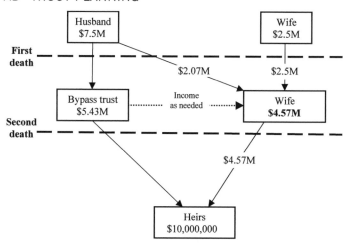

FIGURE 7.2
NEW PORTABILITY OF ESTATE TAX EXEMPTION

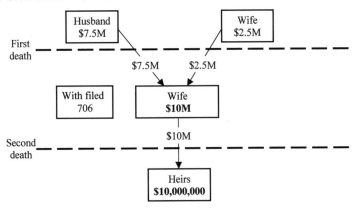

UNLIMITED MARITAL DEDUCTION

One subject that seems to come up frequently is confusion surrounding the "unlimited marital deduction" at the first spouse's passing. American citizens living in Canada can pass an estate of any size to their U.S. citizen spouses without incurring any U.S. estate taxes because of the unlimited marital deduction available at the first spouse's passing. This means the deceased spouse's entire estate (assets titled in his/her name alone or jointly with the spouse) passes to the survivor with no estate tax, no matter how big the estate is. Likewise, a Canadian citizen only, married to a U.S. citizen and passing first, also has an unlimited marital deduction that permits him/her to pass the entire estate to the U.S. citizen with no estate tax. The confusion comes in when a U.S. citizen married to a Canadian only citizen tries to pass the estate to the survivor . . . there is no unlimited marital deduction in this case. The reason is that the U.S. government fears the surviving non-citizen spouse can take the excess assets (the amount above the permitted exemption) out of the country without paying any estate taxes due at the American citizen's death. However, given the estate tax exemption portability, even a non-citizen spouse automatically gets to inherit $5.43M from the U.S.-citizen spouse. Alternatively, the U.S. citizen's estate may elect to take a marital credit under the Canada-U.S. Tax Treaty to shelter an additional amount of the estate equal to almost a whole second exemption.

FIGURE 7.3

UNLIMITED MARITAL DEDUCTION EXAMPLES

	Unlimited	
Dual Canada-U.S. citizen	←————→	U.S.-citizen spouse
	Unlimited	
U.S. citizen	←————	Non-citizen spouse
	$5.43M	
U.S. citizen	————→	Non-citizen spouse

It's important to note that a specifically designed Canadian estate plan is required for Americans in Canada. This is especially true if your estate is greater than the current allowable exemption (U$10.86M) as estate tax is typically due at the death of the U.S. citizen passing assets to a non-citizen, unless the IRS has some way of "attaching" itself to the assets. One way to do this is to establish a Qualified Domestic Trust (QDOT) in the U.S. citizen's Canadian will. This trust holds the excess amount of the estate above the exemption that would be subject to estate taxes at the U.S. citizen's passing and delays the estate tax liability until the Canadian citizen passes. A QDOT provides estate tax deferral at the first death because the trust is considered resident in the U.S., and the IRS can require the trustee to pay any estate taxes owing (attach itself). You should note that estate taxes are in addition to any professional fees, court costs, and probate fees that could consume another 3–10% or more of your estate. The complexity and time required to settle an estate via probate are different for every state and province. Some states and provinces have streamlined probate processes that are very inexpensive to settle even with an attorney, while other jurisdictions are much more complex and lengthy.

CANADIANS AND THE U.S. ESTATE TAX

Believe it or not, Canadians who are non-U.S. citizens or green card holders can be subject to estate tax in both Canada and the United States. How? Based on the value of your assets considered to be "in the United States." The most common types of U.S. assets subject to estate tax include U.S. real estate and tangible personal property located in the United States. However, one "gotcha" that people are often unaware of are stocks in

American companies, regardless of where they are held. For example, if you hold shares of Microsoft or any other U.S. company in your Canadian brokerage account, those are considered U.S. situs and you could be subject to U.S. estate taxes on them. Under the Canada-U.S. Tax Treaty, Canadians are entitled to a prorated exemption against U.S. estate tax based on a ratio of American assets to their worldwide estates. This subject is covered in much greater detail in our companion book *The Canadian in America*.

Advanced Techniques for Large Estates

If you have had the good fortune of accumulating an estate in excess of the federal estate tax exemption, more sophisticated estate planning techniques can be used to reduce your estate taxes at your passing (like the QDOT mentioned previously). These techniques are unique to each person's situation and go beyond the scope of this book. The time to plan is now because, if your estate is big enough and you just want to leave it all to your heirs, you automatically cut the government in on a piece of your estate whether you want to or not. In our experience, most of our clients desire greater control over their estates than a game of Russian roulette with the IRS or CRA. However, determining which technique to use and how to implement it in your situation so it will withstand the scrutiny of an IRS estate tax audit will require competent counsel, who should be interviewed and selected carefully.

Gift Taxes

To prevent you from avoiding estate taxes entirely at your death by gifting away your estate on your deathbed, Congress countered with the gift tax. In general, any gift is taxable unless it meets one of the exclusions. See the "Gifting" section later in this chapter for more details.

Generation-Skipping Transfer Taxes

To ensure that the U.S. government gets paid its estate taxes at every generation, it instituted generation-skipping transfer taxes to prevent you from passing your estate too far down the "family tree." The generation-skipping transfer tax (GSTT) kicks in at the highest marginal estate tax rate (currently 40%) on any amount that passes directly from you to your grandchildren, or indirectly to them through a trust for your children that is not subject to estate tax on your child's death, and is in addition to any estate taxes above. Once again, the government is kind enough to allow you to exclude $5.43 million from the GSTT to pass to the next generation. This means that, without the proper planning, for every dollar in excess of $5.43 million that is passed, 40¢ must be paid to the IRS in GSTT. Since you are in the 40% estate tax bracket as well, you could see 80¢ in taxes for every dollar transferred to the next generation!

State Death Taxes

In general, there can be up to two different death taxes paid to your state of domicile. They include inheritance taxes and estate taxes. However, since you are no longer a resident of any state, these taxes won't apply to you unless you still own real estate in that state. Some states reserve the right to levy death taxes on properties in the respective state, so ensure you understand the implications and how to deal with them in these circumstances.

Income Taxes

Like the deemed disposition tax in Canada, the U.S. citizen or green card holder's executor or executrix must file a final U.S. federal Form 1040 to report any income in the year of death on behalf of the decedent. If not structured properly, things such as IRAs might have to be declared on your final U.S. return along with the taxable portion of your RRSPs/ RRIFs. In addition, you will have to declare any interest, dividends, or realized capital gains in the year up to the point of death as well. These U.S. income taxes (don't forget any applicable Canadian taxes) are in addition to any U.S. estate tax as well.

Common-Law Relationships

Canada has recognized common-law relationships for some time now. In fact, it is an official tax filing status in Canada. There are criteria used to define common-law relationships (see Chapter 3), but of utmost importance is that common-law relationships can be the basis for granting permanent residence in Canada. For example, a Canadian citizen can sponsor an American citizen of either gender to enter Canada as long as they can prove they have a common-law relationship. The sponsored person will receive permanent residence status and eventually Canadian citizenship if desired. The difficulties occur because the U.S. or dual citizen is still subject to U.S. estate and gift taxes since the IRS doesn't recognize common-law relationships for U.S. estate and gift tax purposes. This means there is no marital deduction at death and no increased exemption for gift tax purposes (see gifting section later). In essence, the American citizen(s) are treated as single, and their estate tax situation is the same as that of the "unmarried U.S. citizen" outlined earlier. We've worked with some clients in this area, and one of our recommendations has been that they get married. Then the planning opportunities for married couples outlined above can assist in reducing, deferring, and eliminating U.S. estate tax. Obviously, the client's specific beliefs, goals, and objectives need to be taken into consideration before any plan can move forward.

Same-Sex Marriages

Canada recognizes same-sex marriages as an official tax filing status in Canada under "married." Same-sex marriages can now be the basis for granting permanent residence in Canada. For example, a Canadian citizen may sponsor an American citizen same-sex spouse to enter Canada, and that spouse can receive permanent residence status and eventually Canadian citizenship if desired. The difficulties occur because the American or dual citizen is still subject to U.S. estate and gift taxes. With the Defense of Marriage Act overturned by the Supreme Court in the U.S., the IRS now recognizes same-sex couples, legally married in jurisdictions that recognize such marriages, as being married for federal estate and income tax purposes. Further, these rules apply even if the same-sex married couple are living in a jurisdiction that does not recognize same-sex marriage! This means the IRS extends all of the same estate and income tax laws given to heterosexual couples to "legal" same-sex marriages. This will simplify estate planning greatly for these non-traditional marriages. It is expected that over time same-sex couples will be recognized nationally in the U.S. as having the same status as traditional heterosexual couples today.

THE DOUBLE ESTATE TAX CONUNDRUM

For the American in Canada, there is the potential for double taxation at death on some assets. For example, you are subject to Canada's deemed disposition tax at death on any RRSPs/RRIFs and real estate not considered your principal residence. In addition, you may be subject to estate and/or income taxes in the United States on the same assets.

Fortunately, there are provisions in the Canada-U.S. Tax Treaty that allow a credit against income, profits, and gains paid on American real estate or other appreciated assets as a credit for U.S. estate taxes even though the two taxes are different — an estate tax versus a capital gains/deemed disposition income tax. Until recently, it was unclear whether this provision of the treaty applied to the income tax on RRSPs/ RRIFs and other similar plans at the second spouse's death. A prominent Canada-U.S. estate planning attorney whom we work with raised this issue initially under Article XXVI of the treaty, where Competent Authority assistance can be sought when double taxation results. The U.S. Competent Authority, which consulted with the Canadian Competent Authority, and based on their ruling, agreed that a full tax credit is available for the tax paid on RRSPs/RRIFs against any U.S. estate taxes. The tax court conceded to the U.S. Competent Authority's decision.

However, you may not be out of the woods yet on the double taxation issue because the governments may still be able to double dip. You may still be subject to double income tax on your final IRS income tax return because you may not use the same Canadian income taxes twice against both your U.S. estate and income taxes owing on the RRSP/ RRIF. In addition, you may be subject to estate and/or income tax by the state in which the property is located because the treaty provisions and Competent Authority ruling don't apply. Furthermore, you may be subject to the provincial probate fees outlined earlier. There may also be "income in respect of the decedent" (IRD), depending on your circumstances. Needless to say, there are many gray areas that have yet to play out in tax court. One thing you can do for estate planning purposes in both Canada and the United States is review the beneficiaries on your IRAs and other qualified plans in the United States — 401(k), 403(b), 457 plans, etc. — to ensure they pass according to your wishes or in some cases collapse them and move them to Canada (see Chapter 10). The other thing is to hire a competent, experienced Canada-U.S. estate planning attorney to draft your estate plan taking into account these assets in both Canada and the United States (contact us if you need a referral).

Of equal importance is the fact that the IRS doesn't recognize common-law or same-sex marriages in the U.S. estate tax system. These situations typically require additional sophisticated planning to ensure that your wishes are implemented and to mitigate wherever possible court costs, attorney fees, and taxes.

THE CANADIAN ESTATE PLAN

In Canada, wills are the primary tool used in governing your estate according to your wishes. In the United States, the taxation of living trusts is common because they are "flow-through" entities taxed at your personal rates. This makes them much more popular and effective as an estate planning tool in the United States. However, in Canada, trusts are taxed as a separate entity and are subject to the punishing Canadian trust tax rates (see below). Although Canadians can use trusts for tax and estate planning purposes, the primary use of trusts in Canadian estate planning is accomplished through testamentary trusts created at death in your will.

LAST WILL

A last will and testament provides instructions to the person of your choice (your executor/executrix or personal representative) on what to do with your financial affairs in the event of your death. Your Canadian will simply replaces your "pour-over" will, which is part of most U.S. trust-centered estate plans. If you have children but they are all U.S. residents, making them the executors of your Canadian will adds complexities and potential delays in the settling of your affairs. Likewise, if you have beneficiaries and assets in both Canada and the United States, they can add complexities and potential delays. Ensure that you get the appropriate counseling when considering the executor of your will and which assets should be distributed to which heirs. Simply saying "I want everything divided equally between my heirs" usually isn't the best approach to settling your estate. We generally recommend that your executor be a person you trust who is located near you in Canada to streamline the settlement of your estate.

Many people have asked us if their American wills are valid in Canada. To be valid in a Canadian probate court, your will simply needs to be presented and be properly signed and witnessed. However, if the provisions in your will are unclear, missing, or violate Canadian law, it may be valid, but the provisions may not be executable in Canada. For example, there are differences in domestic law in who takes custody of your children or in disinheriting heirs. Another roadblock is not being able to find the witnesses to your will to validate their signatures, rendering the will invalid. Furthermore, despite popular opinion, a will does not avoid probate (which means "to prove") and thus is more easily challenged by ex-spouses or children from a previous marriage, even if they are in the United States. As long as they can create doubt that your intentions were not as articulated in your will, they can cause long delays in court, and your estate will incur thousands in legal fees to sort it out. During this time period, accounts can be frozen, leaving heirs struggling to meet daily living expenses. In Canada-U.S. situations, you can have double the problems because you may have to settle American "situs" assets, such as a winter home in the United States, in the U.S. probate court first before going through probate in Canada on the same property.

A better question to ask is "What mayhem will I cause in my estate planning by having two wills in different countries?" If you have an American will and a Canadian will with similar provisions (e.g., paying burial fees), you can cause confusion because there can be debate about whether those fees should be paid out of the American or the Canadian portion of your estate. Likewise, there can be conflicting provisions if both wills address real estate but have different dispositive provisions. Proving your U.S. will as valid in a Canadian probate court can become expensive and be ineffective in the end. This all gets very tricky, very quickly, and can have disastrous effects on your estate plan if not drafted in a coordinated fashion.

GENERAL POWER OF ATTORNEY

This document outlines your wishes in managing your financial affairs in the event of your incapacity and gives the person of your choice (your agent or attorney-in-fact) the power to implement your wishes. Such powers may include the ability to pay your bills, vote on corporate stocks, file your tax returns, open your mail, care for your pets, conduct routine banking, converse with your financial or legal advisors, and so on when you are unable to do so. These documents are not as common in Canada as in the United States, but that doesn't diminish their importance. Given that these documents are unique to each province, we typically recommend that your state POAs be replaced with properly drafted documents in your province of domicile. Moreover, your chances of creating conflict in your estate planning increase when you have two valid POAs in two different countries. That being said, if you still have assets in the United States that you own on a sole and separate basis, you should have a POA drafted in the state where your asset is located specifically governing that asset.

HEALTH-CARE DIRECTIVES

Typically, these documents include your living will, health-care, and mental power of attorney documents. Your living will outlines your wishes regarding your health care to physicians and other health-care workers, your family, and the courts in the event you are unable to communicate such wishes because you are brain dead, unconscious, under the influence of analgesics, or terminally ill. This document provides as much or as little control over how far you want life-prolonging procedures to go, specifies which medical procedures you want administered in which circumstances, and alleviates your loved ones from having to make these difficult decisions in such tragic circumstances.

A health-care/mental power of attorney gives the person of your choice (your agent or attorney-in-fact) the power to implement your health-care wishes as outlined. If you go to Canada with U.S. health-care directives, you should have them replaced with documents suited to your province of domicile. Again, each province has its own rules surrounding your POAs, but they are vital in allowing you to control your health care even when you are mentally incapacitated.

ESTATE PLAN IMPLEMENTATION

As mentioned earlier, getting the estate plan documents drafted and executed is only the beginning. You must implement your estate plan properly if your wishes are to be followed. Unfortunately, a spouse doesn't automatically have the legal authority to undertake these actions on behalf of the incapacitated spouse on his or her solely named account (this is where proper implementation of your estate plan is important). You must file your wills where they can be found, and unless you carry your POAs in your back pocket wherever you go, filing them with a digital retrieval service is recommended. This is important so they are available as necessary for any medical staff to implement your wishes at the time they are needed.

There are a few things to consider in the "titling" of your assets. In Canada, there are several ways to hold property, including sole ownership, joint tenancy, and tenancy in common. How your assets are titled can have an effect on your estate plan because, with certain titling, your assets pass by law versus your estate plan. For example, if you name a beneficiary on your RRSP, it passes automatically to that beneficiary at the RRSP owner's death. For your spouse, the RRSP automatically continues its tax deferral. For other heirs, you can be assured they will receive those funds but the full amount of the RRSP is deemed disposed of on the decedent's final tax return. For IRAs in the United States, it may make sense to name a U.S. beneficiary because he or she can inherit the IRA and eliminate any Canadian taxation of any required distributions from the IRA. If your IRA is left to a Canadian beneficiary, your heirs are eligible to continue any required minimum distributions but they will be subject to Canadian taxation. If minimum distributions have not been started, you can transfer the IRA balance to the beneficiaries on the IRA and then they report the income on their return as they receive it.

GIFTING

Most Americans living in Canada are unaware that the rules surrounding gifting in the United States follow them to Canada. Canadians can gift cash or assets to spouses, children, or others with no gift tax repercussions because that form of tax doesn't exist in Canada. There are other Canadian tax rules, such as the income tax "attribution rules," when gifting to spouses or children in lower tax brackets and the deemed disposition when gifting to a trust (see Chapter 5). You should familiarize yourself with the information below before arbitrarily making any gifts once a tax resident in Canada.

GIFTING TO A NON-CITIZEN SPOUSE

If you are an American citizen living in Canada and your spouse isn't an American citizen, specific IRS gifting rules apply. American citizen spouses have an "unlimited" gifting exemption between them, which means that, during their lifetimes, they can transfer assets back and forth between themselves with no gift tax consequences. However, for gifts subject to U.S. gift tax involving non-American citizen spouses, there is an annual limit of $147,000 in 2015 (adjusted for inflation), as outlined below.

$147,000
Non-citizen spouse ⟷ Non-citizen spouse
Unlimited
U.S. citizen ⟵ Non-citizen spouse
$147,000
U.S. citizen ⟶ Non-citizen spouse

If this limit is exceeded, the IRS has again kindly provided for your convenience Form 709 — United States Gift (and Generation-Skipping Transfer) Tax Return, and you end up using some of your lifetime exemption or paying an attorney to devise other legal means of remaining in compliance. These gifts can occur very innocently, so care must be taken in coordinating the transfer of assets from the United States to Canada. For example, if you sell a home in the United States titled in the name of the American citizen and deposit the funds in a joint account in Canada, you may just have made a gift.

GIFTING TO OTHERS

As mentioned previously, the IRS also has a gift tax that many Americans living in Canada forget about. American citizens are able to gift up to U$14,000 to any one person annually in 2015 (indexed annually for inflation but in $500 increments). Any gifts in excess of this amount require taxes to be paid or a portion of your $5.43 million lifetime gift exemption to be used up (e.g., giving an automobile) as filed on Form 709. The reason behind the gift tax is to prevent American citizens with large worldwide estates from giving away everything during their lifetimes or on their deathbeds to avoid estate taxes. The gift tax often catches many by surprise because of interest-free loans they may have given to children or associates. You need to determine up front if it is a gift or loan. If it's a gift, it must be below the annual exemption, or Form 709 must be filed. If it's a loan, the IRS deems an "imputed interest rate" to the lender at prevailing interest rates required on any amount lent. This must be realized as "phantom income" on your tax return even if no cash is received (interest is gifted to the child using the annual exemption). If the interest exceeds U$14,000 annually in 2014, a gift tax return has to be filed to pay the gift tax or "split" the gift with your spouse. One final point: the gift is not considered income to the recipient, so you don't have to worry about handing a big income tax bill along with your gift.

RECEIVING AN INHERITANCE OR GIFT

We have received countless calls and emails from people desperately thinking that they would lose the inheritance they just received from a Canadian or American relative due to U.S. income or estate/gift taxes. Nothing could be further from the truth. A gift or an inheritance is exactly that; it isn't "earned income," so it is exempt from American and Canadian income tax when given to you. Furthermore, as long as the requisite deemed disposition taxes were paid in Canada when the estate was settled, and the requisite estate taxes were paid in the United States, the inheritance should pass to you free of any Canadian or American death taxes. However, there is one caveat: you should understand the impact of taking possession of the inheritance or gift on your own estate at your passing away, particularly as an American in Canada. Otherwise, you may want to disclaim any inherited amounts to keep them out of your estate. You'll also need to report the inheritance or gift to the IRS on Form 3520 — Annual Return to Report Transactions with Foreign Trusts and Receipt of Certain Foreign Gifts if the gift or inheritance exceeds $100,000. Note that this is not a taxable event but simply a reporting requirement of the IRS. Depending on your situation, there are strategies that can be employed using trusts, disclaimers, or other techniques to ensure that the inheritance is kept out of your estate.

TAXATION OF TRUSTS

A living trust generally owns your assets and provides instructions to the person(s) of your choice (your trustee) on how to handle your financial affairs in the event of your death or incapacity. There are three key roles for any living trust:

1. the grantor puts the assets into the trust (also known as the settlor, trustor, or trust maker);

2. the trustee governs the trust and manages the assets the trust owns; and

3. the beneficiary receives the income and assets from the trust as dictated by the terms of the trust.

When you are alive, you generally occupy all three roles in your own revocable living trust because you put the assets into the trust, you manage them, and any income or distributions from the trust go to you. Difficulties start to arise when each of these roles is located in a different country. For example, when the trustee of a U.S. trust becomes a resident of Canada, the trust also moves to Canada (the trust "situs" moves as well). Now the trust becomes a tax resident for Canadian tax purposes and may become a foreign trust for American tax purposes. Ensure that you get appropriate counseling to understand the implications of having a Canadian trustee, American beneficiaries, and U.S. assets as things get complex. Generally, we recommend that you have your contingent trustee in Canada as well, if possible, to streamline the settlement of your estate.

With this backdrop, the following will allow you to familiarize yourself with the differences in the taxation of trusts between Canada and the United States. In the United States, the taxation of a trust depends a lot on whether the trust is revocable (changeable) or irrevocable (not changeable). If it's revocable, it is simply a "flow-through" entity and taxed at personal marginal income tax rates on your personal return, no separate trust tax return is filed. If it's irrevocable, it is a stand-alone entity that must obtain its own Employer Identification Number (EIN) and usually is required to file Form 1041 — U.S. Income Tax Return for Estates and Trusts. Trusts are subject to the following tax rates (see Table 7.5), except qualified dividends and long-term capital gains, which are taxed at a flat 15%. Furthermore, there are no tax consequences for assets moved into, or out of, a revocable living trust, and in some cases they could last indefinitely. However, the 3.8% NIIT applies.

TABLE 7.5

2015 U.S. TRUST TAX RATES

Taxable Income (U$)	Rate
0–2,500	15%
2,501–5,900	25%
5,901–9,050	28%
9,051–12,300	33%
12,301 +	39.6%

In Canada, trusts are always taxed as stand-alone entities whether you are alive or not. Each trust has its own trust account number and is required to file a T3 trust tax return. If the trust income is retained within the trust, the taxation is simple: all of it is taxed at the highest marginal rate (29% federal plus that of your province, which can total up to 48% +). If the trust income is distributed to its beneficiaries, it is declared on the beneficiaries' tax returns and is subject to their marginal Canadian income tax rates. Moreover, there is a deemed disposition if you move assets into, or out of, a Canadian trust, which means there will be an early collection of capital gains tax for appreciated assets. Like the IRS filing requirements of Forms 3520 and 3520-A for American residents who have an interest in or receive distributions from a foreign trust, if you are a Canadian resident who has an interest in or receives distributions from a U.S. trust, you may have a Canadian tax filing and disclosure requirement as well. CRA Form T1141 — Information Return in Respect of Transfers or Loans to a Non-Resident Trust and Form T1142 — Information Return in Respect of Distributions from and Indebtedness to a Non-Resident Trust will need to be filed as well. Finally, the use of trusts is hampered by the Canadian 21-year rule that states the trust ceases to exist after 21 years, all of the assets are distributed, and the requisite taxes are paid at that time.

Despite their complexity, the use of trusts in American departure and Canadian pre-entry planning may be beneficial and, depending on your circumstances, can produce great income, estate, and gift tax savings. It is a complex procedure and should be undertaken only by attorneys and advisors well versed in Canada-U.S. estate planning.

REAL-LIFE EXAMPLE

We received a desperate call from a woman in California who was the sole trustee on her mentally incapacitated mother's Revocable Living Trust. The investment advisor for the account told her to move the account within 90 days, or it would be frozen (see Chapter 10 for a continuation of this example). Since we are registered to manage investments in both Canada and the U.S., she contacted us to provide help. The problem arose because the trustee had a sibling in Canada who disputed the management of the trust and took the sister/trustee to court. In the process, the Canadian resident sibling was appointed as a co-trustee on the mother's trust at the suggestion of the attorneys to provide further oversight. A red flag immediately went up for me as the attorneys on both sides of the dispute likely had no idea they perhaps had just made this trust taxable in Canada as well, which would have had some very negative tax and compliance consequences for the mother, who needed these funds to sustain her! When a resident of Canada is placed as a trustee on a U.S. trust, the trust tax residency generally comes to Canada as well, which means the trust is now a foreign trust for IRS purposes. After reviewing the details and fact pattern with our network of professionals, by sheer luck the attorneys avoided having this trust become taxable in Canada, because the trust likely did not meet the Canadian trust residency rules of where "mind and management" of the trust still take place. However, if the U.S. trustee decides to resign because she can't co-manage the trust with her sibling, or she becomes an angel, mind and management will move to Canada, and the trust will be subject to the punitive Canadian trust tax rates and the cumbersome IRS foreign trust rules. This will result in higher taxes and professional fees, leaving fewer funds for the mother's care.

YOUR U.S. ESTATE PLAN

In light of the discussion above, good planning can save you a myriad of taxes and headaches while living or moving to Canada. For example, it may be best if you unwind your U.S. revocable living trust prior to taking up tax residency in Canada to avoid the punishing trust tax rates outlined above. This is counterintuitive because, in the United States, you are told to fund your trust. However, before becoming a tax resident of Canada, it may make sense to take everything out of your trust and wind it up. On the other hand, if you have assets remaining in the United States (e.g., a winter home), it may make sense to leave them in your trust to avoid probate in Canada and the United States and to ease the transfer of these assets, particularly to American beneficiaries. And, if you have heirs or charities in the United States, you may want to use your U.S. estate planning to leave your American assets to them. As you can see, it depends a lot on your individual financial situation and what you are trying to achieve. Our companion book, *The Canadian in America*, deals in much greater detail with the issue of owning real estate remaining in the United States when you live in Canada.

REAL-LIFE EXAMPLE

We received a call from an executive transferred up to Canada to head up the Canadian arm of an international company. His tax returns had just been prepared by his Canadian accountant, and he owed tens of thousands of dollars in Canadian taxes. He and his wife were U.S. citizens living in Canada, and just prior to their move their U.S. estate planning attorney had suggested they come in to update their Revocable Living Trust and ensure it was fully funded before migrating to Canada. He launched into his new career in January, and his trust with its $2.5M taxable portfolio remained intact for the entire year, until his tax return was prepared. When the Canadian CPA received all of the 1099s in the name of the client's trust, he prepared a T3 trust tax return instead of a T1 individual return. With both co-trustees moving to Canada, the taxation of the trust moved to Canada as well, and, since none of the income was distributed to them for their use, it was all taxable at the Ontario tax rate of over 49%!

FINANCIAL 8 FREEDOM

And I'll say to myself, "You have plenty of
good things laid up for many years.
Take life easy; eat, drink and be merry."
— LUKE 12:19

In our firm, we use the term "independence planning" in place of the more common term "retirement planning" because of the connotations associated with the term "retirement." We are all saving so we can become financially independent, but the question becomes "Independent to do what?" Retirement is often thought of as stopping work and pursuing an unscheduled life of whatever your heart desires that day. In our experience working with many clients, this generally becomes mundane quickly, and people start looking for more purpose in life, and for ways to stay engaged. In fact, we view retirement not as the closing of a book but as a turning of the page to a new chapter in life. Fortunately, that chapter is blank, and we encourage you to write it so that it is exciting, vibrant, and energizing for years to come.

A big part of our transition process is aimed at determining when you might become independent of work and helping you to understand what you want to do for the balance of your life. This approach creates excitement about the future and enables you to sacrifice now in order to achieve the goals you have set for your future. For you to gain these insights, any transition planning firm should spend ample time understanding what your current and future lifestyle looks like and then determining the cost of that lifestyle on an inflation-adjusted basis over your life expectancy. These financial projections should incorporate the various sources of income you have, make a number of conservative assumptions, add the volatility of returns in financial markets, and then determine how your unique financial situation projects into the future once you are residing in Canada. From there, you can begin to make these critical decisions based on numerical insights, not on opinions, conjecture, or notions.

In the United States, the primary vehicle used to become financially independent is the 401(k) plan. It is one of several major savings vehicles made available by Congress over the years and, with the ever-increasing contribution amounts, sends a clear message that people need to be responsible for saving for their future. 401(k) plans — as well as 403(b) and 457 plans — allow American taxpayers to contribute up to U$18,000 in 2015 for those under the age of 50 and an additional U$6,000 for a total of U$24,000 for those 50 or over. Other additional savings alternatives include IRAs and Roth IRAs, which allow U$5,500 in contributions in 2015 plus another U$1,000 for those over 50 for a total of U$6,500. The questions we are asked most often are "How do we save for our future in Canada?" and "Will we still qualify for some form of American government or company pension when we are living in Canada?" These questions can be perplexing because you may have short earning histories in both Canada and the United States because of your move, which may mean you don't meet the minimum work history in either country to qualify for any government benefits. Once again, proper transition planning can set you on a course that will maximize your benefits because you lived in both countries. Following are some of the independence planning issues you should consider in making your move to Canada.

REGISTERED RETIREMENT SAVINGS PLANS

In Canada, the primary vehicle used to become financially independent is the Registered Retirement Savings Plan (RRSP). Unfortunately, this is the last major savings vehicle left in Canada. It allows Canadian taxpayers to contribute up to 18% of their past tax year's salaries up to the following maximum deduction on the Canadian tax return (see Table 8.1).

TABLE 8.1
MAXIMUM RRSP DEDUCTION

Year	Contribution (C$)
2015	24,930
2016+	Indexed

For 2015, 18% of last year's salary up to a maximum amount of $24,930 (for those earning a salary of C$138,500+) can be contributed to your group or self-directed RRSP. However, if you are making the transition to Canada and want to make an RRSP contribution right away, you'll be unable to because you don't have any salary in the previous year on which to base the 18%. Your current year contribution is calculated as 18% x C$0 salary = C$0 RRSP "room" for the year you enter Canada, so you need to prepare yourself for the fact that you won't have any tax deductible savings vehicle in your first year unless you contribute to a registered plan through your employer (see below). However, here is a planning tip. If you are returning to Canada and have employment income there in the past, you may have RRSP "room" carried over from other years, allowing you to claim a deduction for your RRSP contributions. You will need to contact CRA to get the information or look at your last Notice of Assessment from CRA when you left Canada. Alternatively, you can make the maximum contribution to a U.S. plan before you leave, but be sure you understand the implications of doing so beforehand (see later in this chapter).

Canadian RRSPs have a couple of distinct advantages over IRAs and 401(k) plans in the United States. First, if you don't make your IRA contribution before April 15th of the following year or your 401(k) contribution withheld from your paycheck before December 31st of the current year, those contribution opportunities are gone forever. With RRSPs, any unused contribution room is rolled over indefinitely. This opens up some planning opportunities as you can forgo your RRSP contribution in lower-income years and accumulate it for a high-income year. Then you can make the entire RRSP contribution, plus any rolled-over amounts, in that year and take a large tax deduction. Even more interesting is that CRA permits your RRSP contribution to be made in cash or with other investments/securities! You should understand the tax implications of contributing securities as an RRSP contribution, but it is one way to ensure you get the full deduction of your accumulated RRSP room when you don't have the cash to do so. Contributions to qualified plans in the U.S. must be cash. You are allowed to contribute up to C$2,000 over your allowed RRSP room as well without penalty, but you won't get a tax deduction for it. However, it may still make sense because you have C$2,000 more that can grow tax deferred. The downside is that any growth distributed is taxed as ordinary income versus the more favorably taxed capital gains or dividends. The fact that you won't lose any RRSP contribution opportunities is a real benefit over U.S. qualified plans.

Second, another planning strategy for your RRSP is a spousal RRSP. Since you file separate tax returns in Canada, the higher-earning spouse can end up paying significantly more tax than a stay-at-home spouse, particularly in your golden years. Where possible, you want to split your income so you take "two runs up the tax ladder" rather than one big one. To that end, the spouse who is expected to have the higher income in your retirement years will be the one with the larger RRSP, subjecting more to taxation. With a spousal RRSP, the earning spouse can contribute to the spousal RRSP (like a Canadian only tax resident) and still take the tax deduction, but when the funds are withdrawn they are taxed on the lower-income spouse's return (and avoid taxation in the U.S.) Note that you can defer withdrawals in your RRSP until age 71 (versus age 70½ for an IRA) before you need to convert your RRSP to a Registered Retirement Income Fund (RRIF) and commence minimum withdrawals annually (see later in this chapter).

One note of caution: if you are an American citizen or green card holder living in Canada and still filing U.S. tax returns, you need to understand that the IRS doesn't automatically recognize the tax-deferred status of your RRSP in the United States that CRA does. Furthermore, RRSP contributions are fully deductible in Canada, but you need to ensure that you understand their deductibility on your U.S. return. The new Fifth Protocol of the Canada-U.S. Tax Treaty now permits a deduction on your U.S. 1040 if you are contributing to a Canadian employer's group RRSP plan. See Chapter 5 for more details on the taxation of RRSPs, RRIFs, etc.

TAX-FREE SAVINGS ACCOUNTS

In 2009, the Canadian government created a new type of savings account called a TFSA, similar to a Roth IRA in the U.S. This account allows anyone over the age of 17 to contribute $5,500 in 2015 (indexed for inflation in $500 increments). There is no tax deduction in Canada or the U.S. for contributions to a TFSA, but the investment income earned in the TFSA is tax free (versus tax deferred) on your Canadian return (see Chapter 5 for the taxation of TFSAs in the U.S.). If you cannot make a contribution in one year, your contribution "room" is carried forward and accumulates. A contribution to a TFSA is in addition to any RRSP or pension plan contributions. There are no income limitations or earned income requirements to contribute to a TFSA, and money can be given to a spouse to contribute to a TFSA as well.

Withdrawals from a TFSA can occur anytime and are tax and penalty free, including the earnings. Even better, a withdrawal is first attributed to your contributions, and as a result the withdrawal is added back to your TFSA contribution room and rolled forward. If you want to recontribute that amount to your TFSA in a future year, you can do so. The big problem with TFSAs, if you still file a U.S. tax return, is they are considered fully taxable in the U.S., so you should plan this carefully (see Chapter 5 for more details).

MONEY PURCHASE REGISTERED PENSION PLANS

Another savings alternative is a Money Purchase Registered Pension Plan (RPP) available through your employer, similar to the 401(k) plan in the United States. RPPs allow the following maximum contributions (see Table 8.2).

TABLE 8.2

MAXIMUM RPP CONTRIBUTION

Year	Contribution (C$)
2015	25,370
2016	Indexed

Any contributions you, or your employer, make to an RPP reduces the amount you can contribute to an RRSP because doing so creates a "pension adjustment" that reduces your RRSP room (you don't get both). Any pension contributions by you reduce the amount of RRSP room for that year because the Canadian government wants to cap the total amount of RRSP tax-deductible contributions at C$25,370. If you leave or retire from your employer, you don't have access to these funds. Your only choice is to roll them into a Locked-In Retirement Account (LIRA).

LOCKED-IN RETIREMENT ACCOUNTS

Most Americans will realize they are in another country if they find themselves with one of these accounts. LIRAs are exactly that, "locked-in," because the federal and provincial governments don't trust you to roll a LIRA into an RRSP and leave it there for your retirement. They feel the need to "help" you save for your future even though they don't provide any restrictions on how you invest them, and if it's a company like Enron you could lose all of your funds anyway. We have seen hardship caused by these rules because retirees aren't able to access any of these funds when they need them to fund their retirement lifestyle. This is particularly true for those who don't have other sources of income. We are working with a client who spent his entire life working in Canada and was fortunate to retire early from a firm "downsizing." He had put some funds away into an RRSP, but the bulk of his wealth was in his RPP. His only choice at retirement was to roll over C$1 million into a LIRA and wait until he reached the eligible age to begin withdrawals. In the meantime, he was healthy and wanted to travel, golf, and enjoy his golden years with his wife, but they were restricted by their lack of cash flow.

LIRA accounts have caused all kinds of hardship for retirees in Canada, and a movement has progressed across Canada to change these rules to add more flexibility in accessing these funds in retirement. Universally, the federal government and all provinces will permit you to access your LIRA if you have shortened life expectancy, financial hardship, or just a small amount in your LIRA (generally $10,000 for those under age 65 and $20,000 for those 65 and older). For everyone else, there are limits on how much you can get access to at any one time. Here is a summary of the rules for unlocking LIRAs in provinces where they exist for residents of Canada.

Alberta — If you are 50 or older, you can make a one-time withdrawal of up to 50% of the value of your LIRA. To avoid taxation on the withdrawal, you can transfer those funds to an RRSP. If the remaining balance in the LIRA is small enough, you may be able to collapse the entire account.

British Columbia — No unlocking exemptions exist except for shortened life expectancy and small amounts.

Manitoba — If you are 55 or older, you can make a one-time withdrawal of up to 50% of the value of your LIRA and roll it into an RRSP.

New Brunswick — If you are 55 or older, you can unlock up to three times the maximum annual withdrawal amount for a Life Income Fund (LIF — annuitized LIRA) up to 25% of the value in the account.

Newfoundland and Labrador — No unlocking exemptions exist except for shortened life expectancy and small amounts.

Nova Scotia — No unlocking exemptions exist except for shortened life expectancy and small amounts.

Ontario — When you roll your LIRA into a LIF, you have 60 days to make a one-time withdrawal of up to 50% of the value of your LIRA and roll it into an RRSP at any time.

Quebec — No unlocking exemptions exist except for shortened life expectancy and small amounts.

Saskatchewan — If you are 55 or older, with your spouse's consent, you can roll the entire balance of your LIRA into a RRIF, but you must designate your spouse as the beneficiary.

Federal plans — If you are 55 or older, you can make a one-time withdrawal of up to 50% of the value of your LIRA and roll it into an RRSP.

If you decide to return to the U.S. and become a non-resident of Canada, you can generally unlock the entire amount of your LIRA (see our companion book *The Canadian in America* for more details).

DEFERRED PROFIT SHARING PLAN

A less common plan is the Deferred Profit Sharing Plan (DPSP). It is offered by some employers to supplement an RPP or group RRSP. Only the employer contributes to the plan based on a certain percentage or fixed dollar amount of the profits the firm generates, up to a maximum of C$12,685 in 2015. The funds go into an account in your name and aren't taxed until they are withdrawn. Similar to your RPP or group RRSP, any contributions create a pension adjustment that reduces your RRSP room for that year. DPSPs generally have a vesting period of two years or so, depending on your employer. However, once you are vested, you have access to these funds and can withdraw them as necessary. You will pay tax on any amounts withdrawn, but you won't pay the 10% early withdrawal penalties as you would in the United States.

CANADA PENSION PLAN/QUEBEC PENSION PLAN/OLD AGE SECURITY

In Canada, there are two government pension plans similar to Social Security in the United States: the Canada Pension Plan (CPP), or Quebec Pension Plan (QPP) if you reside in Quebec, and Old Age Security (OAS). By moving to Canada, you'll be eligible to collect these two pensions, which we discuss in more detail below. For the details surrounding the taxation of these government pensions, see Chapter 5.

QUALIFYING FOR CPP/QPP

When you enter Canada and begin working, you'll make payroll contributions to CPP and Employment Insurance (see Chapter 5 for more details). If you make at least one contribution to the system, you qualify for a CPP/QPP benefit as early as age 60, with full benefits payable at age 65. You can obtain an estimate of your future CPP/QPP benefit by asking the Social Development Canada branch in your province of residence for a statement (1-800-277-9914) or creating a My Service Canada Account (servicecanada.gc.ca/eng/online/mysca.shtml) and obtaining your Statement of Contributions to ensure all of your earnings are captured. In 2015, the maximum CPP payment you can receive is C$1,038.33 per month (C$12,459.96 annually) at age 65 (adjusted every January for the CPI). Unlike Social Security, however, there is no spousal benefit for the non-contributing spouse. However, because you file separate tax returns in Canada, CRA gives you the choice to split your CPP/QPP (and company pensions) between spouses so that the higher-income (working) spouse can pay less tax. You do this when you file for your benefits, and as long as you are both over the age of 60 you can split your CPP between your returns.

Determining when to collect your benefits can be tricky now that new rules have been brought in to increase the penalty if you collect before age 65, but you get a retirement "credit" if you delay collecting until after age 65. If you collect your CPP early (at age 60), it is reduced by 0.58% per month in 2015 and will reach the maximum of 0.60% per month in 2016. Full retirement age is 65, so you will end up with a 34.8% reduction in your benefits if you collect early in 2015, and 36% in 2016. However, you no longer have to stop working to begin collecting. There is also a retirement credit added to your benefits if you delay taking CPP after age 65. For each month you delay payment, your benefit will increase by 0.70% per month (that's 8.4% per year!). This means that, if you wait until age 70 to collect CPP, you will receive 42% more than if you collect it at age 65. You can see the Canadian government is trying to incent people to wait on collecting CPP by penalizing them 36% if you collect early but rewarding them 42% if they wait. As a result, if you don't need the money and have longevity in your family tree, it may be worthwhile to wait before collecting. Either way, it is worthwhile having a financial advisor run some numbers with an understanding of your other sources of income to determine the best age to maximize your CPP benefits.

One interesting twist for Americans in Canada is that each spouse has to qualify for CPP on his or her own record. There is no automatic spousal benefit like Social Security in the United States (see below). However, if you work after collecting CPP, you no longer have to pay any CPP premiums after age 65 if you elect not to. If you work after collecting Social Security, you still have to pay into Social Security, but your benefit goes up as well.

QUALIFYING FOR OAS

Unlike CPP, OAS is based purely on the time you live in Canada, not whether you worked in Canada. To qualify for full OAS benefits at age 65 (no early collection), you must have lived in Canada for at least 40 years after reaching the age of 18. For example, if you move to Canada when you are 25, you will qualify for full OAS benefits at age 65. This means that both the working and the non-working spouse will qualify for a benefit. In 2015, the maximum OAS payment per person is approximately C$6,764.88 annually (adjusted quarterly for the CPI). But what happens if you make the transition to Canada and don't live there for 40 years before age 65? You still qualify for partial OAS benefits, but you must have lived in Canada for at least 20 years after reaching the age of 18. If you have lived in Canada for less than 20 years after reaching the age of 18, the Canada-U.S. Social Security (Totalization) Agreement comes into play and qualifies you for partial benefits. For each year you lived in the United States, it counts as one year of eligibility toward OAS in Canada. Your benefits are based on the actual amount of time you have lived in Canada, but you are now eligible for some benefits instead of losing them altogether because you moved to Canada after the age of 18. There is a two-step process at work here: first, determining if you are eligible for any benefits at all; second, determining what your benefit amount is and using the Totalization Agreement as needed to maximize your benefits.

As with CPP, the government is providing incentives to collect OAS later in life to keep the system solvent. As a result, for each month you delay taking OAS after age 65, your benefit increases by 0.6% per month (that's 7.2% per year!). This means that, if you wait until age 70 to collect OAS, you will receive 36% more than if you collect it at age 65. Again, we recommend you sit down with someone who looks at your entire tax liability (remember the clawback), cash flow, and retirement situation to see if it makes sense to wait to collect OAS and CPP.

The Totalization Agreement is an executive agreement between the United States and Canada signed on August 1, 1984. An executive agreement is different from the Canada-U.S. Tax Treaty because it doesn't require the formal approval of U.S. Congress or Canadian Parliament. The purpose of the Totalization Agreement is to provide employers and employees with relief from double payroll taxes and to "totalize" the payroll taxes you pay in both Canada and the United States to receive partial benefits in both countries for which you may not otherwise qualify. The United States currently has totalization agreements with 17 other countries, while Canada has agreements with 42 other countries.

If you move to Canada for a period of time and then return to the United States, be aware of the difficulty in proving you lived in Canada to qualify for OAS. With CPP, the government has a record of how much you paid into the system and can calculate your benefits. OAS, however, doesn't require payment into the system — it is simply based on the amount of time you have lived in Canada. To keep people who don't qualify for OAS from defrauding the system, the proof of residency standards have increased. In one case, we had a stay-at-home mother who applied for benefits but couldn't prove she had lived in Canada. We helped her to gather some further documents so she would qualify. Some things you may want to consider using as proof include:

- your spouse's tax returns (if divorced) since they will have your name and SIN;
- old passports showing exit from and entry to Canada;
- driver's license records;
- utility bills/records that have your name on them; and
- property tax bills that have your name on them.

U.S. SOCIAL SECURITY

Many people have contacted us concerned that if they move to Canada they will lose their Social Security benefits. If you qualify for these benefits, you will receive them simply by applying for them no matter where you live in the world. In fact, the American government can deposit your Social Security benefits directly into your Canadian checking account if requested to do so. The exchange rates used are competitive, and the convenience is tough to beat. For the taxation of Social Security in Canada, see Chapter 5.

One of the political "hot potatoes" being juggled in the United States is what to do with Social Security. Based on the latest projections, the system is set to run out of money around 2042. However, some subtle changes have been made to extend the life of Social Security. Until 2001, the age when you could receive full retirement benefits was 65. Now the full retirement age is based on the year you were born, as outlined in Table 8.3.

TABLE 8.3

SOCIAL SECURITY FULL RETIREMENT AGE

Year of Birth	Full Retirement Age	% Benefits Reduced if Collected at Age 62
1937 or before	65	20.0
1938	65 and 2 months	20.8
1939	65 and 4 months	21.7
1940	65 and 6 months	22.5
1941	65 and 8 months	23.3
1942	65 and 10 months	24.2
1943 to 1954	66	25.0
1955	66 and 2 months	25.8
1956	66 and 4 months	26.7
1957	66 and 6 months	27.5
1958	66 and 8 months	28.3
1959	66 and 10 months	29.2
1960 or later	67	30.0

Your benefits are reduced by 5/9ths of 1% for each month you collect Social Security before your full retirement age. As the table above illustrates, extending the age to receive full benefits had the effect of penalizing folks in the year of birth by 30% if collected early. The general consensus is that both the Medicare and Social Security systems in the United States need significant change to make them sustainable for the next generation. In fact, Medicare has six times the deficit that Social Security does. As outlined in Chapter 2, Medicare Part B is a "means tested" premium (the more you make, the more you pay), and each year the premiums have gone up significantly for those who are means tested. We believe that a means tested Social Security benefit is on its way in the United States, similar to the OAS recovery tax ("the clawback") in Canada, where the more you make the less you'll get (discussed in Chapter 5). In addition, we expect the contributions into the system to be increased as well.

In making the transition to Canada, you may wonder if you are eligible for any U.S. Social Security benefits. The initial answer is "no" unless you establish the necessary "quarters of coverage" that make you eligible, which most folks have done. To qualify for Social Security retirement benefits, you must establish at least 40 quarters of eligibility in the United States. To establish four quarters of eligibility in 2015, you must earn income of U$4,880. If you earn the minimum income amount for at least 10 years, you'll establish the 40 quarters of eligibility and can begin collecting Social Security benefits.

The question is "What if I didn't establish the 40 quarters before I left?" This is where the Canada-U.S. Totalization Agreement can get you qualified for benefits provided you have at least six quarters of eligibility established in the United States. For each year you live in Canada, it counts as one year toward Social Security. Your benefits are still based on the amount you paid into the Social Security system, and this amount will be nominal given your short earning history in the United States. In 2015, the maximum Social Security payment you could receive is U$2,663 per month (U$31,956 annually). Since you are splitting your earning years between Canada and the United States, it's rare that you'll qualify for the maximum Social Security benefits. However, similar to CPP/QPP, if you pay into Social Security, you still receive some benefits.

In addition, Social Security offers a spousal benefit. If only one spouse qualifies for a Social Security pension benefit, the other spouse receives half of the spouse's pension benefit automatically (the reward for the stay-at-home parent) even if they are living in Canada. Some effective planning can be done with those moving to Canada whereby one spouse pays into the Social Security system and qualifies for benefits while the other spouse automatically qualifies for half of the amount without having contributed one nickel to the system. Further, there are various collection strategies you can employ depending on your spouse's benefit, your tax bracket, and your retirement situation to maximize your Social Security benefits. Again, we recommend you sit down with someone who looks at your entire tax liability (remember OAS and CPP), cash flow, and retirement situation to see if it makes sense to wait to collect your and/or your spouse's Social Security benefits.

WINDFALL ELIMINATION PROVISION

When it comes time to apply for your Social Security benefits, you may be surprised to find out that, because you are collecting CPP when living in Canada, your Social Security benefits will be reduced due to the "Windfall Elimination Provision" (WEP). This is a confusing set of rules that can affect your benefits, but it depends on your individual circumstances.

Here's how it works. To calculate your Social Security benefit, Social Security uses a percentage of your average earnings over the 35 years of highest earnings. Since some Americans living in Canada have a much shorter earning history in the United States, they qualify for a smaller Social Security benefit (because a number of their 35 years have zero as their earnings amount since they were working in Canada). Now here's the rub: the smaller your average earnings over your 35-year history, the more Social Security aims to replace those average earnings (the smaller your average earnings, the more Social Security benefits will replace them). Generally, lower-paid workers get a Social Security benefit that equals about 60% of their pre-retirement earnings, while the average replacement rate for highly paid workers is only about 28%. For example, the lowest-earning workers (up to U$9,000 per year) receive a Social Security benefit that equals 90% of pre-retirement-covered earnings, while the average replacement rate for the highest-earning workers (up to $95,000 per year) is about 25%. You, however, will have unusually low average earnings for Social Security purposes because you didn't contribute for most of the 35-year "look back" period, so you can see where the problem comes in. Why? Because you were working in Canada, contributing to CPP, and becoming qualified for CPP benefits. CPP aims to replace about 25% of pensionable earnings on which your contributions are based. Again, CPP will drop eight of your lowest years in calculating your average contributions. As a result, the Social Security Administration calls this a "windfall" that accounts for the fact you are getting full CPP benefits and are not entitled to the more generous Social Security benefits provided for those with lower average earnings over the 35-year period (some don't think this is fair treatment, but we have to disagree). The Social Security agent then declares the Windfall Elimination Provision and reduces your Social Security benefits to take this "rub" into account (see Figure 8.1).

However, before accepting the agent's declaration, there are a few things you should know to make sure the Windfall Elimination Provision is properly applied to your situation. First, the provision was written for U.S. federal government workers and some state workers (e.g., police officers) who did not have to contribute to the Social Security system (it was voluntary). Even though it was written for these folks, like it or not, the Social Security Administration has made it official policy, giving it broader application to those who work abroad. Second, the provision doesn't apply if you use the Canada-U.S. Totalization Agreement to qualify for either CPP or Social Security benefits. Section 215 of the Social Security Act contains this rule that is little known among front-line Social Security staff. In fact, for most agents, your application may be their first (and last) to take into account CPP benefits (but don't let them include OAS or any other company pensions!). You need to ensure the proper application of this rule to your situation, or you could find your benefits unnecessarily reduced. One way to ensure that the rules are being applied properly to your situation is to file for Social Security benefits using Form SSA-2490-BK — Application for Benefits under a U.S. International Social Security Agreement. This form will be routed through the Office of International Programs and ensure a higher level of processing. At this writing, the form wasn't available online, so you'll have to call the Social Security Administration or visit a local office to obtain a copy but we provide a copy in Figure 8.2. And third, if you fully qualify for CPP benefits in Canada and Social Security benefits in the United States, the Windfall Elimination Provision applies, and only your Social Security benefits will be reduced. Take heart, however; you still come out ahead of someone who qualifies in either the U.S. Social Security system or the Canada Pension Plan system because both systems aim to replace more of the lower earner's wages . . . another advantage for those moving between the countries.

FIGURE 8.1

HOW THE WEP RULES APPLY

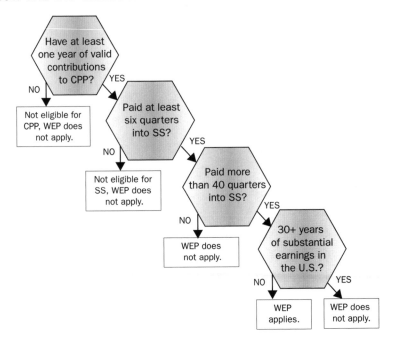

FIGURE 8.2

SOCIAL SECURITY ADMINISTRATION FORM SSA-2490-BK

SOCIAL SECURITY ADMINISTRATION

Form Approved
OMB No. 0960-0448

APPLICATION FOR BENEFITS UNDER A U.S.
INTERNATIONAL SOCIAL SECURITY AGREEMENT

(Do not write in this space)

If the worker is living, this application should be completed by or on behalf of the worker. If the worker is deceased, this application should be completed by one of the worker's survivors who is claiming benefits under the provisions of the international social security agreement.

PART I

Complete Part I in all cases.

1. (a) Print name of worker (First name, middle initial, last name)

   (b) U.S. Social Security Number

   — — — / — — / — — — —

2. Provide the following information about the worker's social security credits (coverage) and last place of residence in the foreign country.

   (a) Use columns (1) - (5) to enter information about the worker's periods of employment or self-employment in the foreign country. *(If additional space is required, enter the information in Remarks -- item 19.)*

(1) Dates Worked (From - To)	(2) Name and *Address of* employer or self-employment activity	(3) Type of Industry or business	(4) Social Insurance Number used while working	(5) Name of Agency to which contributions paid

   (b) Use columns (1) - (4) to enter information about the worker's periods of coverage under the foreign social insurance system which are not based on employment or self-employment (e.g., coverage for voluntary contributions, deemed or equivalent coverage, periods of military service, illness, etc.)

(1) Dates Covered (From - To)	(2) Type of coverage	(3) Social Insurance Number used for this coverage if different than shown in item 2(a)(4)	(4) Name of Agency to which contributions paid (if any)

   (c) Enter the worker's last place of residence in the foreign country:

   (City and State or Province)

PLEASE REMOVE PAGE 1 OF THIS FORM BEFORE COMPLETING THE REST OF THE APPLICATION. AFTER APPLICATION IS COMPLETED AND SIGNED, STAPLE DETACHED PAGE TO APPLICATION.

Form SSA-2490-BK (4-2004) EF (8-2006) (Formerly SSA-2490-F4)
Destroy Prior Editions   Page 1

SOCIAL SECURITY ADMINISTRATION FORM SSA-2490-BK

Form Approved
OMB No. 0960-0448

APPLICATION FOR BENEFITS UNDER A U.S.
INTERNATIONAL SOCIAL SECURITY AGREEMENT

(Do not write in this space)

If the worker is living, this application should be completed by or on behalf of the worker. If the worker is deceased, this application should be completed by one of the worker's survivors who is claiming benefits under the provisions of the international social security agreement.

PART I

Complete Part I in all cases.

1. (a) Print name of worker (First name, middle initial, last name)

   (b) U.S. Social Security Number

   _ _ _ / _ _ / _ _ _ _

2. Provide the following information about the worker's social security credits (coverage) and last place of residence in the foreign country.

   (a) Use columns (1) - (5) to enter information about the worker's periods of employment or self-employment in the foreign country. *(If additional space is required, enter the information in Remarks -- item 19.)*

(1) Dates Worked (From - To)	(2) Name and Address of employer or self-employment activity	(3) Type of Industry or business	(4) Social Insurance Number used while working	(5) Name of Agency to which contributions paid

   (b) Use columns (1) - (4) to enter information about the worker's periods of coverage under the foreign social insurance system which are not based on employment or self-employment (e.g., coverage for voluntary contributions, deemed or equivalent coverage, periods of military service, illness, etc.)

(1) Dates Covered (From - To)	(2) Type of coverage	(3) Social Insurance Number used for this coverage if different than shown in item 2(a)(4)	(4) Name of Agency to which contributions paid (if any)

   (c) Enter the worker's last place of residence in the foreign country:

   (City and State or Province)

SOCIAL SECURITY ADMINISTRATION FORM SSA-2490-BK

3.	I apply for all benefits for which I am eligible under the provisions of the social security agreement between the United States and ⟶	Name of country

4. This application may be used to claim benefits from the U.S. and/or the foreign country shown in item 3. Check (X) the block(s) indicating the type of benefit(s) for which you are applying under the country(ies) from which you are claiming the benefit(s).

BENEFIT CLAIMED FROM FOREIGN COUNTRY

Type of Benefit Claimed From Foreign Country:

☐ Retirement/Old-Age   ☐ Survivors   ☐ None

☐ Disability or Sickness/Invalidity   ☐ Other (Specify) _____

BENEFIT CLAIMED FROM THE UNITED STATES

(a) Are you presently receiving benefits from the United States? ⟶	☐ Yes *(If "Yes" answer (b) below.)*	☐ No *(If "No" answer (c) below.)*
(b) If you are already receiving U.S. benefits, do you wish to file for a different type of U.S. benefit? ⟶	☐ Yes *(If "Yes" answer (d) below.)*	☐ No *(If "No" go on to item 5.)*
(c) If you are not presently receiving U.S. benefits, do you wish to file for U.S. benefits at this time? ⟶	☐ Yes *(If "Yes" answer (d) below.)*	☐ No *(If "No" go on to item 5.)*

(d) Indicate the type of benefit you wish to claim from the United States:

☐ Retirement   ☐ Disability   ☐ Survivors

INFORMATION ABOUT THE WORKER

5. (a) Print worker's name at birth, if different from item 1(a)

(b) Check (X) one for the worker ☐ Male ☐ Female	(c) Enter worker's social insurance number in the foreign country if different than shown in items 2(a)(4) or 2(b)(3)

(d) If the worker's Social Security number in either the United States or the foreign country is not known, enter the worker's parents' names:

Mother's name (First name, middle initial, last name, maiden name)

Father's name (First name, middle initial, last name)

(e) Enter the worker's citizenship (Enter name of country)

6.	Do you want this application to protect an eligible spouse's and/or child's right to Social Security benefits? ⟶	☐ Yes	☐ No

7.	(a) Was the worker or any other person claiming benefits on this application a refugee or stateless person at any time?	☐ Yes *(If "Yes" answer (b) below.)*	☐ No *(If "No" go on to item 8.)*

(b) If "Yes" enter the following information about the person:

Name	Dates of refugee or stateless status

Form **SSA-2490-BK** (4-2004)   EF (8-2006)   Page 3

SOCIAL SECURITY ADMINISTRATION FORM SSA-2490-BK

PART II

Complete Part II ONLY if you are claiming benefits from a foreign country.

8. If you are applying for sickness or disability/invalidity benefits, enter the date you became disabled. Otherwise enter "N/A."	Date *(Month, day , year)*

9. (a) If you are applying for retirement/old-age benefits, have you stopped or do you plan to stop working?	☐ Yes *(If "Yes" answer (b) below.)* ☐ No *(If "No" go on to item 10.)*
(b) If "Yes," enter the date you stopped or plan to stop working.	Date *(Month, day , year)*

10. (a) Are you applying for foreign social security benefits under a special system that covers a specific occupation (e.g., miners, seamen, farmers)?	☐ Yes *(If "Yes" answer (b) and (c) below.)* ☐ No *(If "No" go on to item 11.)*
(b) What was your occupation in the foreign country?	
(c) Did you perform the same type of work in the U.S?	☐ Yes ☐ No

INFORMATION ABOUT THE APPLICANT

Complete item 11 ONLY if you are not the worker. If you are the worker, leave this question blank and go on to item 12.

11. (a) Print your name (First name, middle initial, last name, maiden name)	(b) What is your relationship to the worker?
(c) Enter your U.S. Social Security number	(d) Enter your social insurance number in the foreign country *(if none or unknown, so indicate)*

ADDITIONAL INFORMATION ABOUT THE WORKER

12. (a) Enter worker's date of birth (Month, day, year)	(b) Enter worker's place of birth *(City, state, province, country)*

13. If the worker is deceased, enter the date and place of death	(a) Date (Month, day, year)	(b) Place *(City, state, province, country)*

14. (a) Was the worker in the active military or naval service of the U.S. (including U.S. reserve or U.S. National Guard active duty for training) or a foreign country after September 7, 1939?		☐ Yes *(If "Yes" answer (b) thru (c) below.)* ☐ No *(If "No" go on to item 15.)*

(b) Enter the name of country served and dates of service:	Country	Dates of Service
		FROM: *(Month, day , year)* TO: *(Month, day , year)*

(c) Has anyone (living or deceased) received, or does anyone expect to receive, a benefit from any U.S. Federal agency based on the worker's military or naval service?	☐ Yes *(If "Yes" answer (d) below* ☐ No *(If "No" go on to item 15*

(d) If "Yes" enter the following information for each person: *(If additional space is required, enter the information in Remarks -- item 19)*

Name	U. S. Agency	Claim No.

Form **SSA-2490-BK** (4-2004)   EF (8-2006)   Page 4

SOCIAL SECURITY ADMINISTRATION FORM SSA-2490-BK

15.	(a) During the past 24 months, did the worker engage in employment or self-employment covered by the U.S. Social Security system?	☐ Yes	☐ No
	→	(If "Yes" answer (b) and (c) below.)	(If "No" go on to item 16.)

List the periods of work covered by the U.S. Social Security system and the name and address of the employer or self-employment activity

(b) Name and address of employer or self-employment activity	Work Began (Month-Year)	Work Ended (Month-Year)

(c) May we ask any employer listed above for wage information needed to process this claim? →	☐ Yes	☐ No

INFORMATION ABOUT DEPENDENTS FOR WHOM BENEFITS ARE CLAIMED

16.	(a) Are there any children of the worker who are now, or were in the past 12 months, unmarried and: →	Under age 18	☐ Yes ☐ No
		—OR—	
		Age 18 or over and a student or disabled	☐ Yes ☐ No

If either block is checked "Yes", enter the information for each child. NOTE: Children include natural children, step-children and adopted children plus grandchildren living in the same household as the worker.

(b) Name of child	(c) Relationship to worker	(d) Sex (M or F)	(e) Date of birth (Month, day, year)

17. The spouse, widow or widower of the worker may be eligible for a benefit. In addition, a former spouse of the worker may be eligible as a divorced spouse, widow or widower. Provide the following information about any spouse or former spouse of the worker.

	SPOUSE	FORMER SPOUSE	FORMER SPOUSE
(a) Name (including maiden name)			
(b) Date of Birth (Mo., day, yr.)			
(c) Date of Marriage (Mo., day, yr.)			
(d) Date of Divorce (if any) (Mo., day, yr.)			
(e) Country of Citizenship			
(f) Social Insurance Number in foreign country			
(g) U. S. Social Security Number (if any)			

Form **SSA-2490-BK** (4-2004)   EF (8-2006)   Page 5

SOCIAL SECURITY ADMINISTRATION FORM SSA-2490-BK

18.	(a) Has the worker, or any other person listed on this application, ever previously applied for U.S. Social Security benefits or social insurance benefits from the country shown in item 3 of this application?	☐ Yes *(If "Yes" answer (b) thru (f) below.)*	☐ No *(If "No" go on to item 19.)*

If "Yes" enter the information requested for each person. l*(If additional space is required, enter the information in Remarks -- Item 19.)*

(b) Name	(c) Type of benefit (e.g., Retirement)

(d) Claim Number	(e) Amount of benefit (if benefit awarded)	(f) Agency which approved or denied claim

19. REMARKS *(You may use this space for any explanations. If you need more space, attach a separate sheet.)*

Form SSA-2490-BK (4-2004)   EF (8-2006)   Page 6

SOCIAL SECURITY ADMINISTRATION FORM SSA-2490-BK

PRIVACY ACT NOTICE

Statutory Authority: This form requests information under the authority of Section 203(a) and 233 (d) of the Social Security Act as amended (42 USC 405(a) and 433 (d)).

Mandatory or Voluntary: While it is not mandatory, except in circumstances explained below, for you to furnish the information on this form to Social Security, no benefits may be paid under an international agreement on social security unless an application has been received. Your response is mandatory where the refusal to disclose certain information affecting your right to payment would reflect a fraudulent intent to secure benefits not authorized by the Social Security Act.

Purpose: The information on this form is needed to enable Social Security authorities in the U.S. and the foreign country you listed on page 3 of this application to determine if you are entitled to benefits under an international agreement on social security.

Effect: Failure to provide all or part of this information could prevent an accurate and timely decision on your claim and could result in the loss of some benefits.

Use of information: Information from this form will be forwarded to the Social Security authorities of the foreign country you listed on page 3 of this application to help them locate information about the worker's periods of coverage under that system. It will also serve as an application for benefits payable under the foreign laws as well as under U.S. laws if the intent to claim benefits under that system has been indicated in item 4 of this application form. The Social Security Administration cannot be responsible for assuring the confidentiality of information provided to a foreign social insurance agency. In general, that country's rules of confidentiality will apply. The information may also be used (1) to facilitate statistical research and audit activities necessary to assure the integrity and improvement of the Social Security programs, and (2) to comply with Federal laws requiring the exchange of information between the Social Security Administration and another U.S. government agency.

We may also use the information you give us when we match records by computer. Matching programs compare our records with those of other Federal, State or local government agencies. Many agencies may use matching programs to find or prove that a person qualifies for benefits paid by the Federal government. The law allows us to do this even if you do not agree to it.

Explanations about these and other reasons why information you provide us may be used or given out are available in Social Security offices. If you want to learn more about this, contact any Social Security office.

I hereby authorize the United States to furnish to the competent social insurance agency of the other country all of the information and evidence in its possession which relates or could relate to this application for benefits. I also authorize the agency(ies) of the other country to furnish the Social Security Administration or a United States Foreign Service post all of the information and evidence in its possession which relates to this application for benefits.

I declare under penalty of perjury that I have examined all the information on this form, and on any accompanying statements or forms, and it is true and correct to the best of my knowledge. I understand that anyone who knowingly gives a false or misleading statement about a material fact in this information, or causes someone else to do so, commits a crime and may be sent to prison, or may face other penalties, or both.

SIGNATURE OF APPLICANT	Date (Month, day, year)
Signature (First name, middle initial, last name) (Write in ink) **SIGN** ▶ **HERE** ▶	Telephone number(s) at which you may be contacted during the day ___ ___ ___ (Area Code)

Mailing Address (Number and street, Apt. No., P.O. Box, or Rural Route) (Enter resident address in "Remarks" if different)

City and State	ZIP Code	Country (if any) in which you now live

Witnesses are required ONLY if this application has been signed by mark (X) above. If signed by mark (X), two witnesses to the signing who know the applicant must sign below, giving their full addresses. Also, print the applicant's name in the Signature block.

1. Signature of Witness	2. Signature of Witness
Address (Number and street, City, State, and ZIP Code)	Address (Number and street, City, State, and ZIP Code)

Form **SSA-2490-BK** (4-2004)   EF (4-2004)   Page 7

U.S. COMPANY PENSIONS

Fewer and fewer people ask us how a move to Canada will affect their current U.S. company pension plans as just 17% of American workers are eligible for such plans. Again, if you have paid into the plan and are eligible for benefits, you don't suddenly become ineligible (unvested) for benefits because you move to another country. Your pension benefit amount remains, and in fact you may even get it paid directly into your Canadian bank account if you wish. The taxation of these pensions is discussed in greater detail in Chapter 5. The problem with these "defined benefit" pensions is that they are paid in American dollars and are most likely not adjusted for inflation. You are thus exposed to a couple of risks. First, you introduce currency risk into your financial situation because, when you move to Canada, you need Canadian loonies to fund your retirement expenses. Since your American pension is paid in American dollars, your pension amount will fluctuate based on the currency exchange rate, leaving you short one year and with an excess in another year. Second, you face inflation risk since many defined benefit pensions are not adjusted for inflation; they pay the same fixed dollar amount or only partially adjust it to inflation. As a result, you see a gradual decline in your spending power over your lifetime. By the time it starts to affect you, you are generally unable to return to work to supplement it. Look at your retirement plan options: given a move to Canada, you may be able to take the "commuted value" of the pension and roll it to an IRA instead. This typically gives you a host of benefits and reduces your risks.

U.S. RETIREMENT PLANS

In the United States, there is a proliferation of "qualified" plans (versus "registered" plans in Canada) that you may have taken advantage of to save toward your financial independence. They include IRAs, Roth IRAs, SEP-IRAs, simple plans, 401(k), Roth 401(k), 403(b), and 457 plans. One of the most popular questions we field is "What happens to these plans? What should I do with them?" Generally, they maintain their tax-deferred status in Canada except for Roth 401(k)/IRAs which can lose their tax-deferred status. For the taxation of these plans, see Chapter 5. To find out which options you have in moving these accounts, see Chapter 10. One thing you should be aware of is that, if you are a U.S. citizen or green card holder, you can still contribute to these plans, even while resident in Canada. Whether you contribute or not depends on your individual situation and your longer-term financial goals and objectives. Also, it depends on which plan you contribute to whether you'll be able to deduct these contributions on your Canadian tax return (see Chapter 5 for more details), so ensure you seek the necessary counsel beforehand to see if your circumstances apply.

EMPLOYEE BENEFIT PLANS

Several employee benefits may be available to you if you leave the United States to work with a larger employer in Canada. Similar to the United States, Canada has stock option plans and retirement compensation arrangements. We provide a brief discussion below so you can familiarize yourself with them.

RESTRICTED STOCK UNITS

To retain key people, many companies now use restricted stock units (RSUs). Employees are granted RSUs but cannot do anything with them until certain conditions are met (i.e., partial vesting occurs every six months over a two-year period). After the "trigger" is met, the employee vests in the RSUs. At that point, the stock is no longer restricted, and the employee can keep the stock or sell it. Since the "risk of forfeiture" is now gone, the stock is immediately taxable as ordinary income based on the market value of the stock at the time of vesting. As a result, there is little incentive to keep the stock after vesting. In some cases, an 83(b) election can be taken in the U.S. to recognize the income at the time of the grant, versus the time of the vesting, if the stock has appreciated significantly. This may offer some better tax results in the U.S., but in Canada it is still taxed as employment income included on your T4. Restricted stock awards are another less common form of executive compensation with rules different from RSUs. For example, in Canada RSAs are immediately taxable at the time of grant, versus the time of vesting, which can put a cash flow strain on the employee because there is tax due but no stock vested to sell.

STOCK OPTIONS

Stock options were a common form of compensation for employees in both Canada and the United States because they allow employees to participate in the movement of the employer's stock without having to commit any of their own funds. However, with securities regulators fining many companies for illegal activities surrounding stock options (e.g., back-dating), many companies have abandoned them in favor of RSUs with the advent of mandatory stock option expensing by the corporation. Taxation of these options is complex when you are moving to Canada, and it is beyond the scope of this book since each situation is unique with regard to granting and vesting in the option prior to, or after relocating to, Canada. Following are a few general insights into stock options that may be helpful.

In the United States, there are two types of stock options, and the difference between them is related to how they are taxed on your U.S. return.

- Non-qualified stock options (NQs): the primary difference from the incentive stock options below is that, when the NQ is exercised, the difference between the exercise price and the fair market value of the stock is considered ordinary wage income.
- Incentive stock options (ISOs): they offer some terrific tax opportunities if circumstances permit. When the ISO is exercised, the difference between the exercise price and the fair market value of the stock is considered ordinary, short-term capital gain income if the stock is sold within a year of exercising. However, if the ISO is exercised and the stock is held for longer than one year, all of the gains are considered long-term capital gains and are taxed at the long-term capital gains rate of 15% (plus any NIIT as applicable). However, you have to be careful of the alternative minimum tax (AMT) in the United States because the exercise of an ISO is considered income for AMT purposes. This means you may owe a

boatload of tax even though you haven't sold a single share of stock.

In Canada, the difference between NQs and ISOs is not recognized; all stock options are taxed the same whether issued in the United States or Canada, whether ISOs or NQs. However, stock options in Canada are generally taxed more favorably since they qualify for a 50% deduction of the amount between the exercise price and the fair market value of the stock at exercise. This means that only half of the gain is taxed but at the higher Canadian marginal tax rates. Another opportunity you have with stock options in Canada is the ability to defer the stock option income upon exercise (not available on your U.S. tax return if you are required to file one). This can be an effective strategy if you want to defer the income to a lower tax year. There are annual filing requirements and annual limits on how much you can defer, so you should seek competent Canada-U.S. tax planning advice.

Note that stock options granted to you for employment in the United States are generally taxable there even after you move to Canada. Given the complications of the different types of options listed above, a cautious approach is warranted when exercising them because you may have to declare the stock option income on your U.S. return as well as your Canadian return, creating a double tax situation. It is important to note that even if you live in Canada, stock options exercised from a U.S. employer are taxable in the state those options were initially granted as well. You will receive a W-2 for non-qualified stock options you exercise and both federal and state taxes are withheld. This means you have to file a non-resident return in that state as well.

We highly recommend that you exercise options with great caution, or you could cause devastating tax effects that many incurred in the popping of the tech bubble in 2000. In fact, it may make sense to exercise your options after you have entered Canada. The most recent tax treaty and technical interpretation from the CRA provides further direction on the taxation of stock options between Canada and the United States that may be helpful by allocating the gains between the Canadian and American returns based on the amount of time spent in each country. These new sourcing rules can be very beneficial, so competent advice is recommended.

DEFERRED COMPENSATION/RETIREMENT COMPENSATION ARRANGEMENTS

Deferred comp plans, for short, are usually offered to senior-level executives in the United States to allow them to defer portions of their salaries (in addition to any retirement plans the company may have) into a plan they can collect after they retire from the company. The idea is to reduce the amount of taxable income now, when the executive is in a high tax bracket, until later, when he or she is assumed to be in a lower tax bracket. There are different types of deferred compensation arrangements in the United States depending on the company and its objectives for the plan. Most have the executive pay the payroll taxes up front, and when the plan distributes the income it is taxed just like wages. These plans may be subject to the company's creditors, so there are some risks associated with the tax deferral provided. Distributions from deferred comp plans are fully taxable in Canada and on your U.S. return as applicable. A foreign tax credit is available to offset any double taxation.

Similar to deferred comp plans in the United States, Canada has the Retirement Compensation Arrangement (RCA). With these plans, the employer typically puts an amount into the employee's RCA. At the time of the contribution, the contribution (and any future earnings) are subject to a 50% refundable tax that must be remitted to CRA. Once the employee has retired from the firm and begins taking withdrawals out of the RCA, the distributions are taxable as ordinary income in both Canada, and the U.S. with an offsetting foreign tax credit available. In addition, CRA returns $1 of tax for every $2 withdrawn from the RCA. Although the RCA allows for some tax deferral, 50% of all contributions to the plan (and ensuing income) stay with CRA. When they are returned to the employee, there is no interest paid. In essence, CRA gets an interest-free loan. In Canada, all amounts withdrawn from the RCA are fully taxable on your tax return. If you have a U.S. tax filing obligation as well, all amounts withdrawn are fully taxable, but proper tax planning will ensure that offsetting foreign tax credits mitigate your tax liability.

SMARTEN 9
UP!

An investment in knowledge always
pays the best interest.
— BENJAMIN FRANKLIN

EDUCATION ACCOUNTS IN THE UNITED STATES

In the United States, there are several different ways of saving for your child's education and using tax benefits to support those improving themselves through education. These include Coverdell education savings accounts, Uniform Transfer to Minors Act (UTMA) accounts, and state college savings plans (more commonly known as Section 529 plans after their place in the Internal Revenue Code). Like any good parent, you started one of these plans with the intention of funding your child's education. But what happens to these plans when you move to Canada? What should you do with them? We address each of them below.

COVERDELL EDUCATION SAVINGS ACCOUNT

This plan allows you to put U$2,000 after tax away annually per beneficiary. These funds can be used for tuition, books, computers, Internet connections, and actual living expenses. These expenses can apply from kindergarten through to university. The good thing about these plans is that, if they are used to pay for qualified education expenses, even in Canada, the withdrawals are tax-free on your U.S. return. The bad news is that CRA doesn't recognize the tax deferral the IRS does. As a result, these accounts are fully taxable on your Canadian return. Depending on your circumstances, you may want to consider collapsing these accounts or using up the balances in them before taking up tax residency in Canada.

UTMA ACCOUNT

The Uniform Transfer to Minors Act account allows you to deposit an unlimited amount of funds, but be aware of the U.S. gift tax implications (see Chapter 7). If you are required to file U.S. tax returns (for American citizens or green card holders), be aware that the first U$1,050 in income in 2015 from the account is tax-free, with the next U$1,050 taxed at your child's marginal tax rate of 10%. When the income in the account exceeds U$2,100, the excess income is taxed at your highest marginal tax rate (as much as 39.6%) until each child reaches age 18. This is known as the "kiddie tax" and is intended to prevent people from avoiding taxes by simply giving their money to their children to be taxed at their lower tax bracket (similar to the attribution rules on capital gains in Canada). Funds withdrawn need to demonstrate that they were taken out for the benefit of the child only and must not be used for "normal" expenses that you as a parent are expected to provide (food or rent). Also be aware that your child gets unrestricted access to the entire UTMA account at the age of majority for the state in which the account was set up (normally 21), so if he or she chooses to buy a Corvette don't blame us!

In Canada, these accounts are fully taxable each year. However, given the titling on the account, any interest or dividends will be taxed on your child's Canadian tax return, allowing you to avoid putting the income on your return. Furthermore, CRA doesn't care how much you withdraw and how you use the funds.

STATE COLLEGE SAVINGS PLANS

Section 529 plans are state-sponsored programs that have become very popular. Every state now has a plan. These plans allow you to make after-tax contributions that can be invested in a wide range of mutual funds. When it comes time for withdrawals for education expenses (room, board, books, tuition), everything (dividends, interest, capital gains) is withdrawn tax-free at the U.S. federal level if you, or your child, attends an "eligible" institution. In addition, there are some great estate tax planning advantages to these plans that may be applicable in your situation. Most importantly, you retain full control of the funds and can change beneficiaries at any time with no tax or other implications.

One question we are often asked is "Can Section 529 funds be used for a Canadian education?" To maintain their tax-free withdrawal status in the United States, the funds have to be used for qualified expenses at an "eligible" institution. Such an institution must participate in the Federal Family Education Loan Program administered by the U.S. Department of Education. Institutions apply and, if approved, are assigned a unique "school code." Since many Canadian (and foreign) institutions have applied, you can go to http://www.fafsa.ed.gov and see whether your Canadian institution is eligible. Our last check showed there were over 100 Canadian institutions approved, including all of the major provincial universities. However, when you become a tax resident in Canada, be aware that these accounts no longer maintain their tax-deferred status, and the earnings must be declared annually on the tax return of the person whose name is on the account.

REGISTERED EDUCATION SAVINGS PLAN

In Canada, the primary means of saving for your child's education is the Registered Education Savings Plan (RESP). It allows you to contribute a lifetime maximum of C$50,000 (after tax) for each child. If you contribute C$2,500 or more, the Government of Canada will contribute another C$500 to the account (20% match) through the Canada Education Savings Grant up to a lifetime maximum of C$7,200. If your income is below C$43,953 in 2014, your grant is C$600; if your income is between C$43,954 and C$87,907, your grant is C$550. These plans are a terrific way for you to begin accumulating funds toward your future education expenses. The funds inside RESP's grow tax deferred from a Canadian perspective until needed for education expenses, and any withdrawals of the gains, income, or grant amounts are taxed as ordinary income to the student (who is typically in a lower tax bracket than the contributor). Your original contributions are withdrawn tax-free.

If you are required to file U.S. tax returns, you run into some unexpected complications with RESPs. RESPs don't automatically retain their tax-deferred status with the IRS. Furthermore, unlike RRSPs, there is no treaty election, IRS form, or revenue procedure to continue the deferral. As a result, you have to declare the income inside the RESPs each year on your U.S. tax return until collapsed, along with Form 3520. Fortunately, CRA will permit you to withdraw funds for "qualified education expenses," including those at a qualified U.S. university. From an American standpoint, any withdrawals should be tax-free as well because you have been declaring the income annually on your U.S. tax return. However, this asset will be included in your estate for estate tax purposes and could be subjected to the punishing estate taxes outlined in Chapter 7.

One thorny issue arises if you decide to move back to the United States, leave an RESP in Canada, but are unable to use it for education expenses. CRA rules state that as a non-resident you can't withdraw any earnings on your original contributions to an RESP for any purpose other than "qualified education expenses." This means that, even if you are willing to pay the Canadian taxes and penalties, you still can't get the earnings out — only your original principal can be withdrawn (tax-free), and you will have to return all of the grant money received to the Government of Canada. RESPs require some planning to ensure that there will be someone in your family (or among relatives) to benefit from these plans; otherwise, the earnings can be left on "Island Canada" indefinitely. We believe this rule was an oversight by CRA in drafting the laws surrounding RESPs and non-residents of Canada, but we are not sure when, or if, it will be addressed (this issue is dealt with in greater detail in our companion book *The Canadian in America*).

There are no provisions to roll your RESP into any education account in the United States and maintain the tax deferral from a Canadian or American perspective. Moreover, if you have young children who won't be attending a postsecondary institution any time soon, there are income declaration requirements outlined above but also various reporting requirements on your U.S. return, such as Form FinCEN 114 — Report of Foreign Accounts, Form 3520 — Annual Return to Report Transactions with Foreign Trusts and Receipt of Certain Foreign Gifts, Form 3520a — Annual Information Return of Foreign Trust with a U.S. Owner, and

Form 8938 — Statement of Specified Foreign Financial Assets when you leave your RESPs in Canada. And the filing requirements of your state of domicile are another matter that need to be considered. Finally, it will be difficult to manage the investments in your RESP because your financial institution will only allow you to sell investments to avoid the ire of the U.S. Securities and Exchange Commission (see Chapter 10 for more details).

AMERICAN TAX INCENTIVES FOR EDUCATION

If you move to Canada but still have to file a U.S. tax return, you should familiarize yourself with the various income tax credits and deductions that may be available to you, or your child, to offset some of your education expenses.

AMERICAN OPPORTUNITY CREDIT

This tax credit is worth a total of U$2,500 for each of your children in the current tax year. You are eligible to take this credit for up to four years of undergraduate studies for a maximum credit of U$10,000 per child. You are eligible for a U$2,500 tax credit if you pay at least U$2,500 in college expenses each year, which is relatively easy to do. There are income restrictions to be aware of in qualifying for this credit, and it is available only for up to four years of undergraduate studies. You use IRS Form 8863 to claim the American Opportunity Credit, but you'd better hurry, as Congress has approved this credit only to 2017, after which it will expire.

LIFETIME LEARNING CREDIT

This tax credit is worth U$2,000 annually for each tax-paying family as long as there is a child or parent in school full or part time upgrading his or her skills. There are income restrictions in qualifying for this credit, and you can select only between the Hope Scholarship and the Lifetime Learning Credit in any one year.

There is some coordination that needs to take place between these credits and withdrawals from a Section 529 plan, so it is prudent to seek some advice when freeing up the cash to pay college expenses. For example, you can take either the American Opportunity Credit or the Lifetime Learning Credit but not both in one year. However, if you pay all college expenses with tax-free funds from a Section 529 plan, those are not eligible expenses for either credit.

STUDENT LOAN INTEREST DEDUCTION

This is an "above the line" deduction (don't have to itemize) on your tax return for any interest paid on student loans. The maximum deduction is U$2,500, but there are income restrictions on your eligibility for this deduction that you should determine beforehand.

TUITION AND FEES DEDUCTION

There is a deduction of up to U$4,000 for college tuition and related expenses, but there are income restrictions on whether you qualify or not. Furthermore, you can't take the deduction if you take one of the credits outlined above.

CANADIAN TAX INCENTIVES FOR EDUCATION

As in the U.S., there are many different tax incentives available to you or your child in Canada to offset your education expenses. They include the tuition, education, and textbook amounts, the employment amount, the public transit pass amount, and the student loan interest credit. Other expenses — such as lab fees, examination fees, computer fees, and most health and athletic fees — become credits on your Canadian return. The education amount is C$400 for each month you were full time in school, C$120 if you attended part time. Your educational institution will issue Form 2202 or 2202A — Tuition, Education, and Textbooks Amounts Certificate, which outlines the months you were in school full or part time and the amount of eligible tuition. The textbook amount gives you a credit of C$65 per month of full-time schooling and C$20 for part-time education. The employment amount gives you a credit for the lesser of C$250 or the total employment income you declared on your tax return. The public transit pass gives you a credit for the amounts you spend on monthly or annual public transportation. What is interesting about these credits is that, if you can't use them all (because your income is so low), they can be transferred to the higher-income parent, who can use them. Alternatively, they can be carried forward to a later tax year when your income is higher (you're working) until used up. Similar to the U.S. deduction, any student loan interest can be deducted by the student, and any unused amounts can be carried forward for up to five years. You should also keep track of your moving expenses because legitimate expenses incurred in moving to get educated are deductible on your Canadian return.

KEY DIFFERENCES

There are several key differences in the school systems between Canada and the United States.

- In Canada, junior high runs from grades 7 to 9. In the United States, it is typically grades 7 and 8 and is called middle school.
- In the United States, K-12 school generally starts in early or mid-August and runs through May, with longer breaks in between. In Canada, school generally starts in early September and runs through June, with shorter breaks.
- Based on our experience and feedback from others, U.S. undergraduate classes tend to be easier than Canadian undergraduate classes, but U.S. graduate classes tend to be more difficult than Canadian graduate classes.
- In the U.S., belonging to a fraternity or sorority is more common than in Canada.
- In the U.S., you "graduate" in grade 8 (out of middle school) and again in grade 12 versus Canada when you typically graduate in grade 12 only.
- In the U.S., prom is a far bigger event, with a lot of pomp and circumstance, than in Canada.

There are some linguistic differences in education circles you should be aware of as well (see Table 9.1).

TABLE 9.1

LINGUISTIC DIFFERENCES IN EDUCATION

Canada	United States
Grade 9 or first year of university	Freshman
Grade 10 or second year of university	Sophomore
Grade 11 or third year of university	Junior
Grade 12 or fourth year of university	Senior
Junior high	Middle school
University	College
Diploma	Associates degree
Marks	Grades

MONEY DOESN'T 10
GROW ON TREES

Fortunes are made by being highly concentrated,
but fortunes are preserved by being highly diversified.

— ANONYMOUS

Americans making the transition to Canada typically leave some investment accounts or IRAs in the United States, thinking they'll just continue managing them as they always have. The reason most often given
for leaving these investments in the United States is the tax that would
have to be paid upon withdrawal (see Chapter 5). What folks don't realize
is that it's not "business as usual," and there are complications with
accounts in the United States when you are residing in Canada. If you
decide to move the investment assets to Canada, there are other complications and unforeseen obstacles to overcome. Following are some of the
things you should consider in the area of investment planning.

KEEPING ACCOUNTS IN THE UNITED STATES

Relocating to Canada is often followed shortly by a notice from your
brokerage firm saying that it can no longer hold your accounts and
that you must move them immediately because you are now a resident of Canada based on the change of address form you submitted
(you submitted one, didn't you?). This notice may come from an
overzealous compliance officer who doesn't know what to do with a
Canadian address on an American account or a brokerage firm that

isn't registered in Canada. In reality, there is no legal reason for you to move your qualified plans anywhere since American financial institutions can continue to hold these accounts for non-residents of the U.S. However, securities rules cause more complications with regular, taxable brokerage accounts, so you may find that you can't place any "buy" trades in the account (only sales are permitted). In some cases, you may be forced to transfer the account to another institution or liquidate the entire account and close it.

To get around this issue, some American expatriates attempt to "trick" their financial institutions and securities regulators by providing an American address of a family member or friend or a post office box number. This tactic can lead to several problems.

- If you are using the services of an investment manager to manage your account, you are no longer permitted to do so. Since you are now a resident of Canada, your investment manager must be registered in your province of residence in order to render any investment advice to you. As a result, your investment manager will need to get registered in your province of residence (which can be a costly, difficult process) and meet the proficiency requirements. This will all come to light when you put a Canadian address on your account. Despite recent efforts, there is no national regulator in Canada, and there remains a patchwork of regulations for each province that makes getting registered even more difficult and expensive (see later in this chapter).
- You won't receive your monthly investment statements or other important information (proxy voting, notification of annual meetings, class action settlements, etc.) in a timely fashion because you'll be reliant on your family/friends to send such information to you when it's convenient for them.
- Your confidentiality and/or identity could be compromised if your information ends up at a "trusted" friend's or relative's house.

NON-U.S. TAX FILERS

- For non-residents of the U.S. who are not required to file a U.S. tax return, any dividends and interest paid into your brokerage account won't have the correct withholding taken as required by the Canada-U.S. Tax Treaty. The reason is that your financial institution believes you are still living in the United States. This creates a compliance issue with the IRS if you are being issued 1099 slips on this income instead of Form 1042S slips, requiring you to file a Form 1040NR tax return with the IRS to remit the correct withholding. To further complicate things, you must also declare this income on your Canadian tax return (see Chapter 5).
- Lump-sum IRA withdrawals will most likely have the incorrect withholding taken as required by the Canada-U.S. Tax Treaty, and you'll end up remitting more withholding than required by the IRS.

U.S. TAX FILERS

- When you put a U.S. address on your brokerage account, the financial institution will issue Form 1099 tax slips to the tax authorities for any taxable income. Since most U.S. tax filers file a federal 1040 tax return, there isn't a problem. What they often forget is that the 1099 tax slip is also sent to the state tax authorities for the address on the account. Eventually, you will receive some "hate mail" from the state wondering why you are not paying state tax on your investment income and not filing tax returns with that state! If you file a return with the state as a resident, you will have to declare your worldwide income on your state return, but most states do not recognize foreign tax credits, nor do they follow the Canada-U.S. tax treaty like the federal government does, and this may make your RRSPs and other accounts fully taxable in that state. Alternatively, you will have to write a letter to the state tax authorities explaining and proving you are not a resident of that state for tax purposes.
- Americans retain the right to vote when living abroad, which

generally goes through the state where they last resided. Overseas voting documents ask U.S. citizens if they have the intention to return to the state or remain abroad for an extended period of time. If you have the intention to return, even after living abroad for a long time, the state can assess state income taxes for the years you have been away, based on your intended domicile, not residency. There is case law supporting this.

- The issue of domicile can also create problems in estate planning. With your U.S. address on your brokerage account, that state can make a case that your estate should be settled there in the event you become an angel. If your estate is not set up appropriately for that state, or that state's estate tax laws are not favorable, you could end up subject to unnecessary estate taxes, probate, and estate settlement fees. Added to the settlement costs for your estate in Canada, it could become expensive (see Chapter 7 for more details).

Also overlooked are the restrictions on trading in your American IRAs and other qualified plans while you are a resident in Canada. For reasons we still haven't solidified, American brokerage firms prohibit Canadian residents (even though you are an American citizen filing U.S. tax returns annually) from making trades in these accounts. Despite hours of research, we are unsure if it's because of fears of insider trading and proper accounting of the income in these accounts for SEC purposes, or if it's because of Canadian protectionist actions as lobbied by the Investment Dealers Association (we have heard that the Ontario Securities Commission is prohibiting such transactions). We continue to explore this matter to see why only Canada and Australia must abide by such silly rules. Any other country in the world, except those on the Department of State's "black list" (e.g., Iran, Libya, Cuba, etc.) is able to open accounts and manage them in the United States while living in those countries. It seems absurd that the two largest trading partners in the world can't find a solution to this problem, particularly when there are hundreds of thousands of American citizens living in Canada with IRAs stranded in the United States. To further complicate things, the regulatory environment in Canada is disjointed because there is no national regulatory body; each province runs everything individually, with a board of each province's representatives attempting to coordinate things. Either way, if your U.S. investment manager wants to render advice to you, he or she needs to be registered in your province of domicile. The Securities Exchange Commission has recently undertaken initiatives to review the activities of foreign investment managers doing business in the U.S. and domestic investment managers conducting business abroad. To avoid many of these difficulties, it's best if you set up your account and invest in it how you want before you leave for Canada. Once you are there and have a Canadian address on the account, it will be frozen, and you'll no longer be able to conduct any trades. Alternatively, you can hire our firm to manage the account for you as we are registered to manage investments in both Canada and the U.S.

If you are able to keep your accounts in the United States (most brokerage firms are no longer permitting Canadian residents to hold brokerage accounts), be aware of a couple of difficulties. First, as a Canadian resident, you are subject to Canadian taxes on your worldwide income. Your American investment manager/broker likely doesn't know the Canadian tax implications of the transactions he or she is undertaking and as a result could be conducting investment trades and handing you an unnecessary tax bill on your Canadian return in the process. Research has shown that expenses in the investment vehicle and tax efficiency are the two key determinants of investment returns. We recommend that you retain an investment manager well versed in the tax rules in both countries and how the Canada-U.S. Tax Treaty applies to your situation to ensure that your tax liability is mitigated where possible. Another common area overlooked is the difficulty experienced with brokerage accounts in the United States if the account holder dies while resident in Canada. Typically, the probate process has to be endured twice, once in the United States and once in Canada, and there is the potential for double taxation (see Chapter 7 for more details).

REAL-LIFE EXAMPLE

We received a desperate call from a woman in California who was the sole trustee on her mentally incapacitated mother's account. The investment advisor for the account told her to move the account within 90 days, or it would be frozen. This was a big problem because as trustee she was using the account to pay her mother's bills and in 90 days would no longer be able to do so! Since we are registered to manage investments in both Canada and the U.S., she contacted us to provide help. The problem arose because the trustee had a sibling in Canada who disputed the management of the trust and took the sister/trustee to court. In the process, the Canadian resident sibling was appointed as a co-trustee of the mother's trust at the suggestion of the attorneys involved to provide further oversight despite no discrepancies being found. When the investment advisor was asked to provide duplicate statements to the co-trustee/sibling in Canada, it realized there was a "Canadian control person" on the brokerage account and immediately issued the notice to move the account. Unfortunately, we were unable to assist her in this situation for the same reason, which meant the only option was to remove the Canadian resident sibling as a trustee or have the account frozen. This meant more attorney fees and delays as the 90 days were counting down quickly.

SETTING UP ACCOUNTS IN CANADA

When you begin moving your investments to Canada, you need to select a financial institution. You may approach one in your local area that you have never heard of about setting up an account. Without a doubt, the representative there will be more than happy to get you set up and recommend several "great" investments (review Chapter 13). Following are some things to consider.

WHERE TO SET ACCOUNTS UP

A common question our firm fields is "Where should I set up an investment account in Canada?" We believe the best value for the dollar is at one of the large discount brokerage firms. They offer lower commission rates, a wide array of lower-cost mutual funds, and exceptional Internet-based services. The custodian of choice for our clients' investments in Canada is National Bank Correspondent Network (NBCN) Institutional, making it one of the largest discount brokerage firms in Canada. It offers discounted transaction and trading rates and virtually every institutional mutual fund available, and it has fixed income and stock desks. For our clients in the U.S. or those with investments remaining there, we use TD Ameritrade Institutional. Again, it offers discounted transaction and trading rates as well as a wide range of institutional mutual funds and an experienced fixed income desk. There are other financial institutions available, but we encourage you to do your research and select an investment firm that upholds the fiduciary responsibility to you (see Chapter 12).

SOCIAL INSURANCE NUMBER

For those making the transition to Canada and wanting to open an account as a Canadian resident, they must have a Social Insurance Number to put on the account application form (see Chapter 5). This number ensures that any income from the account can be tracked for Canadian income tax purposes. With the tragic events of 9/11, the federal governments in both countries have determined that the best way to fight terrorism is to restrict the access terrorists have to money. As a result, you'll contend with a lot of scrutiny and paperwork before opening an account. The institution may ask for your employment status, employer's name and address, immigration status, passport number, and country to determine exactly who is opening the account. In our experience, it can be an unusually lengthy process.

TITLING YOUR ACCOUNT

The other question you'll see on the account application form asks how you want the account titled: joint tenancy with rights of survivorship, tenancy in common, tenancy in the entirety, sole and separate property, etc. Most Americans have no idea, so they check any box or don't check one at all, and the brokerage firm uses its default (normally joint tenancy with rights of survivorship). In reality, the option selected can have pro-found estate planning effects on your family in the event one of you dies or becomes incapacitated. You will also be asked to designate a primary and contingent beneficiary. These are decisions that shouldn't be taken lightly. See Chapter 7 for further details on this issue.

U.S.-DOLLAR ACCOUNTS

Another big question we get is "Can I set up a U.S.-dollar account in Canada?" The resounding answer is "Yes! You can open a U.S.-dollar account in Canada!" In the United States, it's impossible to open a Canadian-loonie account at most American financial institutions. The bottom line is that U.S. brokerage firms just aren't capable of opening and managing Canadian-loonie-denominated accounts effectively because there just isn't sufficient demand for them.

MOVING INVESTMENTS TO CANADA

Another confusing and potentially frustrating area often encountered is moving your U.S. investments to Canada. Let's dispel a common myth right off — yes, it's possible to move some U.S. investments to Canada without having to sell them first. However, as we have personally experienced, the simplest transfers can take months for the unwary. Following is some information to consider when moving your investments to Canada.

MOVING YOUR IRA

Our firm is often asked "Can I move my IRA to Canada? If so, how? In a lump sum? In stages? Using the required annual minimum withdrawal amount? Spouse's first? This year or next?" Unfortunately, the answers to these questions require considerable thought, a current understanding of financial markets, and a thorough understanding of your unique financial situation to determine the Canadian tax implications, U.S. tax implications, and which IRA(s) to withdraw first. The other thing to consider is "When a prudent withdrawal strategy is developed, what will be done with the money?" There simply is no general answer for everyone, but usually it's better to transfer these assets to Canada for purposes of estate planning, tax planning, currency exchange, and simplification of life. The answers depend, again, on your individual financial situation, your U.S. tax residency, and your overall goals and objectives. However, proceed with caution. A U$100,000 lump-sum IRA withdrawal could mean as much as U$45,000 in tax — that's a lot of money where we come from. Some proper planning is certainly in order.

FACT: MOVE YOUR IRA TO AN RRSP

One common myth we often dispel is the ability to move a U.S. IRA — or 401(k), 403(b), and 457 plans — to a Canadian RRSP. Interestingly enough, this can be done, though the reverse can't (see below). If you leave the U.S. and give up your tax residency status, it's possible to move your IRA to an RRSP in Canada at a favorable tax rate. However, this strategy is less favorable for an American citizen or a green card holder living in Canada because they are considered U.S. tax residents and are required to file U.S. tax returns annually. As a result, any withdrawals from an IRA are subject to the marginal tax rates in the United States (up to 39.6%) plus an additional 10% early withdrawal penalty for those making lump-sum withdrawals prior to age 59½. In addition, any amounts are taxable in Canada on your Canadian T-1 tax return.

However, if you are a non-resident of the United States for tax purposes, it's possible to move your IRA to a Canadian RRSP very tax effectively. We caution you in advance that you'll need to exercise much patience in educating your financial institution since this may be the first (and last) time it does this. That's why we recommend you work with a supervisor or someone who has done this type of transfer before where possible. Part of the problem is that you have a Social Security Number on the account, but the institution doesn't know if you are a U.S. citizen or green card holder. At first, when you try to collapse your IRA and move it to Canada, your custodian will state that there's a 30% withholding tax (plus 10% early withdrawal penalty for those under the age of 59½) that must be remitted to the IRS. What your financial institution doesn't know is that the Canada-U.S. Tax Treaty has provisions that can reduce your withholding. To begin, you need to fill out and file IRS Form W-8BEN — Certificate of Foreign Status of Beneficial Owner for United States Tax Withholding with the trustee of your IRA (the financial institution). Of particular importance is Part II of the form, where you fill in the appropriate treaty section that reduces your withholding to just 15%! Furthermore, because you aren't a tax resident of the United States, the 10% early withdrawal penalty no longer applies. If your trustee still doesn't get it right, he or she won't be able to get any of your excess withholding back from the IRS. You'll have to file Form 1040NR — U.S. Nonresident Alien Income Tax Return with the IRS to get it back. The only drawback is that you have to wait until the next calendar year after the withdrawal to get your refund.

From a Canadian perspective, your IRA withdrawal is fully taxable on your Canadian return because, as a Canadian tax resident, you are required to declare your worldwide income. To reduce this taxable amount, the Canada Revenue Agency allows you to make a lump-sum contribution to an RRSP for any foreign retirement arrangement payments received. Once your check arrives from your U.S. financial institution (less the 15% withholding sent to the IRS), take it to your RRSP custodian and deposit it into your RRSP. Your custodian will issue you an RRSP contribution slip that you put on your Canadian tax return for that year, but it will be short the 15% withholding. At this point, you have to determine whether you will take this as taxable income in Canada or whether you have other cash elsewhere to contribute to your RRSP to get the full deduction for the total amount withdrawn from your IRA in the U.S. All contributions to your RRSP must be done in the year of the IRA withdrawal or within 60 days of the following calendar year, or the entire IRA withdrawal will be taxable on your Canadian return as well! You are eligible to take the 15% withheld in the United States as a foreign tax credit on your Canadian return, so some double taxation will be mitigated. Overall, this is a complex, time-consuming, tricky undertaking with many potential landmines, so we encourage you to seek the right advice to assist you in implementing this as part of your overall financial plan.

Despite the complexities outlined above, there may be situations where leaving your IRA in the United States is the most prudent thing to do. For example, you may be returning to the United States in the near future and want to continue the tax deferral. Alternatively, it may make sense to do staged withdrawals of your IRAs over a longer period of time for foreign tax credit planning purposes or to take advantage of lower income tax years. Our point here is that you shouldn't just collapse and move these registered accounts to Canada without thinking the process through from beginning to end.

MYTH: MOVE YOUR RRSP TO AN IRA

Another common myth we often dispel is the ability to move a Canadian RRSP to an American IRA in a tax favorable fashion. The current rules and regulations simply don't allow a Canadian RRSP to be rolled into an IRA while maintaining the tax-deferred status in both countries. Your only alternative is to collapse the RRSP, pay ordinary marginal tax rates on your Canadian return, and transfer the cash to the U.S. See our companion book *The Canadian in America* for more details on moving your RRSP to the United States.

SPECIFIC TYPES OF INVESTMENTS

Following are some of the things you need to consider in moving specific types of investments to Canada.

- **Stocks:** most individual stocks traded on an exchange in the U.S. can be moved to a Canadian brokerage firm and sold when requested (you can even keep them in a U.S.-dollar account). However, you may be better off selling them while still in the U.S. account because transaction costs are generally lower in the U.S. than in Canada. Moreover, be aware of which currency you want because stocks listed on both a Canadian and a U.S. stock exchange (e.g., Bell Canada) will be sold in the currency of the account that holds the stocks. For example, if you transfer a U.S. stock to a Canadian-loonie account in Canada and sell it, the proceeds will be in Canadian dollars. Likewise, any dividends paid will be issued in Canadian dollars. I did this personally with my wife's company stock that we moved to Canada. The other factor to consider is holding U.S. stocks in Canada may subject you to U.S. estate taxes as a non-tax filer in Canada as these are considered U.S. situs assets (see Chapter 7 for more details).
- **Bonds:** again, most individual U.S. bonds can be transferred wholesale to a Canadian brokerage account and sold when requested. However, these bonds will appear on your statement in Canadian dollars unless you have set up a U.S.-dollar account with your Canadian financial institution. As with stocks, the proceeds of the sale or any interest paid will be in

Canadian dollars and will be considered U.S. situs for U.S. estate tax purposes.

- **Mutual funds:** despite valiant efforts, we have been unable to transfer a single mutual fund from the U.S. to a Canadian financial institution or mutual fund company. Even U.S.-based mutual fund companies won't permit you to transfer mutual funds from their U.S. headquarters to their Canadian subsidiaries (e.g., Dimensional Fund Advisors). I personally tried to move the Templeton International Stock fund and the Templeton International Growth fund (both denominated in U.S. dollars) from Templeton's U.S. headquarters to the Canadian subsidiary to no avail. After countless phone calls and written requests, I gave up, sold the mutual funds, and moved the cash to Canada. Before selling, analyze and understand the tax implications of doing so as well as the deferred sales charges that may be involved. Without proper planning, moving mutual funds can cost you dearly.
- **Exchange Traded Funds (ETFs):** these mutual funds that trade like stocks have taken the investment world by storm because of their low expenses ratios and tax efficiency. There is a proliferation of ETFs here in the U.S. and some in Canada. We have found it possible to move U$ ETFs to a U$ account in Canada. However, it is impossible to move C$ ETFs to the U.S.
- **Cash:** moving cash is the easiest way to bring your investment portfolio to Canada. Liquidation of the portfolio avoids a myriad of issues, but you should analyze and understand the tax implications of doing so first. The quickest way to move your cash to Canada is to wire it from your bank or brokerage firm using a discount currency exchange firm that will convert your U.S. dollars into Canadian loonies and wire them into your Canadian brokerage or bank account as desired. Whatever you do, don't attempt to take a large amount of cash with you when you leave the United States through a border crossing (see Chapter 4 for more details).
- **Partnerships/unit trusts:** these investments offer you a double whammy because generally you can't move them to Canada,

and they tend to be difficult to sell (illiquid). You end up stuck with this investment orphaned in the United States, which forces you to keep an account open there, and any income it produces is subject to U.S. taxes. Overall, they add a lot of complexity to your life.

- **Income trusts:** these structures are less popular because of the negative tax consequences in Canada. Investing in income trusts still makes sense if you are a U.S. tax resident because the income will be classified as qualified dividends (15% maximum tax rate) versus ordinary interest income.

LOBBYING YOUR BROKER

Occasionally, we have witnessed shameful behavior when your broker/ investment manager turns from being "Dr. Jekyll" when your investments are under his or her management to being "Mr. Hyde" when you tell him or her that it's in your best interests to move them to Canada. In some cases, managers even put their clients in class "B" back-end loaded mutual funds before they leave for Canada to guarantee their commissions! Typically, these are people with whom you have had a long relationship and have treated you well, but when it no longer suits them they suddenly forget that your interests need to come first (that's the difference between a fiduciary standard versus a suitability standard as outlined in Chapter 13). They just don't understand they cannot render investment advice to a resident of Canada without being registered as an investment counselor/portfolio manager in Canada. This is in violation of Canadian securities rules even if the investment assets are located in a U.S. account. We have also seen top-notch investment managers cooperate with their clients to help them meet their needs in expeditiously moving these assets to Canada, particularly if there are regulatory compliance requirements they are no longer able to meet. In fact, many financial advisors have simply referred out the relationship to us because they knew the client would be better served by our unique specialty. You need to be cognizant of any changes in your investment manager and understand what is going on so you can be proactive in expediting the process of moving your assets to Canada.

First, your investment manager may be compensated for the assets housed with the firm. Typically, at the end of the month, a "snapshot" is taken for the purpose of compensation, so the manager will try to delay the transfer of assets at least until then. Second, investment managers typically get compensated more for stock holdings in your portfolio or loaded mutual funds, and they don't want to lose that recurring revenue stream! No doubt you'll see some foot dragging. Third, your investment manager simply won't understand why it's in your best interests to withdraw your IRAs or move your other qualified plans to Canada. As Americans, we are trained from birth to put money into an IRA or 401(k) and never take it out, so when the request is made it's very "countercultural." To ensure the expeditious movement of your investments, we recommend the following.

1. If possible, initiate the transfer from your Canadian brokerage firm, not your U.S. investment manager. You want to use your Canadian firm to initiate a "pull" strategy versus relying on your U.S. manager to initiate a "push" strategy.

2. If necessary, have a nice but firm conversation with your investment manager; make it clear that you are doing this and that there's no changing your mind.

3. Follow up, follow up, follow up. Create a sense of urgency about this move, and keep hounding your investment manager for an update/the status of the transfer so the message is clearly sent.

4. Be sure to obtain the name of your investment manager's supervisor so that, if your investment manager is suddenly "on vacation" or "out of the office," you have a backup person to keep moving the transfer forward.

5. Document, document, document. Keep track of all phone calls, the date and time, the subject, the person you talked to, and the outcome.

6. Email your broker, and if necessary cc the manager, so that everything is documented. Investment management firms are required to maintain all email records for regulatory purposes, so a clear history is built and can be referred to in resolving disputes.

INVESTING IN CANADA

There are several differences between the United States and Canada when it comes to investing your money. Unfortunately, for most Americans making the transition to Canada, they are unaware of these differences and end up making some costly mistakes or paying too much for the same thing they can get elsewhere. This is typically the result of an over-zealous broker, a smooth-talking mutual fund provider, or an annuity salesperson. Following are some of the things you need to consider before investing your hard-earned dollars in Canada.

INVESTMENT EXPENSES

The U.S. is known as one of the most inexpensive places in the world to invest, far below the expenses seen in Canada. This is important because the investment research has shown that investment expenses and tax efficiency are two key determinants of portfolio returns. Interestingly enough, these are two factors we can directly control. Competition in the U.S. financial services industry continues to put pressure on brokerage fees, commission rates, and mutual fund expenses. Coupled with the advent of index funds and exchange-traded funds, these factors have reduced investment expenses far more in the U.S. than in Canada (although that is changing . . . but slowly due to the large industry lobbying efforts). The most insidious thing about these fees is that most investors don't even know they are paying them unless they look at a prospectus sent to them (most don't because they trust their advisors, who don't voluntarily disclose them). Most mutual funds in Canada typically have a 2–3.5% expense ratio compared with an average of 0.25–0.75% in the United States. For example, C$100,000 in Canadian mutual funds can cost you easily 2–3.5% or C$2,000–$3,500 per year (on top of any deferred sales charge), while a no-load U.S. mutual fund has an expense ratio of approximately 0.25–0.75% or U$250–$750 per year or less. In addition, there is a much larger selection of low-cost mutual funds in the United States with expense ratios around 0.10% or less for an S&P 500 Index fund. Not only are the costs of the mutual funds much higher, but the cost to hire an investment manager is also much higher in Canada than in the U.S. In the U.S., the typical investment manager will charge 1% of the first $1M in assets under management, with a declining percentage for each additional million. In Canada, we have seen the same fees start at 1.25% and go as high as 2% on the first $2M in assets under management. Canada's high investment costs relative to the world have been publicly condemned by the World Trade Organization, but lobbying efforts in the industry have left much unchanged and investors paying the price. In the meantime, we encourage you to tread carefully when investing in Canada, hire an investment advisor, and check the investment expenses before you leap. Also be sure you hire an advisor who does not run you afoul of the IRS PFIC rules, as outlined in Chapter 5.

OTHER DIFFERENCES

- **Money market "sweep"**: dividends or interest payments, maturing bonds, or investment sales are paid in cash into your account. In Canada, this cash generally sits in an account earning "savings" account interest rates until you choose to invest the cash in a money market mutual fund. These money market funds in Canada may have a deferred sales charge and/or a high management expense ratio, so understand the instrument before investing. In the United States, any cash in your account is typically "swept" on a daily basis into a money market mutual fund automatically. The nice thing is that these are low-cost funds that allow you to take money out at any time, penalty free. As a result, you earn the higher money market rate starting the same day your cash hits the account versus a savings account rate, which on average can be 3% less.
- **Mutual funds**: some investors in the U.S. have researched and become familiar with the different mutual fund families

in the United States, such as Vanguard, PIMCO, American, Dimensional Fund Advisors, etc. In Canada, however, few such funds exist. The question then becomes "Which mutual fund families should I use in Canada?" Altamira? MacKenzie? AIM? CI? Royal Funds? There are close to 2,000 mutual funds you can select from in Canada, but it will take you a while to determine which mutual fund is right for your unique circumstances. However, as outlined in Chapter 5, if you remain a U.S. tax filer, you could run afoul of the IRS PFIC rules, which have some negative tax consequences.

TAX-PREFERENCE INVESTMENTS

There are several tax-preference investment alternatives you may have in the United States that may no longer be appropriate for you in Canada.

- **Municipal bonds:** if you purchase bonds issued by the municipal governments in your state of residence, the interest is both federal and state tax-free (if applicable). However, when you become a tax resident of Canada, CRA doesn't recognize this as tax-free income, and it is fully taxed. As expected, the interest rates on tax-free bonds are typically lower than those on fully taxable bonds because of their tax-free status. This means you now own a lower-yielding bond that is fully taxable at the higher rates in Canada at both the federal and the provincial levels.
- **Federal U.S. obligations:** interest from U.S. government bonds, T-bills, etc. is tax-free at the state level (if applicable) but still taxable at the federal level. When you become a tax resident of Canada, these bonds are fully taxable on both your federal and your provincial tax returns.
- **Exempt money market:** these money market mutual funds invest only in federal or municipal government short-term paper and provide the tax benefits outlined above. Again, they will be fully taxable in Canada.
- **Annuities:** you are allowed to make a one-time or an ongoing contribution to a fixed, variable, or equity indexed annuity,

and the earnings grow tax deferred. However, when you move to Canada, CRA doesn't recognize the tax deferral in the annuity, and it becomes fully taxable every year on your Canadian T-1 tax return.

- **Life insurance:** there are many insurance policies in Canada and the United States that allow part of your premium to pay for the life insurance with the balance going toward investments. Fortunately, these investments maintain their tax-deferred status in Canada. If you withdraw the cash value, any amount above your premium payments made is taxable in both Canada and the United States, but offsetting foreign tax credits should mitigate any double taxation.

We have seen many complex schemes and financial products added to people's lives to reduce their income taxes. We are all for legal tax optimization techniques used to your benefit. However, sometimes the simplest strategies are the best. For example, if you buy a low-cost, tax-efficient, exchange-traded fund and never sell it, how much tax will you pay? What are the expenses associated with this strategy? Correct, none. You just got tax deferral at a fraction of the expense and complexity of some sophisticated tax strategy concocted by a tax attorney! Good advice from an advisor held to a fiduciary standard is typically your best bet.

OUR INVESTMENT PHILOSOPHY

We believe in two simple principles when it comes to investing.

1. Grandma was always right: don't put all of your eggs into one basket. In other words, diversify, diversify, diversify. Why? Because of the second principle.

2. Nobody can predict the future!

Based on these principles, our firm doesn't try to outguess short-term market movements or pick hot managers, stocks, or sectors. We don't try to determine when to be in the market or when to be out of it, because the investment research has concluded that accurate predictions can't be made on a consistent, long-term basis (for those who think they can, is it luck, or is it skill?). Instead, our intention is to capture market returns as efficiently and effectively as possible by remaining invested in a broadly diversified portfolio tailored to meet your investment goals and your tolerance for the ups and downs of financial markets. This approach includes an analysis of your long-term projections, current and projected tax situations, current investment portfolio, foreign tax credit inventory, and of course the lifestyle you want now and in the future. In other words, we manage your investment portfolio in an integrated approach to your comprehensive financial plan. We spend time where the investment research suggests, on asset allocation based on long-term economic trends.

As mentioned earlier, research has shown that the costs of investing along with the tax efficiency of the portfolio are two key determining factors in portfolio returns. As a result, a combination of tax-efficient index funds, exchange-traded funds, and other low-cost vehicles (read no-load) will form the core of your portfolio, with some asset class adjustments as warranted. Our custom-made tools allow us to analyze your Canadian and American investments, consolidate them in one currency for analysis, and determine the right investment strategy to achieve your desired lifestyle.

Our firm believes in a broadly diversified investment portfolio that starts with the four basic asset classes: cash, stocks, bonds, and hedging strategies. Stocks are further broken down into domestic (American and Canadian) and foreign (the rest of the world, including Europe, Asia, and emerging markets). They are further broken down into large cap and small cap as well as growth and value. Bonds are also broken down into domestic and foreign. They are broken down further to include short-term, medium-term, and long-term bonds. Hedging strategies consist of asset classes that move out of sync with stocks and bonds. They include real estate, natural resources, energy, precious metals, and other strategies not correlated to these other asset classes as they become available.

Finally, our firm believes in a disciplined approach, and this is where we help our clients the most. This means investing when you have the money and selling when you need it again. There is a big difference between speculating and investing, and it's important to note the chasm between them. We find that people invest in one of three ways: by fear, by greed, or by objective. When investing by fear, the slightest drop in financial markets has these speculators selling out of everything, creating tax and transaction costs, and waiting on the "sidelines" till things improve. Investing by greed leads them to buy when the market is up, resulting in the acquisition of overpriced securities that correct to normal P/E ratios. Investing by objective looks at the rate of return your portfolio needs to achieve to reach your objectives and structures the portfolio to achieve those objectives over the long term while taking into account your tolerance for market fluctuations. We believe in a low-cost, tax-efficient approach to investing driven by market research coming out of the institutional world. We are approved by Dimensional Fund Advisors to use their Nobel prize–winning mutual funds in both Canada and the U.S. These funds are not available to the public and are only available through a highly selected group of investment managers.

Our annual retainer service starts by developing an investment policy statement. This document uses your transition plan to outline further details of how your portfolio should be structured. It provides the guidelines on how the portfolio will be governed to meet your objectives. Once the policy is agreed to by all involved, the portfolio is implemented. You should never have anyone invest your money unless you have a written investment policy statement beforehand. Of course, any plan must be monitored closely. As a result, we conduct quarterly reviews of the portfolio, rebalancing it and managing taxes as necessary. The portfolio information is downloaded daily into portfolio accounting software used to determine the performance of the portfolio, which in turn enables better decision making. We provide quarterly reporting and rebalancing and are available to answer your questions as the markets move through their natural cycles. If you are interested in having your investments managed in the context of your Canada-U.S. transition plan, we'd be happy to assist you. We are able to offer a comprehensive, coordinated approach to investing in both Canada and the United States since we are registered investment advisors in the United States and investment counselor/portfolio managers in Canada. We can provide a coordinated solution for you from the inception of your move to Canada, all the way until you are resident there.

11 THE BUSINESS OF BUSINESS

Today or tomorrow we will go to this or that
city, spend a year there, carry on business
and make money.
— JAMES 4:13

For business owners, there are more options under their control when moving to Canada than for non-business owners. For example, your business can be a ticket to legal immigration status in Canada. However, business entities also add a lot of complexity to your situation, and there can be many hazards in leaving the United States without getting the requisite planning done. In our experience, business entity planning requires a longer lead time than individual planning and the proper team in place to adequately design and implement the appropriate strategies before entering Canada. However, if you do this correctly, you can reap huge rewards from both a Canadian and an American perspective.

IMMIGRATE TO CANADA

If you are running a "qualified" business in the United States that has been operating for at least one year, you may be able to use it to qualify for immigration status in Canada, though this is becoming more difficult. To qualify under the new Start-Up Visa, you will need to work with a Canadian private sector organization that specializes in start-ups (see Chapter 3 for more details). Once you succeed in securing the necessary funding and approval, you and your family are admissible to Canada with permanent residence status. Once you hold permanent residence for five years, you are eligible to apply for Canadian citizenship. As you can see, you could be discarding a golden opportunity to move to Canada if you inadvertently sell or wind up your business beforehand.

INCOME TAX IMPLICATIONS

By now, you have an understanding of the personal tax implications when you move to Canada. However, when you add a business to the mix, the complexity increases dramatically. It has been our experience that your current, trusted team of advisors, whom you have worked with for many years, are typically incapable of addressing the Canada-U.S. issues adequately when you move to Canada. In fact, some clients have told us that their advisors said it simply couldn't be done because of the complexity and discouraged them from attempting a move to Canada altogether. They were told they should just stay in the United States because the taxes in Canada are too onerous. In fact, structured properly, business owners in Canada can pay less tax than in the United States! A move can be done, though, and depending on your individual circumstances, the savings in time, effort, and money can be significant. You just have to understand that your current advisors need to join or be replaced by a new team led by a competent Canada-U.S. transition planner to coordinate the activities of the team. In addition, the sooner you put this team in place in anticipation of your move, the more fruit the planning process can bear. Following are some of the issues to be aware of when moving to Canada when you own a business in the United States.

U.S. TAX FILING REQUIREMENTS

When you move to Canada with a business remaining in the United States, you can end up in a double or triple tax situation fairly easily. First, because the entity is conducting a trade or business in the United States, you must file the requisite U.S. tax return and pay any taxes in the United States. Second, if you have a U.S. filing requirement as an American citizen or green card holder, you must declare any income from "flow-through" entities (e.g., Limited Liability Companies [LLCs],

Sub-Chapter S-Corporations) or dividends/wages from C-Corporations on your personal tax return as well. As you can see, the potential for double and triple taxation increases in these situations.

In the United States, there are different tax forms depending on the entity. For example, C-Corporations file Form 1120 — U.S. Corporation Income Tax Return, while corporations that have taken the S-Corporation "flow-through" election file Form 1120-S — U.S. Income Tax Return for an S Corporation. With the S-Corporation, each shareholder receives a Schedule K-1 outlining his or her share of the "pass-through" from the corporation, and this share must be declared on the individual tax return(s). Since C-Corporations are already double-taxed in the United States (at both the corporate level and the personal level for amounts distributed as wages or dividends), adding Canada to the mix creates the potential for a third layer of tax (see the simplified example below). Don't forget, U.S. corporations must file Form FinCEN 114 — Report of Foreign Bank and Financial Accounts as well or be subject to a U$10,000 penalty.

As an American citizen or resident who is a shareholder, officer, or director of a foreign corporation (i.e., a business in Canada), you must file Form 5471 — Information Return of U.S. Persons with Respect to Certain Foreign Corporations with your U.S. personal income tax filing, which is due April 15th each year. This is simply a reporting requirement (versus a tax return), but if not completed the penalties can be up to U$10,000 for each year the form wasn't filed. The IRS estimates the average time to prepare the form (exclusive of the requisite bookkeeping) at about 50 hours, but the actual time can be much longer for the uninitiated. Form 5471 appears to be deceptively simple since it's only four pages long, but there are also several worksheets and schedules that must be prepared along with 15 pages of instructions that will test your patience.

Any income taken out of the Canadian corporation as wages or dividends must also be reported on your individual 1040 tax return in the United States because you are required to declare your worldwide income on your U.S. tax return. Proper tax preparation should allow you to take offsetting foreign tax credits to avoid double taxation, but you still have to be aware of the other effects the income may have on your itemized deductions, personal exemption, and marginal tax bracket.

CANADIAN TAX FILING REQUIREMENTS

As a Canadian resident holding Canadian corporate entities, you quickly face complex tax filing requirements. Since the business is located in Canada, you must continue filing Canadian corporate tax returns on CRA Form T2 — Corporate Income Tax Return. Any income withdrawn as wages or dividends has to be declared on your Canadian individual T1 tax return. If you are required to file U.S. tax returns as well, this income must be declared on Form 1040, and tax must be paid in the United States as well.

Another issue to be aware of is that, once a U.S. tax filer has Sub-Part F income to report from a foreign corporation, the corporation thereafter must switch to a calendar year. This change can cause complications because, if the Canadian corporation has a fiscal year such as June 1st, you may have to pick up 18 months of income on that return spread out over five years, whereas it is common to operate on a fiscal year end (mid-year) in Canada. This difference causes complications because you have to reconcile your books twice to get the appropriate numbers together for your tax preparer. In addition, reconciling your personal wages, dividends, and varying currency exchange rates from the corporation to align with the mandatory calendar tax year for your individual tax returns in Canada and the United States makes things complicated.

As a Canadian tax resident owning a business in the United States, you are required to declare your worldwide income on your Canadian return. This includes all income from your U.S. entity, putting you in a double or triple tax situation that may or may not be offset with foreign tax credits (see the simplified example below). There are a number of onerous Canadian tax filing requirements as well. For example, Canadian individuals, corporations, trusts, and partnerships are required to file Form T1135 — Foreign Income Verification Statement annually with their respective returns and declare any foreign holdings and the income generated from them.

When you leave the United States, the shares of your business are subject to the step-up in basis mentioned in Chapter 5. This means, for Canadian purposes, that the cost basis of the shares of your company is equal to their fair market value on the day you enter Canada. To substantiate this with CRA, you should get a business valuation done just prior to entering Canada. If you sell your company after entering Canada, your Canadian cost basis will likely be much higher than your U.S. cost basis if a tax return is still required.

Another tax filing requirement you should be aware of is the need to collect and remit Goods and Services Tax (GST) for the federal government or the Harmonized Sales Tax (HST) for your respective province for any goods and services your business sells in Canada. The GST is a flat 5% sales tax on most goods and services sold in Canada. The HST is different in each province and is a combination of the GST and that province's sales tax (see Chapter 5 for more details). The HST must be collected in the provinces of New Brunswick (13%), Newfoundland and Labrador (13%), Nova Scotia (15%), Ontario (13%), and Prince Edward Island (14%). You will need to register and get a GST number to start. This number will be used to track and remit all GST/HST owed. You will need to file Form GST34-2 — Goods and Services Tax/Harmonized Sales Tax (GST/HST) Return for Registrants annually, and there are requirements to file electronically depending on your business. This is a complex area, and many firms are set up in Canada to assist you in remaining compliant in this area.

One planning alternative you should be aware of is the onetime C$800,000 small business capital gains exemption on your company shares offered by CRA. If you are able to structure your business and other financial affairs appropriately, you may be able to include your spouse and double the capital gains exemption to offset the first C$1.6 million in capital gains when you sell your Canadian business or move back to the United States. Unfortunately, the rules for this exemption are very specific and complex, so competent counsel should be retained before such an undertaking.

Some people neglect to do the requisite planning beforehand, and when they realize their situations they start playing tax games with both tax authorities. In our experience, this is akin to playing Russian roulette with the tax authorities, and it's inevitable that you'll commit tax suicide. We don't recommend you do it without seeking the appropriate counsel beforehand to ensure that you understand your risks. We have also seen people undertake tremendous planning where most of the taxable portions of the business can be paid out as a dividend subject to a 15% withholding and used as a foreign tax credit on their U.S. returns. The key is having the right team in place and enough lead time to get the planning done.

Table 11.1 is a summary of the corporate tax rates in both Canada and the United States.

TABLE 11.1

FEDERAL CORPORATE TAX BRACKETS

Canadian Taxable Income		U.S. Taxable Income	
C$0 +	15%	U$0-50,000	15%
Derived as follows:		50,001–75,000	25%
General corporate rate	38.0%	75,001–100,000	34%
Less federal abatement	(10.0)	100,001–335,000	39%
Equals	28.0	335,001–10,000,000	34%
Rate reductions	(13.0)	10,000,001–15,000,000	35%
Equals	15.0	15,000,001–18,333,333	38%
		18,333,333 +	35%

For small businesses in Canada, there is a small-business deduction of 17%, which reduces the tax rate to just 11%. There are also provincial corporate tax rates that range from 10% to 16% that are in addition to federal rates. Likewise in the U.S., state and local governments may also impose taxes ranging from 0% to 12%, but the business gets a deduction for them.

CANADIAN BUSINESS ENTITIES

Compared with the United States, there are fewer business entities in Canada that are "flow-through" for tax purposes, but that is slowly changing. This means that any income generated by the company flows through to your personal tax return in Canada (and the United States as applicable) and avoids the higher corporate income tax rates or being taxed twice, as with corporate dividends. Following are some of the most common business entity types in Canada.

- **Corporations:** this is a common corporation that files a T2 Corporate tax return, is subject to Canadian corporate income tax rates, and offers liability protection. This is how most large "blue-chip" corporations in Canada are structured. In essence, companies in Canada have a "Ltd." label, which is equivalent to "Inc." in the United States or "PLC" in the United Kingdom. These organizations have shareholders (common, preferred, etc.), typically issue bonds, and need to file minutes of annual meetings to ensure compliance.
- **Numbered companies:** most Americans are unfamiliar with this term. In Canada, a numbered company is simply a company incorporated with a number as its name (e.g., 54321 Canada Ltd.). To avoid searching for name availability, the federal (or provincial) authority assigns the number (and name) automatically. A provincial numbered company is named 12345 Alberta Ltd. Another term you probably aren't familiar with is "holdco." This is typically a corporation set up to hold investment management accounts for Canadian tax and estate planning reasons.
- **Unlimited liability corporations (ULCs):** this entity issues shares to its shareholders, and all income is passed through to those shareholders to be taxed on their individual returns. This is an increasingly popular business entity in Canada because it avoids the federal corporate income tax rates and can pass through gains or losses that are taxed at the personal level only. Currently, only Nova Scotia and more recently Alberta offer these types of entities. The Fifth Protocol of the Canada-U.S. Tax Treaty mitigated the tax benefits of these entities in the U.S.
- **Partnerships:** there are many different kinds of partnerships in Canada, and which one to use depends on your needs. For example, there are general partnerships and limited partnerships. A partnership is a separate legal entity and issues T5013 tax slips to its partners. This income must be declared on both the Canadian and the American tax returns as applicable.

When establishing a business entity in Canada as a U.S. citizen or green card holder, you must be aware of the IRS Controlled Foreign Corporation (CFC) rules. A common strategy in Canada is to leave retained earnings inside the corporation and invest them as a tax-deferral technique. A problem arises in that the portfolio income is taxed directly in the hands of the shareholder in the U.S. There is a "mismatch" of the foreign tax credits on the U.S. return, which creates a double tax situation. Further, the shareholder does not get the preferred tax rates on income such as dividends and capital gains and instead is taxed at regular marginal tax rates. As a result, the lack of planning can lead to the following accumulation of taxes.

13% — Canadian corporate tax
39.6% — U.S. federal personal tax
3.8% — U.S. net investment tax

All told, the cumulative tax rate could be up to 56.4% on every $1 of income. If you add state tax (like California at 10%), the total could be over 65%!

Understanding what you are trying to build helps you to determine which of these tools to use in your situation and depends on your individual financial circumstances, the type of business you want to set up, and what you intend to do with the business over the long term. Needless to say, it's best to do some planning beforehand to select the appropriate entity and get it set up appropriately to avoid complications later.

A SIMPLIFIED EXAMPLE

We have seen many business entity structures that made sense to the client when presented by a Canadian accountant or attorney but in reality made no sense given a full understanding of the rules in both Canada and the United States. Figure 11.1 is one business structure we worked on, and it provides a vivid illustration of what the wrong structure can do. A husband and wife living in Canada each owned half of the shares of 1234 Canada Inc., a Canadian corporation. Inside this corporation were three investment properties, one located in Canada and two in the United States. 1234 Canada Inc. owned U.S. Holdings Inc., an American C-corporation. U.S. Holdings owned two investment properties located in the United States. This structure was recommended by the clients' Canadian attorney to "protect them from U.S. liability issues" while they lived in Canada, but this "cross-border expert" created a multilayered tax situation for the clients that they weren't aware of until it was explained to them.

FIGURE 11.1

SAMPLE BUSINESS STRUCTURE

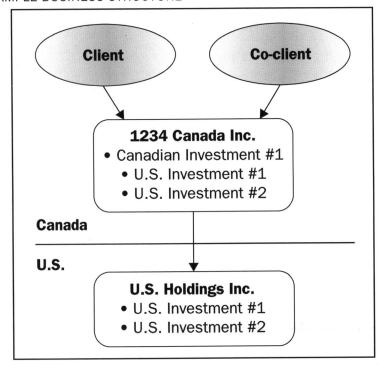

Here is the tax situation for U.S. Holdings Inc.

- **Tax #1:** All income generated by the two investments inside U.S. Holdings Inc. must be declared on IRS Form 1120 — U.S. Corporation Income Tax Return and taxed at American corporate rates, which can be as low as 15% and as high as 39.6%

(on taxable income over U\$100,000) plus state tax (as high as 12.3%, but it depends on which state[s] the corporation operates in or derives income from).

- **Tax #2:** Since U.S. Holdings Inc. is owned by 1234 Canada Inc., all dividends moved up to 1234 Canada Inc. are subject to a 5% non-resident withholding by the IRS.
- **Tax #3:** All the dividends received from U.S. Holdings Inc. will be declared on a Canadian T2 corporate tax return and taxed at Canadian corporate rates at 15%. There will be a foreign tax credit for the 5% withholding but not for the tax paid in the United States by U.S. Holdings Inc.
- **Tax #4:** Any income from U.S. Holdings Inc. distributed as a salary from 1234 Canada Inc. would flow through to the clients' personal tax returns at Canadian rates of 30–45% or more, but 1234 Canada Inc. would get a deduction, so an additional layer of taxes won't occur. However, if distributed as a dividend, the dividend tax credit applies, but no deduction is available to 1234 Canada, so some double taxation still results.
- **Tax #5:** Since both clients were American citizens, they are required to file U.S. Form 1040 tax returns each year. All income declared on their Canadian personal T1 tax returns as wages or dividends needs to be declared on their U.S. returns, but foreign tax credits should mitigate the bulk of the double taxation.

Note that these taxes are primarily cumulative, with little or no offsetting foreign tax credits, for an aggregate tax rate of 60–70% or more! For every dollar of income generated inside U.S. Holdings Inc., only 30–40¢ was actually ending up in the clients' pockets. Even more tragic is the fact that the damage was already done, and little could be done to avoid the steep income tax bill on the income and gains already accrued on the U.S. investments. The clients had no clue this was happening, and with the successful investments they had made they were essentially helping to eliminate the annual deficits in both countries! They had a U.S. accountant preparing their American tax returns and their trusted Canadian accountant preparing their Canadian tax returns, yet the attorney who had devised the structure wasn't coordinating tax preparation on both sides of the border. The clients were trying to do it themselves, but given the complexity it's no surprise they didn't catch the fact they were paying these levels of tax on the same income either. With the requisite planning, the clients would have realized more of the fruits of their investments and had an appropriate structure to mitigate the tax liability at both the corporate and the personal levels in both the United States and Canada.

We will briefly explain the taxation of the investments inside 1234 Canada Inc., but as you can see double taxation can be avoided for the most part because offsetting foreign tax credits and deductions are available.

- **Tax #1:** The IRS reserves the right to tax any trade or business income connected to the United States (except as exempted by the Canada-U.S. Tax Treaty) plus fixed income such as dividends and interest. Because a Canadian (foreign) corporation held the American investments, any income produced by these two investments must be declared on IRS Form 1120F and taxed at U.S. corporate rates, which can be as low as 15% and as high as 39.6% (on taxable income over U$100,000) plus state tax (as high as 12.3%).
- **Tax #2:** Any income generated by any of the properties held by 1234 Canada Inc. is declared on a Canadian T2 corporate tax return and taxed at Canadian corporate rates at 15%. For the two properties in the U.S., a foreign tax credit is available for the tax paid on the U.S. corporate tax return.
- **Tax #3:** Depending on where the work is performed, any income distributed as a salary from 1234 Canada Inc. may be declared as Canadian source and flows through to the clients' personal tax returns at Canadian rates of 30–45% or more. However, 1234 Canada Inc. would get a deduction for those wages paid, and double taxation would be avoided. Yet you have to consider any payroll taxes you may owe in Canada or the United States on those wages. If distributed as a dividend,

however, the dividend tax credit applies, but no deduction is available to 1234 Canada Inc., so some double taxation still results.

As this simplified example vividly illustrates, the taxation of business entities in Canada can become extremely complex when spanning the border. No wonder so many accountants and tax lawyers simply throw up their hands and declare "It just can't be done." We are thankful for the network of professionals proficient in these transactions who have assisted our clients over the years. They have a thorough knowledge of this area and have a number of strategies and techniques that can be deployed as needed to address most business issues. We have personally witnessed this planning save hundreds of thousands of dollars and countless hours of frustration. The best thing you can do? Hire the appropriate team three to four years in advance of your move to start the planning.

12 NORTHERN EXPOSURE

By the time the sun is hot tomorrow,
you will be delivered.
— 1 SAMUEL 11:9

For some folks, remaining in the United States during the winter months before heading north to Canada for the warm summer months suits them just fine. Unlike their "snowbird" counterparts seeking to escape the winter cold, these "sunbirds" seek to escape the summer heat, particularly in the southern states when it can get unbearably hot. Owning property in Canada offers many benefits, including a fixed place to go and a potential increase in your investment. Despite these benefits, people aren't generally prepared for the potential tax, estate planning, and paperwork nightmare that comes with having a property in Canada. This complexity needs to be considered in your overall decision to buy a second home in Canada. This chapter aims to clear up a lot of confusion surrounding owning property in Canada while remaining a resident of the United States.

RECREATIONAL PROPERTY

For properties in Canada that are used exclusively for personal use, there are several issues to consider. For example, there are several options in how you title the property, tax implications when buying or selling it, and disposition issues at your death.

OWNERSHIP

The titling of your property can be confusing. For sole ownership, you have two types: freehold, which gives you unlimited time and use of the property within legal limits, and leasehold, in which you don't own the property but just lease it for your use for a specified time. When more than one owner is involved, you have joint tenancy and tenancy in common. Joint tenancy is when you own the property in equal portions to all other owners. If one of the "joint tenants" dies, there is a "with rights of survivorship," where the deceased person's portion is automatically added to the other owners' portions equally until the last one to die owns the entire property. With tenancy in common, ownership doesn't have to be equal (one person owns 10%, another 50%, and another 40%), and when an owner dies that portion goes to the deceased's estate, not to the other owners. This means that a new owner — who may not get along with the others — can now be involved with the property.

Many people have asked us about the best way to take title to their property in Canada. Some alternatives include holding it directly (jointly or individually), through a business entity, or through their living trust. There are pros and cons with each, and it depends a lot on your individual circumstances (tax situation, current estate plan design, your desires for the property, etc.). For many Americans, the use of trusts in estate planning is common in the United States because they are viewed as flow-through entities for U.S. tax purposes (see Chapter 7). In Canada, trusts are viewed as a separate tax entity with punishing tax rates. Many U.S. estate planning attorneys emphasize that you must fund your trust. This means titling all possible assets in the name of your trust, including your second home. But how do you do this in Canada? It isn't easy. In our experience, if you have already bought your home in Canada, titling it in the name of your U.S. trust after the fact is all but impossible. It seems that attorneys and government land title registries just don't know what to do when it comes to a U.S. trust. Besides, there is a "deemed disposition" for Canadian purposes when you retitle your property in the name of your living trust. Our advice is to buy the property in the name of your U.S. trust at the outset, or you will have to consider another means of governing the property according to your wishes. This approach will allow you to avoid probate in Canada and the United States as well as the

Canadian deemed disposition tax when you die. One problem, though, is the 21-year trust rule in Canada; after 21 years, the trust no longer exists, and everything has to be distributed for tax purposes. This means you have a deemed disposition in Canada on the property after 21 years. You should note that in Canada, attorneys conduct most real estate transactions, while in the United States a title company does so. There are also tax issues that we address below.

Generally, it's a bad idea to own your property inside a C-Corporation because of the adverse tax consequences. In addition, there are onerous tax filing requirements such as IRS Form 5471. Many attorneys still recommend corporations for "liability purposes," but they may be unaware of the other consequences, so tread carefully. Another alternative is to hold the property in some type of a business entity such as a Sub-Chapter S-Corporation, a partnership, or a Limited Liability Company (LLC). Again, which entity you use depends on your individual circumstances, and there are pros and cons to each.

Sometimes the simplest solution is the best, just holding the property jointly or individually. Again, it depends on your circumstances and the future Canadian and U.S. tax and estate implications that will govern how you hold the property. As always, we recommend you get competent advice as we turn our attention to the tax implications for "sunbirds."

TAX ISSUES

There are several tax issues to consider when you buy and sell your second home.

Buying Your Second Home

The first tax to consider when you are buying your second home is the Goods and Services Tax in Canada, affectionately known as the GST. It's a federal sales tax of 5% levied on the "supply" of real property (and most other consumable goods) in Canada. When you purchase property in Canada, you may have to pay the GST depending on the individual circumstances surrounding your purchase. For example, if you are purchasing a new home, GST must be paid, but you may be eligible for a partial rebate depending on the size of the home. If you are purchasing a pre-owned home from someone who used it personally, no GST is owed.

There is no GST on the purchase of land, but there may be GST if you build a home or renovate one. As you can see, there is no simple answer, and getting the right professionals to assist you is recommended.

If you are purchasing a second home in the Maritimes, an additional sales tax called the Harmonized Sales Tax (HST) of 8% may be required. Unfortunately, this tax is in addition to the GST outlined above. Some provinces also charge a property purchase or transfer tax, as does British Columbia. In that province, this tax is due every time the property changes hands, and it is 1% on the first C$200,000 and 2% after that. There are certain exemptions, but they depend on your individual circumstances.

Selling Your Second Home

When the time comes to sell your second home in Canada, there are some tax consequences to consider. CRA reserves the right to tax property in Canada. As a non-resident of Canada selling Canadian real property, you are subject to a flat 25% withholding tax on the gross sales price. This means that, if you sell a property in Canada for C$200,000, C$50,000 will be withheld and remitted to CRA by your attorney. However, if you file Form T2062 — Request by a Non-Resident of Canada for a Certificate of Compliance Related to the Disposition of Taxable Canadian Property, you can reduce the amount withheld to 25% of the net gains only. This means that, if you get an approved T2062 from CRA before or shortly after the sale of your real property, you only have to remit C$200,000 less C$100,000 original cost of the property = C$100,000 gain multiplied by 25% = C$25,000. You declare the sale proceeds less the adjusted cost basis that result in your taxable gain. This gain is declared on a non-resident T1 tax return. In Canada, only half of your gain is taxed at ordinary marginal income tax rates (see Chapter 5), and since you have paid some amount on the initial sale of the property you could get a refund on any overpayment by filing a non-resident T-1 tax return.

Since you are a U.S. tax resident, you must declare the sale of this second home as part of your worldwide income on your U.S. return as well. This will be considered a long-term capital gain subject to a flat 15% tax rate in addition to any state income taxes owing. This can lead to double taxation. If you're getting proper tax preparation, the tax you pay in Canada will become a foreign tax credit on your U.S. return to offset some or all of the double taxation (but not necessarily on your state tax return). Further, be aware that your capital gain/loss will have to be adjusted for currency exchange purposes.

Transferring Your Second Home

In some cases, you may succeed in getting an existing property titled in the name of your trust. However, you should understand the tax consequences of doing so first. As outlined above, the United States views a revocable living trust as a flow-through entity to your personal return. In Canada, however, a trust is viewed as a separate taxable entity (see Chapter 7). This means that, when you try to move your Canadian recreational property into your U.S. trust, CRA considers this a "deemed disposition," and any capital gains accrued to that point are reported and the requisite taxes need to be paid. This is where good planning up front — getting your property titled correctly when you purchase the property — is probably your best option.

INVESTMENT PROPERTY

When you purchase a home in Canada for investment purposes (to rent out or to "flip"), you still have to contend with the ownership and tax implications outlined above. There are additional issues to consider.

CANADA

As outlined above, CRA retains the right to tax all Canadian-source capital gains on real property. However, if you are generating rental income, you are required to appoint an agent in Canada to ensure that any taxes owing are paid. If you don't pay the taxes, your agent residing in Canada must do so. This way CRA has assets and people it can attach itself to for any claim of taxes owing. To appoint an agent, you need to file Form NR6 — Undertaking to File an Income Tax Return by a Non-Resident Receiving Rent from Real Property or Receiving a Timber Royalty each year with CRA. The NR6 needs to be filed before January of each tax year, or before your first rent payment is due. Once approved, this option allows you to remit 25% withholding tax on the net income each month (if any) when rent is collected. If you don't file an NR6 in a timely fashion, you are subject to a 25% withholding tax on the gross rental income, which could lead to a significant cash flow problem. You must also file a Section 216 tax return each year to properly account for your expenses against any rental income, which may result in a refund or a balance owing. Finally, if capital cost allowance is taken on the Canadian return, there could be a nasty "recapture" at the sale of the property for which you should plan. Recapture is the taxation of the cumulative capital cost allowance taken on the property over the years, all in the year of sale. All of this is captured on a T1 non-resident tax return, where the final tax liability is determined. This is dealt with in greater detail in our companion book *The Canadian in America*.

The other issue you have to contend with if you are buying and selling homes or raw land on a speculative basis is turning capital gain income into ordinary income. If you have no intention of moving into the home and simply plan to capture some gains in a rapidly rising housing market, CRA may classify all the gains as ordinary income taxed at the marginal tax rates in Canada. Remember, if classified as capital gains, only half of the gains are subject to the marginal tax rates, so if you don't do it right you could be doubling your taxable income. The key determinants of how these gains are taxed are your intention when you purchased the property, how quickly you sold it, and the facts and circumstances surrounding the transaction.

UNITED STATES

Since you are required to report your worldwide income on your U.S. tax return, the rental income you derive from Canada must be reported as well, after converting the income to U.S. dollars. This income can lead to double taxation because of the 25% withholding you paid to CRA. Proper tax planning and preparation can recoup some of the tax paid to Canada as a foreign tax credit on your U.S. return. Interestingly enough, you must depreciate the rental property on your U.S. return, while claiming capital cost allowance is optional in Canada. Again, when it comes time to sell the property, there is the "recapture" of the depreciation on your

U.S. tax return in the year of sale, which can lead to a nasty tax surprise. Proper tax planning can make this a much easier transaction.

ESTATE PLANNING

Owning property in multiple jurisdictions causes unique estate planning issues that must be dealt with in advance. By far, this is one of the most neglected areas we see with sunbirds owning property in Canada. As outlined above, your best approach may be to buy your Canadian property in the name of your U.S. trust at the outset. If you own the property outright, you may want to consider getting a separate Canadian will drafted to govern just that property in Canada, but make sure it's coordinated with your U.S. will so they don't conflict with each other. A business entity may better suit your needs as well; it just depends on your tax, ownership, and estate planning circumstances and what you are trying to achieve.

In Canada, there is no estate tax per se; instead, there is the deemed disposition at death (see Chapter 7 for more details). Depending on how the property is owned, Canadian taxes may be owed at the first or second spouse's death, as outlined above. In addition, there may be the provincial probate fees applicable in the province where the property is located (they are listed in Chapter 7).

As an American citizen or tax resident, you must also consider U.S. estate and gift taxes (see Chapter 7). For the calculation of U.S. estate taxes, your worldwide estate is considered, including your Canadian leisure or investment property. At your death, you'll have Canadian deemed disposition taxes and possibly U.S. estate taxes. This is where it's important to know how to apply the Canada-U.S. Tax Treaty to avoid the double taxation that may occur at death. You may also face probate in the United States and its attendant costs and delays. Coupled with probate in Canada, it could be an expensive proposition.

MAYDAY! MAYDAY! 13

Plans fail for lack of counsel,
but with many advisors they succeed.
— PROVERBS 15:22

Having read this book, you may feel like crying out "Mayday!" ("Día de mayo!" if you speak Spanish.) Indeed, you may feel overwhelmed by all of the things to consider in your move and the amount of time you have to address them. Don't panic; although limited, help is available. You have to decide what you are going to do and where you want help. Some folks may want to delegate most of the tasks involved, while others may want to do most of the work on their own just using this book. We encourage you to determine this up front since it will help to guide you in the relationship you are seeking. This chapter outlines some of the things you need to consider in your search for a Canada-U.S. transition planner, and be sure to use the checklist provided in Appendix C.

SELECTING A TRANSITION PLANNER

Today, it seems, everyone is calling himself or herself a "financial planner" or "financial advisor." In our opinion, no industry has so pillaged a term and created such confusion as the financial services industry with the term "financial planner/advisor." Any relationship has trust as its under-pinning. This trust requires a strict upholding of the fiduciary standard (versus a suitability standard). The word fiduciary is defined as "of or relating to a holding of something in trust for another." This means your interests are put ahead of the financial planner's, even if you are leaving the firm. With a suitability standard, the product simply needs to be suitable to you (leaving lots of room for the recommender to serve his or her own needs), not necessarily the best thing for you. Essentially, the financial product salesperson doesn't have to disclose that he or she is recommending a particular financial product because of a quota to meet, a bonus for selling it, or a contest to win — it just has to be suitable. Do you see the chasm between these two standards?

An example may help. We fielded a call in 2014 from a sales representative in Canada who found our website and needed some help with an American client living in Canada. The client had U$450,000 in an IRA in the United States that this salesperson had convinced the client to withdraw and put into a Canadian RRSP because she'd heard it could be done. We explained to the representative that the client would pay ordinary income tax (up to 39.6% plus a 10% penalty plus 3.8% NIIT) to the IRS on the amount withdrawn because Americans must file U.S. tax returns annually, no matter where they live. The salesperson replied, "This is a big commission I am not going to forgo." We challenged her to do the right thing for the client because a loss of U$200,000 + in taxes could likely devastate the client's financial projections. We tried to explain further that she wasn't doing the best thing for the client and that it would be best if she referred that client out. Her response was "I am doing the best thing for the client with the products I am able to sell!" and promptly hung up on us. We had tried for half an hour to save this client from some bad and costly advice. Now let us be clear that caveat emptor applies because the client didn't do the requisite research to find an advisor that met their needs. On the other hand, we believe the salesperson bears the responsibility to fully disclose the hidden fees, expenses, and, yes, our cautionary advice to her regarding this client. As long as the product is suitable, she is off the hook. But can she honestly say she put the client's interests ahead of her own? Particularly when we pointed out the issues to her and how she was potentially damaging the client? It just didn't matter — she saw an opportunity to make some money and serve her own needs. In our opinion, she took advantage of the trust the client had placed in her to benefit herself.

Our firm believes the best way to fulfill the fiduciary responsibility to you is to be fee-only (no product sales, no commissions, payment only from you, the client). This puts us firmly on your side. The planning process should start by having a conversation about you and what you are trying to achieve, not about a particular product, your investments, or a tax-saving strategy that "fits" into your situation. From there, our role is that of a quarterback to coordinate the bevy of attorneys, insurance agents, accountants, investment managers, and other professionals to ensure that your best interests are served at all times. The key is to focus everyone on the achievement of your goals and objectives. As a result, your American stockbroker's or CPA's interests and preferences should be secondary to your needs when moving to Canada. Here are the things to consider in selecting a Canada-U.S. transition planner.

COMPETENCE

The first step in hiring any Canada-U.S. transition planner is to look for the Certified Financial Planner™ designation in both Canada and the United States. The license to use the CFP® designation is issued annually by the Certified Financial Planner Board of Standards in the United States and the Financial Planners Standards Council in Canada. To hold these designations, one must complete course requirements and a comprehensive exam. In addition, there are work experience requirements (three years) that must be met in the financial services industry before use of the designation will be granted. Maintaining these designations requires meeting continuing education standards to ensure the licensee is current with the changing rules and regulations. Most important, however, is the requirement to abide by a strict code of ethics. An undergraduate and a graduate degree (preferably on both sides of the border) should be considered an asset as well as the Tax and Estate Practitioner (TEP) designation given by the Society of Trust and Estate Practitioners.

The next thing to look at is the experience of the transition planner you are considering. Ask if he or she works on a consistent basis in the Canada-U.S. planning arena. Some people call themselves "cross-border" planners, but under further probing it comes to light that they have helped a friend three years ago when he moved to Canada or that the bulk of their clients have no international issues at all. Ask about their current clientele and if they themselves have made the move. There is nothing like having someone with the practical experience of having made the move to help you with your move. If he or she hasn't walked in the shoes you are about to put on, run — don't walk — away. We have seen the negative side of so-called experts, and it ends up costing you twice (a good example is tax preparation: you pay once for the initial work and again to adjust or amend your returns to bring you into compliance), plus there is usually little recourse for a job poorly done, and you will be fortunate to get a refund of your tax preparation fees or any penalties or interest the tax authorities assess. When it comes to transition planners, be careful you are getting what you pay for!

Unfortunately, there is no formal professional training in Canada-U.S. transition planning. It has to come with practical experience, "on-the-job" education, and a comprehensive network of professionals. This means that competent Canada-U.S. transition planners are in very short supply, and there are very few people who can competently write a comprehensive financial plan for your transition to Canada. It often comes down to knowing which questions to ask and how to get effective answers. In addition, there are many potential gray areas to consider in any U.S.-Canada move, and often the judgment and experience of a good transition planner are worth more than the fees paid. In the tax preparation arena, there are more people who can competently deal with Canada-U.S. tax issues and how the treaty between the two countries applies. As always, we recommend you choose your professionals carefully and demand full disclosure of their compensation.

PLANNING PROCESS

The next thing to focus on is the process the transition planner will follow in developing your financial plan. Lack of a well-defined process typically indicates a poor planning approach and, subsequently, poor results. Our years of experience in Canada-U.S. transition planning have led to a very defined process that has proven itself successful many times. As a result, our process isn't something we alter or try to find a shortcut around. There are too many small details in any U.S.-Canada move that can create havoc with your unique financial situation. In considering any transition planner, ask if he or she has a planning process. If so, is it designed for a U.S.-to-Canada transition? In our experience, we have seen many Canadian planners who are approached by someone with Canada-U.S. issues not even ask about immigration status, citizenship, or assets in the United States! These are critical issues that need to be taken into account in the planning. Does the process focus on you and what you are trying to achieve, or is it on a particular product, on tax savings, or on an investment system? Any transition plan starts with a thorough exercise setting goals and objectives. This is time consuming but necessary to establish the context in which to place individual U.S.-Canada financial decisions. Ask how much time will be spent understanding your needs and your unique financial situation and how the conversations will be documented. In our experience, this process typically requires two meetings of two to three hours each to fully understand your situation.

Once the process is complete, ask if a custom-tailored, written report will be issued. Ask to see a sample transition plan. It's important to note the difference between a myriad of colored charts produced by most planning, insurance, or investment software and a financial plan containing detailed analysis of every aspect of your financial situation. Be sure that specific recommendations will be given on all aspects outlined above, from cash management and income taxes to Canada-U.S. issues in estate planning.

CLIENT RELATIONSHIP

Another important attribute in selecting advisors is whether you can work with them or not. Ensure that you understand they know whom they are going to serve (you!). Ask if you'll be working directly with a principal of the firm or with an associate. If an associate, how does the company assign one to you? Is it random, or is there a personality assessment to find the best fit in the firm? When did that associate make his or her U.S.-to-Canada move? When you call in, who will take your call? Is this person technically competent, or does he or she have to ask someone more senior for every answer? Do you share a common heritage? If not, you'll find that the "associate" will typically be your "parrot" to someone senior in the firm (whom you met in the first meeting and haven't seen since) who really knows the answers. This can be a frustrating, time-consuming process for you. Is this person fun to work with? Is he or she a "fit" with the way you like to work (in person, via email, etc.)? You should also know, once your plan is complete, who is going to assist you with implementing it and how much that will cost. Be sure you have a detailed understanding of the recommendations being made, the pros and cons of each, and how each will be implemented. Overall, your transition to Canada shouldn't be a laborious task, and your consultations should offer healthy interactions that any good relationship is expected to provide.

NATURE OF THE FIRM

It's prudent to ask some difficult questions about the firm you are considering. For example, ask about the number of clients lost and gained in the past couple of years. If you get an answer at all, you should ask why people are leaving the firm to glean further insights into your potential relationship with it. If there have been many new clients, ask if the firm is on a big marketing push, for you may be lost in the shuffle.

Another difficult question to ask is whether there has been a high rate of employee turnover. If so, it's difficult to retain someone who has an intimate understanding of you and your financial situation, because new "associates" constantly need to be brought up to speed (usually by you because the partners are too busy). A lack of consistency in the relationship can lead to things missed. Also, if there is turnover, you need to ask yourself "Why isn't this firm able to keep its top employees? Are its hiring practices suspect? Is it just desperate to staff up to handle its marketing growth?"

Find out the strategic direction of the firm and what it is trying to achieve; you'll gain insights into the motivation of a relationship with you (are you just a fee, or does the company want to help you build a better life?). If there is no limit to its growth, this may indicate a focus on fees rather than on a relationship with you. Get some details about the principals of the firm, such as their ages, retirement/succession plans, and so on. Look for principals who are committed to their business over the long term and certainly for as long as you intend to have a relationship with them. You should ask for two or three references of clients who have been with the firm (for varying time periods, starting with relatively new to several years) to get a broad perspective on what it's like to work with this firm. How big is it, and how many relationships does it currently have? How many relationships does it have per associate? Per principal? The higher the client-associate ratio for relationships, the more difficult it will be to service you. If you visit the firm, is there a sense of organization or chaos? Ask to see the office of the person you'll be working with. Are there files stacked all over the floor, desks, and shelves, or is everything relatively clean and in order? Do they return your initial call or email promply? A chaotic firm can mean little or no time to service your needs and one focused on fees rather than clients.

Another area to consider is the agreement you'll sign with the prospective firm. Ask for a sample agreement, and be sure you understand the details. Is the agreement long and complicated, with the fee buried deep in the agreement or not present at all? Do you understand how the fee is calculated for your situation? Is this an objective or subjective process? Does the fee seem reasonable for services rendered, and how does it compare with other fee quotes? You should also watch for agreements that lock you in for a defined period of time or levy penalties if you want out before the expiration of your agreement. This is all good for the advisor and bad for you. Why would you want to be cemented in a relationship that isn't working? Why can't the advisor earn your business and keep it voluntarily rather than force you into a contractual relationship? Does the financial planner get all or most of your money up front and therefore leave little incentive to continue servicing you afterward? Ask for an estimated completion date for your financial plan. Asking some pointed questions will ensure that you have an advisor you can trust to uphold the fiduciary responsibility to you.

REGULATORY COMPLIANCE

By law, anyone rendering financial advice must be registered with the appropriate government authority. In the United States, this means your transition planning firm must be a registered investment advisor with the Securities and Exchange Commission or with the appropriate authority in the state where it is located. In Canada, any advisor must be registered with the appropriate provincial authority in the province where you'll reside. In the United States, you should ask for a Client Disclosure Brochure, which is required by the regulator and should be provided when you inquire about the firm's services. This document must be updated and filed annually, and it contains everything about the financial advisory firm you are considering, including the backgrounds of the professionals employed, the services offered, and how they are compensated. You'll also be able to check for any disciplinary hearings or other issues that may be important to you.

You should also check with industry regulators and associations for more information on the firm you are considering. Most of this can be done online with the Securities and Exchange Commission (www.adviserinfo.sec.gov/) or for any commission folks at finra.org/Investors/ToolsCalculators/BrokerCheck/. You should also confirm the license to use the CFP® designation at the CFP Board of Standards in the United States (www.cfp-board.org) and the Financial Planners Standards Council (www.cfp-ca.org) in Canada. You can also check the background of the licensee, how long he or she has held the license, and whether there have been any disciplinary hearings (and the outcome). Another thing to consider is the advisor's involvement in professional associations. They are a good source of information on the person you are considering to become your trusted financial advisor. In the United States the equivalent is the National Association of Personal Financial Advisors (www.feeonly.org). There is also in the United States the Financial Planning Association (www.fpanet.org), where you can check membership, involvement, standing, and so on.

COMPENSATION

Another important thing you should know is how your transition planner is compensated. This is a controversial subject in the industry, so our intention here is to arm you with the information you need to make an informed decision and pick the planner right for you. Whether they tell you or not, all transition planners get paid . . . nobody works for free. There are basically four methods of compensation.

- **Commission-only:** the person gets paid commissions and trailers from financial products sold to you; this is the most common method of compensation in the industry and is evidenced by a focus on your investments and the disclaimer that the person can't offer tax advice.
- **Fee-offset:** advice is rendered for a fee, but if you purchase a financial product afterward the commissions or trailers are reduced by the fee you have paid up front.

- **Fee-based:** this is a combination of a fixed fee for advice rendered and then commissions and trailers for any products sold to you. In our opinion, it's really "double-dipping," and it's telling how the financial plan typically recommends products for which the person will earn a commission on as well.
- **Fee-only:** you pay a fee for advice rendered, and there is no other source of third-party compensation (no commissions, trailers, etc.), similar to how you work today with an accountant or an attorney.

Let us say up front that our firm is a fee-only financial planning firm, and therefore we are disclosing our bias toward fee-only planning. We believe this method of compensation removes as many conflicts of interest as possible from the relationship with you and puts any firm more solidly on your side in rendering advice in your best interests (upholding the fiduciary responsibility to you). When compensation comes from the sale of financial products to you, it creates an inherent conflict of interest because there is generally a quota to meet or a sales contest to win. Unfortunately, this is perfectly legal in our society because of two very different standards for financial product salespeople versus true financial advisors. In the case of financial product sales, there is a suitability standard, which means that the product has to be suitable to your situation in order to avoid the ire of the regulator. With a fiduciary standard, the regulator requires your interests to come ahead of your advisor's, which means that the advice rendered should be as conflict-free as possible. We suggest you demand full disclosure and ensure you understand, in dollar terms, how much it will cost to implement any recommendations provided. You should carefully discern between:

- a financial product salesperson, who renders advice about a particular product;
- a financial planner, who renders advice on specific technical topics such as taxes or investments;
- a financial advisor, who renders comprehensive financial advice based on an understanding of your entire financial situation and what you are trying to achieve; the focus is on

you and your financial goals, not on a particular financial product, technical area, or strategy; and

- a transition planner, who is a financial advisor who specializes in your transition from the United States to Canada.

We have provided a checklist in Appendix C you can use to help you determine exactly what type of advisor you are considering.

It has been our experience that a transition planner well versed personally and professionally in Canadian and American financial matters is typically the best person to assist you with your move to Canada. It really takes a comprehensive understanding of both sides of the border and continual practice in this area to render the best advice to you.

To save a few dollars, some people believe their American certified public accountant (CPA) and their Canadian chartered accountant (CA) are all they need to competently cross the border. We have seen American CPAs do things for U.S. tax, estate planning, or liability protection purposes with no idea of the consequences in Canada. Double or even triple taxation is the result when the client moves to Canada. We have seen Canadian CAs and American CPAs prepare tax returns with no understanding of CRA or IRS compliance issues. When the first piece of "hate mail" arrives from the IRS or CRA and is presented to the "cross-border tax professional," suddenly calls are no longer returned, or the response "We don't deal with Canada-U.S. tax issues" is given. We have seen some folks try to save money by having a Canadian CA complete their Canadian start-up return and their American CPA complete their U.S. tax return with no coordination between the two returns for income and foreign tax credits. As a result, extra taxes are usually paid.

We dealt with one situation recently in which an American citizen living in Canada had her U.S. return prepared by the Canadian CA because he prepared both American and Canadian tax returns. We found the CA was aware that the American citizen had to file a U.S. tax return annually. However, when we reviewed the return, we found the CA had improperly taken a treaty exemption and declared that, since the American lived in Canada, no capital gains were to be reported on the U.S. return. This was news to the client, and the CA offered to fix the return, but there were other problems that he admitted he didn't know how to fix.

We have seen immigration attorneys simply file a visa application for an unsuspecting client with no explanation of what it means to take up tax residency in Canada and no understanding of the Canadian and American tax or estate planning consequences such a visa brings when executed. We have seen estate planning attorneys create estate plans costing thousands of dollars that pay no regard to U.S. citizenship issues and IRAs or real estate holdings in the United States. We have seen Canadian "investment managers" trade brokerage accounts with no understanding of the U.S. tax consequences they are causing their clients who now reside in Canada. Come tax time, the unsuspecting client is shell-shocked by the tax bill handed out by CRA or IRS. And, sadly enough, we have often seen people rely on the advice of their current American financial planners to orchestrate their moves to Canada, with dire tax and estate planning consequences and little regard for the fiduciary responsibility owed to them . . . even putting clients into variable annuities before they move to Canada to lock in the commissions and trailers before they lose the relationship. We have seen Canadian financial planners happy to be working with new clients from the United States, but their data collection process doesn't even consider assets in the United States or citizenship or immigration issues. Unfortunately, these people are rendering advice in an area they aren't capable of practicing in . . . a clear violation of principle three of the CFP® Code of Ethics and Professional Responsibility (if they hold the CFP® at all). All of these folks may be welcome on a well-rounded Canada-U.S. transition planning team, but they require a quarterback to coordinate all of the activities and to ensure that all the right questions are being asked, and answered, along the way. Failure to put in place a well-thought-out plan, unique to your individual situation, and have it coordinated effectively can have many unintended consequences and cause you no end of grief. To assist you in selecting the right transition planner to meet your needs, use the handy checklist we have provided in Appendix C.

OUR FIRM

Transition Financial Advisors Group uses the tagline "Pathways to Canada" to clarify that we specialize in helping people to make a smooth transition from the United States to Canada or U.S. citizens and green card holders already living there. To that end, our firm operates best as the "financial coordinator" of your Canada-U.S. transition planning team. Not only does our firm have the educational background to meet your needs (we hold both Canadian and American financial planning and investment designations), but we also have the personal experience in moving back and forth across the 49th parallel. One of the most important things our firm brings to any relationship is empathy with you in the many joys and frustrations you'll experience in moving to Canada. Why? Because we have walked in the shoes you are about to put on. In addition, we share a common American and Canadian heritage and can easily talk about football, American politics, or fishing in Alberta. I enjoy many relationships with other professionals across Canada and the United States who are competent in Canada-U.S. planning matters, and we can bring them onto the team as needed. These people include accountants, attorneys, insurance agents, and government contacts. We have chosen this approach over bringing everything in house so we can select the best people to work with you on your Canada-U.S. transition issues.

Our planning fees are typically based on a sliding scale of your net worth and generally start at U$10,000 and go up from there, depending on your net worth. These financial plans take 50 to 80 hours of time to complete on our part and require an investment of 10 hours of your time participating in the process. Trust us, if we don't believe there is sufficient value in an engagement with our firm, we will not extend an engagement. This approach falls in line with our comprehensive financial planning philosophy because our firm looks at everything related to your move. This may include rendering advice on the tax implications of selling your home or converting it to a rental property or providing advice on your homeowner's insurance policy. Our fee is made known up front and put into an agreement that both you and we sign. The fee is then fixed until the engagement is fulfilled, giving you peace of mind that there are no hidden fees or expenses to surprise you later. Obviously, this is how we feed our families, so we don't render advice for free! When we do have time, we are committed to helping our community through pro bono work, so any work we do for free is done in this area only (budget counseling, teaching, etc.).

In our experience, folks who meet the following criteria will benefit the most from our services:

- desire a close, long-term working relationship versus just a transaction;
- willing to delegate financial matters and have done so in the past;
- have a lead time of three to four months before a move to Canada is scheduled (longer with business entities);
- believe in our comprehensive transition planning approach and willing to follow our proven process;
- willing and able to expediently implement the plan (with our assistance) once completed;
- make friends easily and willing to share of themselves, expecting the same in return;
- comfortable using the Internet; and
- have a net worth of U$2 million or more.

You can contact us for a no-obligation review of your situation and the opportunities and obstacles your unique financial situation presents. Just go to our website and click on the green "Get Started" tab to download our "Introductory FactFinder." Fill it out to the best of your ability and send it to us. We will contact you to set up an appointment, and with your "FactFinder" in hand we can be in a better position to discuss your unique situation. If you have some questions up front you want addressed before submitting your FactFinder, feel free to call or email me at the coordinates below.

Transition Financial Advisors Group, Inc.
— Pathways to Canada
Gilbert, AZ
Phone: 480-722-9414
Email: book@transitionfinancial.com
Website: www.transitionfinancial.com

14 REALIZING THE DREAM

I am a Canadian, a free Canadian, free to speak without fear, free to worship God in my own way, free to stand for what I think is right, free to oppose what I believe is wrong, free to choose those who shall govern my country. This heritage of freedom I pledge to uphold for myself and all mankind. — CANADIAN BILL OF RIGHTS

Now that you have moved, settled in, and begun realizing your lifestyle dream in Canada, there are some differences from the United States you'll notice. Contrary to popular opinion, there are general cultural differences between the United States and Canada that you should be aware of since some of them may be harsh realities. Many of these differences are based on our experiences and those of others we have spoken to who have made the transition to Canada. For example, Canadians typically tend to be more risk averse, conservative in their relationships, and better savers. Americans tend to be greater risk takers, are more comfortable with debt, are more entrepreneurial in business, and overall tend to be more outgoing. As a result, they tend to save less and carry more consumer debt than Canadians, although in our opinion that appears to be changing based on the number of check-cashing/ payday loan stores, stores willing to extend credit, creative financing, and increased comfort with debt we are seeing in Canada. Following is a host of other things you'll find interesting in comparing Canada and the United States.

LAW ENFORCEMENT

In the United States, you have become comfortable with the constant presence of the military (aircraft overhead, equipment on the roads) and military personnel most everywhere you go. There are numerous military branches and locations throughout the country. In Canada, however, you'll rarely see the military or know of anyone who has served except maybe a veteran from the great wars in Europe. In Canada, there are approximately 62,000 regular force members and about 25,000 reserve force members in a population of approximately 33 million.

Here is a snapshot to give you a working knowledge of the military in Canada, which falls under the Department of National Defence and consists of the Navy, Army, and Air Force. There are also four Canadian Forces operational commands: Canada Command (for all routine military and emergency operations within Canada), Canadian Expeditionary Force Command (for international operations), Canadian Special Operations Forces Command (for counterterrorism), and Canadian Operational Support Command (for local support to military at home and abroad).

There is also Public Safety Canada, which contains, under one umbrella, the Canada Border Services Agency, Canada Firearms Centre, Canadian Security Intelligence Service (CSIS), Correctional Service of Canada, National Parole Board, and the Royal Canadian Mounted Police (RCMP). In Canada, you can have provincial police like the Ontario Provincial Police or the marshals in Alberta. There are also local city police officers and in their absence the RCMP. Not so in the United States. Nationally, you have the Secret Service and the Central Intelligence Agency (CIA), which is akin to CSIS, along with the Federal Bureau of Investigation (FBI), the U.S. Marshals Service, the Bureau of Alcohol, Tobacco, Firearms, and Explosives (ATF), and the Drug Enforcement Agency (DEA); in Canada, all of these sectors seem to be managed by the RCMP (seems to make sense). You also have the Highway Patrol and State Police in the United States, and the local Sheriff's Department, which is provincially, state, or county run and funded depending where you are. It becomes confusing, but rest assured there are many people available to write you tickets!

In the United States, there is the Reserve Officer Training Corps (more commonly known as the ROTC), while Canada's equivalent is the Cadets. These are high school and university candidates in training for the military. It is strictly voluntary and is intended to prepare them for the military. Finally, there are the Reserves, which are also found in Canada. These are people who were in the military, have left it, but can be called back in an emergency.

In Canada, you may meet people who have served in the military or have children in the military, particularly with the recent Afghanistan war (remember, Canada didn't go to Iraq). This relates to another phenomenon with which you'll have to become comfortable in Canada, the less visible patriotism there. Canadians could learn a lesson in this area by observing how passionate Americans are about their country. U.S. flags and ribbons are everywhere: hanging from houses, flying on automobiles, hanging in the windows of businesses and pasted on bumpers. Americans' support for their troops is truly amazing. However, something to note is that Canadians wear a poppy on Remembrance Day (Veterans Day). Furthermore, the poem "In Flanders Fields" by Lieutenant Colonel John McCrae is often quoted or read in public ceremonies to commemorate Canadian veterans.

GOVERNMENT

You'll also have to become familiar with the political landscape in Canada if you want to engage in an intelligent conversation at parties. There are four primary parties in Canada: Conservatives (right wing), Liberals, New Democrats (left wing), and Bloc Québécois (separatists) versus essentially two political parties in the United States: the Republicans and the Democrats. In the United States and Canada, your political views basically come down to whether you believe in more government, higher taxes, and more social programs (Democratic) or less government, lower taxes, and a more individualistic view of making it in this world (Conservative). The mayor of your city in the United States is still the mayor in your city in Canada, but your governor becomes your premier, and your president becomes your prime minister (see the "Encyclopedia" section below).

In the United States, you register to vote if you are a citizen over the age of 18, and upon registering you get a voter's registration card that declares your party allegiance and in which precinct you vote. In Canada, voters' registration cards are unheard of. Instead, citizens of Canada over the age of 18 receive a voter registration package in the mail. This form will collect the necessary information from you to see if you are eligible to vote. If you are eligible and want to vote, you'll be added to the National Registrar of Electors. Once you are added to the federal voters' list, there's no need to ever register again. You will also find a place on your tax return where you can be added to the National Registrar of Electors. You can still vote in any elections in the United States if you are an American citizen.

HERITAGE

Most Americans view their heritage as American, while most Canadians know they are of German, Ukrainian, Polish, etc. descent. Canadians typically know about their family heritage and how their ancestors came to Canada. Therefore, prepare to be asked what your heritage is (like my American-born wife, who had no clue). We attribute this difference to the fact that America is a much older nation and has been settled longer. It's common to find fifth- and sixth-generation Americans, while it's common to find first- and second-generation Canadians. I'm a second-generation Canadian born to first-generation Canadian parents who in turn were born to my grandparents from Germany. As Canada wanted to settle its land, it opened its doors to many immigrants, who came to homestead and escape the unrest in Europe. As Canada continues its program of diversity through immigration policies, there's a whole new group of first-generation Canadians emerging particularly from Asia.

Another interesting difference between Canada and the U.S. is their views on integrating immigrants in the culture. In the U.S., the general view is a "melting pot" mentality where unique cultures entering the U.S. are expected to integrate into the existing culture, potentially morphing it slightly. In Canada, most policies are focused on "multiculturalism" where there is a real focus on preserving the culture you came from when you land in Canada. The thinking is with different cultures, new thinking and learning is more likely to occur. In our observation, multiculturalism often leads to more conflict because to preserve one's culture, it imposes on the existing culture. For example, you will find all packaging contains both French and English even out west. This is the government's attempt to help the French preserve their culture in Quebec. It is an interesting phenomenon that is worth watching in both nations.

SPORTS

Another cultural phenomenon is the much different sports scene in Canada. In the United States, you grow up with college football on Saturdays and the NFL on Sundays. If it's not football, it's the NBA or MLB or NCAA "college hoops." You'll have to get used to Canada's passion and "national sport," hockey. In Canada, every Saturday night from 4 p.m. to 10 p.m. you watch *Hockey Night in Canada* with color commentators Don Cherry and Ron MacLean bantering back and forth. It's just how you grow up; hockey is everywhere — in the news, on the radio, and on TV. It's easy to stay abreast of your favorite hockey team or player in Canada from September, when hockey camps open, until June, when the Stanley Cup is awarded. University hockey is popular as well. During the summer months, the Canadian Football League (CFL) and university football are popular. It's a much different game than the NFL in that they have only three downs, yet the field is 10 yards longer and 11.7 yards wider. This makes for more passing and some pretty exciting plays. Another Canadian pastime that you won't see much of in the United States (particularly in the southern states) is curling. This is the recreational sport of choice for many adults and is watched on TV religiously. There are international and Canadian championships and the pinnacle event, the Tim Hortons Brier. Curling is becoming increasingly popular in the U.S. thanks to the Winter Olympics.

FOOD

One of the biggest adjustments we had to make in moving to the United States was the difference in food between the two countries. Yes, food. The following items are hard to find in Canada.

- Poore Brothers potato chips
- Chocolate bars — Hershey's milk chocolate, Almond Joy, Mounds, Baby Ruth, Three Musketeers, Payday, 100 Grand, Milk Duds, Mr. Goodbar
- Malt-O-Meal, WheatChex and Wheaties cereals
- Krispy Kreme donuts
- Chicken-fried steak
- Grits
- Biscuits and gravy
- Aleve pain reliever

Here are some other differences we have found or been told about.

- In the United States, it's considered a social faux pas to give or receive fruitcake. In Canada, fruitcake is considered a delicacy and is found in most wedding cakes and during the Christmas season.
- Nanaimo bars are everywhere in Canada!
- Dairy Queen Brazier is far better in Canada than in the United States.
- Dairy Queen ice milk soft serve is creamier tasting in Canada than in the United States.
- McDonald's offers muffins in Canada, while breakfast burritos are available in the United States.
- KFC is crispier and better tasting in Canada than in the United States.
- KFC gravy is much more flavorful in Canada (where fries and gravy, and poutine, are common) than in the United States.
- The Tim Hortons coffee and donut chain (versus Dunkin Donuts in the U.S.) is a phenomenon that has swept across

Canada. The stores are everywhere, and be sure to work some time into your schedule to wait!
- Earls, Boston Pizza, and The Keg are all great casual dining restaurants in Canada, now making their way to the U.S.
- Ruth's Chris Steakhouse can now be found in Toronto, Mississauga, Niagara Falls, Calgary, and Edmonton.
- Morton's Steakhouse is now in Toronto.

Here is a list of items we can only seem to find in Canada when we are there.

- Perogies, though we have found them occasionally at Trader Joe's
- Butter tarts and crumpets
- Ginger beef — thin strips coated with a slightly spicy, sweet sauce
- Pancake mix — Mrs. Nunweiler's or Coyote brand (nice and hearty!)
- Snacks — all Old Dutch potato chips, Popcorn Twists, Hostess Hickory Sticks and Shoestrings, Hawkins Cheezies
- Chocolate bars — Jersey Milk, Eat-More, Caramilk, Coffee Crisp, Aero, Smarties, Mirage, Wunderbar, Cadbury bars, Oh Henry!, Glosettes, Maltesers, Crispy Crunch, Crunchie, Big Turk, Mr. Big, Mack Toffee, Malted Milk, Neilson (Coconut Fingers, Golden Buds, Macaroons, Slowpokes, Willocrisp), Bridge Mixture, Cherry Blossoms
- Cookies — Dare (Wagon Wheels, Chocolate Fudge, Coffee Break), Christie (Fudgeos, Maple Leaf), Dad's (Oatmeal, Oatmeal Chocolate Chip, Oatmeal Raisin)
- Candy/gum — Thrills, Maynard's Wine Gums
- Sauces/syrups/spreads — Roger's Golden syrup, Summerland Sweets syrups, HP Sauce, E.D. Smith Lemon Spread, Shirriff Caramel Spread, Imperial Cinnamon Spread
- Cereals — Post Shreddies, Muesli, Red River, Sunny Boy, Quaker Harvest Crunch
- Japanese Christmas oranges

- Beverages — Tim Hortons coffee, Red Rose tea, Mott's Clamato juice, Sun-Rype juice, and of course almost all Canadian beers!
- 222's pain reliever

However, here are some things that we, and others, have noted when back in Canada.

- P.F. Chang's Chinese Bistro (Pei Wei is the takeout) is nowhere to be found.
- Good Mexican food and good barbecue food are hard to find.
- Portions are generally smaller in Canada, and eating out is more expensive (before the exchange rate).
- The number of restaurants that offer buffet service all day is much greater in the United States than we have found in Canada.
- The selection in most grocery and retail stores is far less in Canada than in the United States.
- Most "sin" taxes are higher in Canada than in the United States (liquor, wine, beer, cigarettes, cigars, chewing tobacco, gasoline).

If you have something to add to this list, please email us at book@ transitionfinancial.com and tell us about it.

THE POSTAL SYSTEM

- It's a postal code in Canada and a zip code in the United States.
- A first-class stamp costs 49¢ in the United States versus 85¢ in Canada.
- Mailing a postcard costs 34¢ in the United States versus 85¢ in Canada.
- First-class postage for a regular #10 envelope from the United

States to Canada costs U$1.15 and C$1.20 from Canada to the United States.

- It takes approximately 7–10 calendar days for first-class mail to reach Canada from the United States, but it takes approximately 10–14 days for mail in Canada to reach the United States.
- In the United States, a letter mailed for delivery in the same city will typically be delivered the next day, whereas in Canada it can be two to three business days.
- In the United States, mail is delivered on Saturdays. Not so in Canada (it was stopped in 1969).
- If you have friends or relatives in the United States who are mailing out wedding invitations to you in Canada, tell them a Canadian stamp is required for the return postage. Putting a U.S. stamp on a return envelope that originates in Canada isn't recognized by Canada Post (however, such letters have been known to slip by).

THE ENGLISH LANGUAGE

The American version of English is different from the British version used in Canada, so words such as check, labor, harbor, center, and liter become cheque, labour, harbour, centre, and litre. That's why your computer's spell checker may highlight these words as misspelled. Table 14.1 shows other differences in the way Canadians use the English language versus Americans.

TABLE 14.1

CANADIAN VERSUS AMERICAN ENGLISH

Canada	United States
Pop	Soda or Cokes
Caesar	Bloody Mary
Barbecue	Cookout
Housecoat	Robe
Chesterfield	Sofa/couch

Car accident	Car wreck
Holidays	Vacation
Ensuite	Master bath
Dinner	Lunch
Supper	Dinner
Felts	Markers
Chocolate bar	Candy bar
Garbage	Trash
Buns	Rolls
Thongs	Flip flops
Slacks	Pants
Runners	Tennis shoes
Golf shirt	Polo shirt
Squares	Dessert
Garburator	Garbage disposal
Washroom	Restroom
Marks	Grades
Junior high	Middle school
University	College
Floating rate	Adjustable rate
Cutlery	Silverware
Pot holders	Hot pads
Tea towels	Wash towels
Porridge	Oatmeal
Toque	Toboggan hat
Brown bread	Wheat bread
Sucker	Lollipop
Soother	Pacifier
Licking	Spanking
Standard	Stick shift
Needle	Shot
Slippers	House shoes
Eavestrough	Gutter
Cabin	Cottage
Guaranteed investment certificate (GIC)	Certificate of deposit (CD)

THE METRIC SYSTEM

After you move to Canada and are settled in, you'll start talking in terms of liters, celsius, etc. However, when you are talking with your friends and family back in the United States, they'll be talking in terms of gallons, Fahrenheit, etc. The following should help you in these conversations.

- Celsius can be converted to Fahrenheit quickly by doubling the Celsius number and adding 32 (e.g., 20°C x 2 = 40 + 32 = approximately 72°F). For negative numbers, the calculation works like this: -20°C x 2 = -40 + 32 = approximately -8°F.
- If you want an exact conversion, use (°F - 32) x 5/9 = °C.
- The boiling point is 212°F versus 100°C.
- Freezing occurs at 32°F versus 0°C.
- Room temperature is 70°F versus 20°C.
- Body temperature is 98.6°F versus 37°C.
- Mr. Fahrenheit was the only glass blower in his day who could blow a symmetrical, thin cylinder (thermometer) to record temperatures. He set 32°F as his starting point because it was the lowest temperature he could record with his device.
- 100 kmph = approximately 60 mph.
- 1 mile = 1.61 km or 1 km = 0.62 mile.
- 1 inch = 2.54 centimeters.
- 1 meter = 3.28 feet.
- The United States adheres to the metric system for track and field, while Canada uses yards for football.
- 1 liter = 1.06 quarts.
- 1 ton = 1.1 tonnes (pronounced "tawns").
- 1 imperial gallon = 4.5 liters.
- 1 U.S. gallon = 3.8 liters.
- 1 imperial gallon = 0.84 U.S. gallon.
- 1 kilogram = 2.2 pounds.
- 500 grams = 1.1 pounds.

ENCYCLOPEDIA

GEOGRAPHY

- The Russian Federation is the largest country in the world, Canada is second, China is third, the United States is fourth, and Brazil is fifth.
- Canada covers 3,849,674 square miles (9,970,610 square km), of which 291,576 square miles (755,180 square km) are inland water (7.6%), while the United States covers 3,717,811 square miles (9,629,091 square km), of which 181,519 square miles (470,131 square km) are inland water (4.9%).
- Quebec is the largest province, and Ontario is second, while Alaska is the largest state, and Texas is second (note that the Yukon, Northwest Territories, and Nunavut are territories, not provinces).
- Texas is 13,314 square miles larger than Alberta.
- The population of Canada is about 35 million, which is less than the population of California (about 38 million). The population of the United States is roughly 314 million (approximately 10 times that of Canada).
- The largest metropolitan populations in the United States are New York, with approximately 20 million, and Los Angeles, with approximately 15 million. In Canada, Toronto has approximately 4.3 million, and Montreal has approximately 3.3 million.
- Canada shares a 5,527 mile (8,895 km) border with the United States spanning 12 states and is the longest unprotected border in the world.
- The lowest temperature ever recorded in Canada was -81°F (-63°C) in Snag, Yukon, while the highest was 115°F (46°C) at Gleichen, Alberta.
- The lowest temperature ever recorded in the United States was -79.8°F (-62.1°C) at Prospect Creek Camp along the Alaska pipeline 20 miles north of the Arctic Circle.
- In the contiguous 48 states, the lowest temperature was -69.7°F (-56.5°C) in Rogers Pass just west of Helena, Montana,

while the highest temperature was 134°F (56.7°C) in Death Valley, California.

- It's interesting to note that the record low ever recorded in Hawaii was 12°F (-11.1°C).

GOVERNMENT

- In the United States, Congress creates the laws governing the land (legislative branch) and is made up of the Senate and the House of Representatives. In Canada, Parliament is made up of the Senate (upper house), the House of Commons (lower house), and the sovereign (represented by the governor general, who represents the queen in Britain).
- Canada is a constitutional monarchy under the queen, while the United States is an independent republic.
- Canada has a parliamentary-cabinet government versus a presidential-congressional government in the United States. This means that in the United States the president is both the head of state and the head of government. In Canada, the queen (represented by the governor general) is the head of state, while the prime minister is the head of government.
- The Republicans (the GOP, for grand old party — the elephant) are most akin to the Conservatives in Canada (the Tories).
- The Democrats (whose symbol is the donkey) are akin to the Liberals (Grits) in Canada.
- It is a governor who heads the state government in the United States, while in Canada it is a premier who heads the provincial government.
- The Canadian equivalent to the CIA (Central Intelligence Agency) in the United States is CSIS (Canadian Security Intelligence Service).
- The Canada Pension Plan (CPP) can be collected as early as age 60, whereas U.S. Social Security can be collected as early as age 62.
- IRAs must commence distributions at age 70 1/2 while RRSPs

must be converted to RRIFs to commence distributions at age 71.

- Canada is part of the British Commonwealth (along with Australia, New Zealand, and India, among other countries), while the United States is not.
- There are 11 statutory holidays in both Canada and the United States. In the United States, Thanksgiving is on the last Thursday in November versus the second Monday in October in Canada; Memorial Day in the United States is the fourth Monday of May versus Remembrance Day in Canada on November 11th; Victoria Day in Canada is on the Monday lying between May 18th and 24th; and Independence Day in the United States is July 4th versus Canada Day on July 1st. There is a holiday on Good Friday (Friday before Easter) and Boxing Day (day after Christmas) in Canada. You'll enjoy one long weekend every month because there's one statutory holiday every month in Canada.

MISCELLANEOUS TRIVIA

- Both Saskatchewan and Arizona do not change their clocks for daylight savings time. Neither do Hawaii, Puerto Rico, the Virgin Islands, American Samoa, Southampton Island in Nunavut, and parts of Quebec.
- American banks typically don't offer currency exchange services, while Canadian banks do.
- Canadian banks charge a fee for each check, while most American banks offer free checking.
- Americans refer to grades 7 and 8 as middle school, while in Canada grades 7, 8, and 9 are known as junior high.
- Canadian high school is grades 10, 11, and 12; the grades aren't referred to in collegiate fashion as freshman, sophomore, junior, and senior in Canada.
- In NFL football, the field is 100 yards long by 53 1/3 yards wide, and the game has four downs, while the CFL field is 110 yards long by 65 yards wide, and the game has three downs.
- Winnie the Pooh and the zipper were both created in Canada.

- Basketball and hockey were both created in Canada.
- In the United States, the big shopping day is "Black Friday," the day after Thanksgiving, while in Canada it is Boxing Day (the day after Christmas per English tradition). However, U.S. retailers are succeeding in making Black Friday a bigger shopping day in Canada now as well as Cyber Monday.
- In the United States, the biggest newspaper is typically Sunday versus Saturday in Canada.

THE TAX SYSTEM

- Tax filing deadlines are April 15th in the United States and April 30th in Canada for personal taxes.
- There's no such thing as a tax filing extension in Canada.
- In Canada, you get a Social Insurance Number (SIN), while in the United States you get a Social Security Number (SSN).
- One return is filed per married couple in the United States versus one return per person in Canada.
- A W-2 slip in the United States is equivalent to a T4 slip in Canada.
- A 1099-INT or 1099-DIV slip is generally equivalent to a T3 or T5 slip in Canada.
- In Canada, only Quebec has a separate return and collects its own taxes. In the United States, 43 states have separate returns and collect their own taxes (the other seven don't have state income taxes).
- Both Canada and the United States allow a tax deduction for medical expenses but limit it by 3% of net income and 10% of adjusted gross income respectively.
- The closest thing to an IRA in Canada is the Registered Retirement Savings Plan (RRSP); unlike the IRA, RRSP contributions are always deductible.
- In Canada, lottery winnings aren't taxable and are paid out in a lump sum. In the United States, lottery winnings are taxable and are paid out over a 20-year period unless the cash option is requested in advance.
- Both tax systems have an alternative minimum tax.

APPENDIX A

GLOSSARY

AHCIP: Alberta Health Care Insurance Plan

AMT: Alternative Minimum Tax

ATF: Bureau of Alcohol, Tobacco, Firearms, and Explosives (U.S.)

ATM: Automatic Teller Machine

CA: Chartered Accountant (Canada), soon to become CPA

CBC: Canadian Broadcasting Corporation

CBSA: Canada Border Services Agency

CCA: Capital Cost Allowance (Canada)

CFC: Controlled Foreign Corporation

CFP®: Certified Financial Planner™

CGA: Certified General Accountant (Canada), soon to become CPA

CIA: Central Intelligence Agency (U.S.)

CIC: Citizenship and Immigration Canada

CIS: U.S. Citizenship and Immigration Services

CMA: Certified Management Accountant (Canada), soon to become CPA

CMHC: Canada Mortgage and Housing Corporation

COBRA: Consolidated Omnibus Budget Reconciliation Act (U.S.)

CPA: Certified Public Accountant (U.S.)

CPC: Canadian Private Corporation

CPI: Consumer Price Index

CPP: Canada Pension Plan

CRA: Canada Revenue Agency

CSIS: Canadian Security Intelligence Service

DEA: Drug Enforcement Agency

DPSP: Deferred Profit Sharing Plan

DUI: Driving under the Influence

EA: Enrolled Agent with the IRS

EI: Employment Insurance

EIN: Employer Identification Number

ERISA: Employee Retirement Income Security Act (U.S.)

FATCA: Foreign Account Tax Compliance Act

FBI: Federal Bureau of Investigation

FDAP: Fixed, Determinable, Annual, or Periodical income

FHA: Federal Housing Authority

FICO: Fair Isaac & Co.

FIRPTA: Foreign Investment in Real Property Tax Act (U.S.)

FPA: Financial Planning Association (U.S.)

GIC: Guaranteed Investment Certificate

GST: Goods and Services Tax (Canada)

GSTT: Generation Skipping Transfer Tax (U.S.)

HMO: Health Maintenance Organization

IDA: Investment Dealers Association

ILIT: Irrevocable Life Insurance Trust

IRA: Individual Retirement Account (U.S.)

IRC: Internal Revenue Code

IRD: Income with Respect to the Decedent

IRS: Internal Revenue Service

ISO: Incentive Stock Option (U.S.)

ITIN: Individual Taxpayer Identification Number (U.S.)

LIF: Life Income Fund

LIRA: Locked-In Retirement Account

LLC: Limited Liability Company (U.S.)

LMO: Labour Market Opinion

Ltd.: Limited Company

LRIF: Locked-In Retirement Income Fund

MSP: Medical Services Plan (Canada)

NAFTA: North American Free Trade Agreement

NAPFA: National Association of Personal Financial Advisors

NIIT: Net Investment Income Tax

NOC: National Occupation Classification (Canada)

NQ: Non-Qualified Employee Stock Option (U.S.)

NWT: Northwest Territories

OAS: Old Age Security (Canada)

ODB: Ontario Drug Benefit program

OHIP: Ontario Health Insurance Plan

OSC: Ontario Securities Commission

PBGC: Pension Benefit Guaranty Corporation (U.S.)

PEI: Prince Edward Island

PFIC: Passive Foreign Investment Company

POA: Power of Attorney

QDOT: Qualified Domestic Trust (U.S.)

QPP: Quebec Pension Plan

RBC: Royal Bank of Canada

RCA: Retirement Compensation Arrangement (Canada)

RCMP: Royal Canadian Mounted Police

RESP: Registered Education Savings Plan (Canada)

ROTC: Reserve Officer Training Corps

RPP: Registered Pension Plan (Canada)

RRIF: Registered Retirement Income Fund (Canada)

RRSP: Registered Retirement Savings Plan (Canada)

S&P: Standard and Poors (U.S.)

SAP: Simplified Application Process

SEC: Securities and Exchange Commission (U.S.)

SEP: Simplified Employee Pension

SIN: Social Insurance Number (Canada)

SS: Social Security (U.S.)

SSA: Social Security Administration (U.S.)

SSN: Social Security Number (U.S.)

STEP: Society of Trust and Estate Practitioners

TD: Toronto Dominion

TEP: Trust and Estate Practitioner

TN: Trade NAFTA (visa)

ULC: Unlimited Liability Company (Canada)

U.S.: United States of America

U.S. CIS: U.S. Citizenship and Immigration Services

U.S.-VISIT: United States Visitor and Immigrant Status Indicator
    Technology

UTMA: Uniform Transfer to Minors Act Account (U.S.)

VA: Veterans Administration (U.S.)

VWP: Visa Waiver Permanent Program Act

WEP: Windfall Elimination Provision (U.S.)

APPENDIX B

RESOURCES YOU CAN USE

In our digital age, there is a multitude of information that can be obtained with the simple click of a button. Following are a host of websites, publications, and firms of relevance to each chapter in this book. If the link is out of date, feel free to email us at book@transitionfinancial.com and let us know.

CHAPTER 1: CANADIAN ASPIRATIONS
Transition Financial Advisors: www.transitionfinancial.com
Financial Planners Standards Council: www.fpsc.ca
CFP Board of Standards: www.cfp.net
Financial Planning Association: www.fpanet.org
National Association of Personal Financial Advisors: www.napfa.org
Society of Trust and Estate Practitioners: www.step.org

CHAPTER 2: COVER YOUR ASSETS
Alberta Health Care Insurance Plan: www.health.alberta.ca
British Columbia Health Insurance/Medical Services Plan: www. gov
    .bc.ca/health/
Manitoba Health: www.gov.mb.ca/health/

Medicare New Brunswick: www.gnb.ca

Newfoundland and Labrador: www.health.gov.nl.ca/health

Northwest Territories: www.hlthss.gov.nt.ca

Nova Scotia: www.novascotia.ca/dhw/msi/

Nunavat: www.gov.nu.ca/health

Ontario Health Insurance Plan: www.health.gov.on.ca

Port Huron Hospital: www.porthuronhospital.org/Canada

Prince Edward Island: www.gov.pe.ca/health/index.php3

Quebec: www.msss.gouv.qc.ca/en/index.php

Saskatchewan Health: www.health.gov.sk.ca

Service Canada: www.servicecanada.gc.ca

U.S. Medicare: www.medicare.gov

U.S. Social Security: www.ssa.gov/international/payments_
outsideUS.html

Yukon: www.hss.gov.yk.ca

Various Insurance Quotes: www.insurance-canada.ca/index.php

CHAPTER 3: O CANADA!

For a list of immigration attorneys we recommend, see the immigration section of our website at www.transitionfinancial.com.

Citizenship and Immigration Canada: www.cic.gc.ca

Foreign Affairs and International Trade Canada: www.dfait-maeci.gc.ca

Alberta Provincial Nominees: www.albertacanada.com

Province of Quebec: www.immigration-quebec.gouv.qc.ca

U.S. Citizenship and Immigration Services: www.uscis.gov/portal/site/
uscis

U.S. Department of State: www.travel.state.gov/

Immigration Attorneys

American Immigration Lawyers Association: www.aila.org

CHAPTER 4: MOVING YOUR STUFF

Canada Border Services Agency: www.cbsa-asfc.gc.ca

Canadian Import Restrictions: www.beaware.gc.ca

Registrar of Imported Vehicles: www.riv.ca/
Transport Canada: www.tc.gc.ca/eng/menu.htm
U.S. Customs and Border Protection: www.cbp.gov
Canada Firearms Centre: www.cfc-cafc.gc.ca
Explosives Regulatory Division of Natural Resources Canada:
    www.nrcan.gc.ca
American Moving and Storage Association: www.moving.org
EZ Canada Moving: www.ezcanadamoving.com

CHAPTER 5: DOUBLE TAXES, DOUBLE TROUBLE

For a list of Canada-U.S. tax preparers we recommend, see the income tax section of our website at www.transitionfinancial.com or contact our office for a referral.

Government of Canada Financial Consumer Agency: www.ic.gc.ca/eic/
    site/oca-bc.nsf/eng/ca02179.html
U.S. Government Accountability Office: www.gao.gov/products/
    GAO-13-318
FinCEN: www.fincen.gov/forms/bsa_forms
CRA: www.cra-arc.gc.ca

Interpretation Bulletins
IT221R3: Determination of Canadian Residency Status
IT298: Canada-U.S. Tax Convention: Number of Days "Present"
Provincial Income Tax Links: www.ctf.ca/ctfweb/eng
Provincial Sales Tax Links: www.taxtips.ca/provincial_sales_tax.htm
IRS: www.irs.gov
Publication 514: Foreign Tax Credits
Publication 521: Moving Expenses
Publication 527: Residential Rental Property
Publication 597: Information on the United States-Canada Income Tax
    Treaty
Publication 733: Rewards for Information Given to the IRS
Publication 901: U.S. Tax Treaties
Publication 4261: Do You Have a Foreign Bank Account?

Publication 4446: IRS Best Websites, Phone Numbers, and Other
    Useful Info
U.S. Department of Treasury: www.treas.gov/Pages/default.aspx
FBAR filing: http://bsaefiling.fincen.treas.gov/main.html
State Income Tax Links: www.taxsites.com/state.html
State Sales Tax Links: www.retirementliving.com/taxes-by-state

CHAPTER 6: SHOW ME THE MONEY
International Salary Calculator: www.homefair.com/
U.S. Salary Calculators: www.salary.com
Pay Scale Calculator: www.payscale.com
Currency Exchange Rates: www.bankofcanada.ca/rates/
    exchange/10-year-converter/
Currency Fair: www.currencyfair.com
Equifax: www.equifax.com
Experian: www.experian.com
Free Credit Report: www.annualcreditreport.com
FICO Scores: www.myfico.com/
TransUnion: www.transunion.com

CHAPTER 7: TILL DEATH DO US PART

For a list of competent estate planning attorneys we recommend, please
contact our office for a referral.

CRA: www.cra-arc.gc.ca
Publication P113: Gifts and Income Tax
IRS: www.irs.gov/
Publication 950: Introduction to Estate and Gift Taxes
Estate Planning Information: www.estateplanninglinks.com

Estate Planning Attorneys
Wealth Counsel: www.wealthcounsel.com
National Network of Estate Planning Attorneys: www.nnepa.com
American College of Trust and Estate Counsel: www.actec.org

CHAPTER 8: FINANCIAL FREEDOM

CPP/OAS: http://www.esdc.gc.ca/en/pension/index.page
U.S. Social Security: www.ssa.gov
IRS: www.irs.gov
Publication 915: Social Security
Moving.com: www.moving.com/real-estate/compare-cities/index.asp

CHAPTER 9: SMARTEN UP!

CRA: www.cra-arc.gc.ca/tx/ndvdls/sgmnts/stdnts/menu-eng.html
Publication P101: Students and Income Tax
U.S. Department of Education: www.ed.gov
Federal Student Aid Website: www.studentaid.ed.gov
Federal Family Education Loan Program: www.fafsa.ed.gov
College Savings Plans Network: www.collegesavings.org/index.aspx
IRS: www.irs.gov (Publication 970: Tax Benefits for Education)

CHAPTER 10: MONEY DOESN'T GROW ON TREES

Investment Dealers Association (Investment Industry Regulatory
         Organization of Canada): www.iiroc.ca/Pages/default.aspx
Toronto Stock Exchange: www.tmx.com/en/index.html
Montreal Stock Exchange: www.m-x.ca/accueil_en.php
NASDAQ Canada: http://nasdaq.com
Morningstar Canada: http://www2.morningstar.ca
Dimensional Fund Advisors Canada: www.dfaca.com
Blackrock Canadian iShares: ca.ishares.com/home.htm
Securities and Exchange Commission: www.sec.gov
National Association of Securities Dealers: www.finra.org/index.htm
American Stock Exchange: usequities.nyx.com/markets/
         nyse-mkt-equities
New York Stock Exchange: www.nyse.nyx.com
NASDAQ: www.nasdaq.com
Chicago Board of Trade: www.cmegroup.com
Chicago Board Options Exchange: www.cboe.com
Index Funds: www.indexfunds.com
Morningstar U.S.: www.morningstar.com
Dimensional Fund Advisors: www.dfaus.com

Blackrock U.S. iShares: us.ishares.com/home.htm
IRS: www.irs.gov/
Publication 550: Investment Income and Expenses
Publication 551: Basis of Assets
Publication 564: Mutual Fund Distributions

CHAPTER 11: THE BUSINESS OF BUSINESS
CRA: www.cra-arc.gc.ca/
IRS: www.irs.gov/

CHAPTER 12: NORTHERN EXPOSURE
British Columbia's Property Transfer Tax: www.sbr.gov.bc.ca/business/
  Property_Taxes/Property_Transfer_Tax/ptt.htm

CHAPTER 13: MAYDAY! MAYDAY!
Transition Financial Advisors: www.transitionfinancial.com, or call us at
  480-722-9414
Financial Planners Standards Council: www.cfp-ca.org
CFP Board of Standards: www.cfp-board.org
U.S. Securities and Exchange Commission:
  www.adviserinfo.sec.gov/IAPD/Content/IapdMain/iapd_
  SiteMap.aspx
National Association of Personal Financial Advisors: www.feeonly.org,
  or call 1-800-366-2732
Financial Planning Association: www.fpanet.org, or call 1-800-647-6340
FINRA: finra.org/Investors/ToolsCalculators/BrokerCheck/
Society of Trust and Estate Practitioners: http://www.step.org/
  online-directory

CHAPTER 14: REALIZING THE DREAM

For a list of other resources you may find useful, see the trivia section of
our website at www.transitionfinancial.com.

Government of Canada: www.gc.ca/
Elections Canada: www.elections.ca/

Royal Canadian Mounted Police: www.rcmp-grc.gc.ca/index.htm
Canadian Security Intelligence Service: www.csis-scrs.gc.ca/
Ontario Provincial Police: www.opp.ca
Canada Post: www.canadapost.ca/cpo/mc/default.jsf?LOCALE=en
U.S. Government: www.usa.gov
Federal Bureau of Investigation: www.fbi.gov
Bureau of Alcohol, Tobacco, Firearms, and Explosives: www.atf.gov
Drug Enforcement Agency: www.justice.gov/dea/index.shtml
U.S. Military
    Army: www.army.mil
    Navy: www.navy.mil
    Airforce: www.airforce.com
    Marines: www.marines.com/home
United States Postal Service: www.usps.com

APPENDIX C

TRANSITION PLANNER INTERVIEW CHECKLIST

COMPETENCE

1. Do you hold both the Canadian and the American CFP® designations?

2. What other designations, degrees, or training do you have in transition planning?

3. How long have you been practicing specifically in the area of Canada-U.S. transition planning?

4. How long have you been working at the firm? What is your next career step in the firm?

5. What percentage of your clients are Canada-U.S. clients versus others?

6. Tell me about your own personal experiences in transitioning between Canada and the United States.

PLANNING PROCESS

1. Describe in detail the planning process you have to address the needs of my Canada-U.S. transition.

2. How do you determine my goals and objectives for my transition?

3. How do you integrate my goals and objectives into my transition plan?

4. Do you have a written sample plan I can review?

5. Do you undertake comprehensive financial planning including retirement projections, insurance analysis, and investments, or is the focus just tax?

6. Tell me about your investment philosophy and key strategies implemented recently.

CLIENT RELATIONSHIP

1. Tell me about your firm. How long have you been in business? Please provide me with your Form ADV or other regulatory disclosures.

2. How many employees do you have? How many clients per employee? Per principal?

3. What are your assets or net worth under management?

4. Will I be working directly with a principal or an associate? Why?

5. How do you determine the person I will be working with in the firm?

6. How much employee turnover have you had in the past two years? Why?

7. What is your typical client? What is his or her net worth?

8. What are the principals' goals and objectives for the firm in the next five to 10 years?

9. How old are the principals? What are their plans for retirement and succession? When will that take place?

10. What personalities work best with you? Your firm? Why?

11. How many clients have left the firm over the past two years? Why?

12. How many clients have you gained in the past two years? Why?

13. Where do you custody investment accounts? Why? Are there any conflicts of interest I need to be aware of?

14. What are your personal interests?

COMPENSATION

1. How are you paid? When are you paid?

2. How do you calculate your fees? What is my fee in dollars? Specifically, show me the calculations for my fee.

3. How do you ensure that your fiduciary responsibility to me is given the highest priority?

4. Can I see a sample agreement? How long does my agreement last? How can I terminate it?

5. If I need a financial product (insurance, annuity, mutual fund, etc.), where do I get it and how much do you make from it?

PROFESSIONAL AFFILIATIONS AND ASSOCIATIONS

You can consult with the following professional organizations to confirm any credentials or affiliations for the transition planner you have interviewed.

1. Financial Planners Standards Council: the organization that licenses and governs the Canadian CFP designation (www.cfp-ca.org/plannersearch/plannersearch.asp, or you can call 1-800-305-9886).

2. CFP Board of Standards: the organization that licenses and governs the CFP® designation in the United States (www.cfp.net/search/, or call 1-888-237-6275).

3. U.S. Securities and Exchange Commission: this is the regulatory body in the United States that governs financial advisors (www.adviserinfo.sec.gov/).

4. National Association of Personal Financial Advisors: the only organization in the United States and Canada comprised of fee-only financial advisors (www.fee-only.org, or call 1-800-366-2732).

5. Financial Planning Association: the largest association of financial planners in the U.S. (www.plannersearch.org, or call 1-800-647-6340).

6. Society of Trust and Estate Practitioners: the global organization for those practicing advanced trust and estate matters (http://www.step.org/searchuser.pl?n=1000).

APPENDIX D

COMPREHENSIVE CASE STUDY: WORKING COUPLE

John and Jenny Movers hired Transition Financial Advisors to assist them in making a smooth transition to Canada (this account is based on a real-life fact pattern, but all names and numbers have been changed). Following are the financial planning issues, obstacles, and opportunities our proven planning process revealed for the Movers. This is intended not to be blanket advice applicable to all situations but to increase your understanding of the many things that must be taken into account when considering a move to Canada and why most folks are ill-equipped to do it themselves or why their current team of professionals generally needs to be led by a qualified transition planner. Each person's situation is unique and requires a custom analysis to determine the best course of action. As a good transition planner should, we review the following eight areas of planning: customs, immigration, cash management, income tax, financial independence, risk management, estates, and investments; each is part of a comprehensive transition plan guided by your goals and objectives.

BACKGROUND

One day John and Jenny received good news. John's U.S.-based employer accepted his transfer request to move to Alberta from Texas. His employer agreed to pay his current salary of U$100,000 (bonus averaging U$40,000) in Canadian loonies (C$100,000 + C$40,000 bonus). Aged 53 and 52 respectively, married, with no children, John and Jenny are American citizens only. Jenny will resign from her current position as a teacher to pursue employment in Canada. The Movers have a net worth of U$2,650,000 comprised as follows (Table D.1).

TABLE D.1

THE MOVERS' NET WORTH

Asset	Fair Market Value (C$)	Cost Basis (C$)	Titling
American brokerage account	750,000	500,000	Joint
401(k)	450,000	—	John
IRA	300,000	—	Jenny
403(b)	100,000	—	Jenny
Checking/savings accounts	50,000	50,000	Joint
Vested stock options exercise	450,000	200,000	John
Employee stock purchase plan	100,000	30,000	John
Principal residence	600,000	375,000	John
mortgage	-100,000		
Autos (x 2)	50,000	75,000	One each
Personal/ household/jewelry	100,000	200,000	Joint
Total	C$2,650,000		
	C$1,325,000		John
	C$425,000		Jenny
	C$900,000		Joint

LIFE PLANNING

We started by determining where John and Jenny were "going," where they "were" now (net worth, financial circumstances), and how they were going to get "there." The "plan" allowed individual financial decisions to be placed in context and ensured that limited resources were channeled toward achieving their plan. Following is a summary of their intentions.

- John and Jenny would like to remain in Canada for five to seven years and then return to the United States.
- They would like to take advantage of John's employment opportunities in Canada to build their net worth before moving back to the United States.
- The Movers would like to be financially independent when John turns 60 through a combination of work in the United States and Canada.
- When they are independent, they would like to purchase a five-acre piece of land in South Carolina near family with a modest home and a guest retreat.
- When independent of work, the Movers would like to be involved in full-time charitable work and offer their home and retreat at no charge to charity workers.
- They might "sunbird" two to three months per year in Canada after becoming financially independent and moving back to the United States.
- They would simplify their lives wherever possible and lead a relatively simple life.
- The bulk of their estate would go to their respective parents who survive them, some to siblings, and the balance to charitable organizations.

CUSTOMS PLANNING

The Movers wanted to take their Lexus with them to Canada to replace it there later. They were going to sell their Mercedes. We pointed out that their Lexus would require safety modifications to meet the standards in Canada. Furthermore, the odometer and speedometer are denominated in miles, reducing its value in Canada. Given their lifestyle choices, they agreed to sell their car before moving and lease or buy vehicles during their temporary stay in Canada, which would make it easier to register them in Alberta. They completed a full inventory of their personal goods when packing and donated a host of items to charity to get a tax deduction in the United States that they wouldn't get in Canada. Since John's employer was covering all of their moving expenses, there were no out-of-pocket expenses to claim for tax purposes. We informed them that they simply had to show their valid Texas driver's licenses to get Alberta driver's licenses.

IMMIGRATION PLANNING

John's company sponsored him under the skilled worker category. Citizenship and Immigration Canada considers the entire family unit as permanent residents, and as a result everyone received legal working status in Canada. We assured Jenny in particular that in moving to Canada and even taking up Canadian citizenship she would not lose her American citizenship and that dual Canada-U.S. citizenship was possible for them. After about three years of residence in Canada, John and Jenny would be eligible to apply for Canadian citizenship. We explained that there was very little downside to doing so, even if they moved back to the United States, so that became their intention once three years had passed.

CASH MANAGEMENT PLANNING

In moving to Canada, the Movers had concerns about how to move the proceeds of the sale of their U.S. house to Canada (see "Income Tax Planning" below). They were concerned about the "loss" when exchanging U.S. dollars for Canadian loonies. We empathized but educated them on currency exchange and emphasized that their retirement investments should remain in U.S. dollars where appropriate investment vehicles existed. Since they intended to move back to the United States for their financial independence, their future needs would be in U.S. dollars, so converting everything into Canadian loonies and subjecting it to currency exchange fluctuations needed to be considered carefully. We also analyzed the cost-of-living differences between Canada and the United States for the Movers' desired lifestyle. They tracked their expenses for six months in Canada and found that they weren't significantly different.

We recommended a discount currency exchange firm that allowed them to conveniently move their cash to Canada, saving currency exchange costs in the process.

Another issue the Movers had to face was qualifying for a mortgage in Canada since they had no Canadian credit rating. We worked with their lending institution to educate it how to "pull" an American credit report and ensure that it was valued in the loan application process. With the support of John's employer and the "can do" attitude of their lender, the Movers succeeded in getting a mortgage to buy a house (using the house proceeds from the United States as a down payment). Through one of the major banks that owns a bank in the United States, the Movers were able to get a credit card issued in their names as well. We also advised John to pay off the loan on his 401(k) before leaving the United States; otherwise, it would be considered a distribution and fully taxable in both the United States and Canada.

INCOME TAX PLANNING

Key Assumptions
- John's salary: C$140,000
- Capital gains jointly: C$35,000 ($10,000 short term)
- Interest jointly: C$7,500
- Dividends jointly: C$12,500 ($10,000 qualified dividends)
- Standard deduction used for U.S. scenario
- Canada-U.S. exchange rates at parity (C$1 = U$1)
- No tax planning included

TABLE D.2
2013 TAX COMPARISON

Canada	John	Jenny	C$	United States	U$
Federal	$32,224	$239	$34,463	Federal	$26,986
Alberta	13,247	0	13,247	Texas	0
Subtotal	$45,471	$239	$45,710		$26,986
Payroll taxes	3,247	0	3,247		9,079
Total	**$48,718**	**$239**	**$48,957**		**$36,065**

% of income			25.1%		18.5%
Health insurance			0		$4,800
Grand total			**$48,957**		**$40,865**
			25.1%		**21.0%**

In the Movers' situation, the move resulted in a tax cost of C$12,892 in 2013, that would be made up by John's employer's international equalization program. When factoring in health insurance premiums (pre-tax), the playing field is leveled a bit more (C$8,092). However, if the Movers had a mortgage, left a state with no income tax (Texas), and paid Canada's sales taxes versus those in the United States, the table would tilt further toward the United States. However, if the Movers lived in California and moved to Alberta, their tax situation would be as follows (Table D.3).

TABLE D.3
2013 MOVE FROM CALIFORNIA TO ALBERTA

Canada	John	Jenny	C$	United States	U$
Federal	$32,224	$239	$34,463	Federal	$26,986
Alberta	13,247	0	13,247	California	9,766
Subtotal	$45,471	$239	$45,710		$36,752
Payroll taxes	3,247	0	3,247		9,079
Total	**$48,718**	**$239**	**$48,957**		**$45,831**
% of income			25.1%		23.5%
Health insurance			0		$4,800
Grand total			**$48,957**		**$50,631**
			25.1%		**26.0%**

Even with California state tax at U$9,766, it still doesn't tilt the table back in favor of Canada by a factor of C$3,126. As this analysis clearly reveals, it's not a black-and-white decision to avoid moving to Canada for strictly tax reasons.

CANADIAN FILING REQUIREMENTS

John and Jenny would each need to file a Canadian "entry" return by April 30th following the year of entry. On this return, they would be subject to their worldwide income from the time they entered Canada. Our analysis indicated there would be embedded gains of C$70,000 in John's employer's stock and C$250,000 in the joint brokerage account, leading to a "step-up in basis" for Canadian purposes and potential Canadian tax avoided of C$38,025 for John and C$24,375 for Jenny. We told the Movers to apply for Canadian Social Insurance Numbers when they got their approval under the skilled worker category so they'd be able to file their Canadian tax returns, set up bank accounts, and so on.

U.S. FILING REQUIREMENTS

As citizens of the United States, the Movers were shocked to find out they'd be required to continue filing a U.S. 1040 tax return by April 15th and declaring their worldwide income even though they wouldn't be living in the United States. Even though they would qualify for an automatic extension to June 15th because, living abroad, any U.S. tax owing would be due by April 15th. They were relieved that a good portion of their wages earned in Canada would be exempt from taxation in the United States due to the foreign earned income exclusion. In addition, we pointed out that they would be required to file a part-year Texas tax return and include their worldwide income up to the point they moved out of the state to Canada. To clearly demonstrate that they were severing their ties with the state of Texas, the Movers canceled their Texas driver's licenses, sold their home, sold their vehicles, and moved the bulk of their personal goods to Canada. To simplify their lives, they consolidated their banking accounts and all of their investment accounts with one financial institution. At our prompting, the Movers also notified all applicable American financial institutions (brokerage firms, banks, life insurance companies, mutual fund firms, etc.) of their Canadian address but that they were still residents of the United States for tax purposes and not to take any withholding per the Canada-U.S. Tax Treaty. Failure by a couple of financial institutions to follow these instructions was taken into account when the Movers' U.S. tax return was filed.

We outlined to the Movers all of the onerous tax filing requirements in future years surrounding their RRSPs. They were shocked to find out that their RRSPs would be fully taxable in the United States and that a Canada-U.S. Tax Treaty election would be required on the U.S. return annually to defer any taxes in the United States. Moreover, they would have to report all accounts in Canada to the Department of Treasury on an annual basis. Finally, we informed John that, if he exercised his stock options after moving to Canada, he'd have to declare income on both his American and his Canadian tax returns, but offsetting foreign tax credits would be permitted to mitigate the potential double taxation. As a result, he decided to exercise some stock options prior to taking up tax residency in Canada and move those funds into his immigration trust.

INDEPENDENCE PLANNING

In reviewing the Movers' projections, we determined that a move to Canada would enable them to achieve independence from work when John turned 63 because of the higher income taxes in Canada; if they remained in the United States the entire time, their financial projections revealed that John would have to work only until age 59. It appeared they would need a net worth of approximately U$3 million to live their desired lifestyle for the balance of their lives, so a disciplined savings plan was put in place but balanced with their desired lifestyle in Alberta to accumulate another C$500,000 before moving back to the United States.

In reviewing the different alternatives available for retirement savings, both John and Jenny began contributing to their RRSPs when eligible, with any surpluses going into their joint taxable portfolio. This approach set them up well for their pending move back to Canada.

Because both John and Jenny would contribute to the Canada Pension Plan while in Canada, they'd qualify for a CPP retirement benefit at age 60 even if they moved back to the United States. Both John and Jenny qualified for a U.S. Social Security benefit before moving to Canada. However, as a result of their CPP benefit, their U.S. Social Security could be reduced due to the rules of the windfall elimination provision.

Depending on how long the Movers would stay in Canada and if they would become permanent residents, they could qualify for an Old Age Security benefit when they turn 65, even if they return to the United States, due to the totalization agreement.

RISK MANAGEMENT PLANNING

Besides a valid visa, a "must have" before considering a move to Canada is some form of health insurance. The Movers were pleased to discover there was no waiting period for Alberta Health Care coverage once they entered Canada. In addition, new group health benefits in Canada included vision and dental care for both of them. Since John is the primary breadwinner, he has a U$500,000 term life insurance policy. Based on our analysis and the Movers' new financial situation in Canada, the death benefit would be sufficient for Jenny, so no further action was required unless currency exchange rates varied greatly. Likewise, we told the Movers to obtain Canadian property/casualty policies to cover their autos and home in Canada.

ESTATE PLANNING

In preparation for their move to Canada, John and Jenny went to their local estate planning attorney in Texas and had their living trust and wills updated. However, we pointed out that their trust would become a tax resident of Canada because the trustees, themselves, were moving there. We explained that their trust doesn't maintain its flow-through status in Canada and is subject to the punishing tax rates there. As a result, the Movers transferred all possible assets into their name alone and dismantled their revocable living trust before taking up tax residency in the United States. They took our advice and hired a competent Canada-U.S. attorney familiar with American citizenship issues, and they drafted new wills with testamentary trusts for their heirs. We also encouraged John and Jenny to get Alberta health-care directives and power of attorney documents done, which they did.

Using the information and titling provided in the table above, the Movers' U.S. estate tax liability was calculated as zero because they would be eligible for the unlimited marital deduction at the first spouse's death and, given the size of their estate, face no U.S. estate taxes with the exemption at U$5.34M. However, what the Movers were unprepared for was the deemed disposition at death tax in Canada, currently estimated at C$0, at the second spouse's death if they were to die today; however, as they accumulate assets with embedded gains, it would go up.

INVESTMENT PLANNING

In moving to Canada, the Movers were surprised at how few low-cost investment alternatives were available for their RRSPs compared to such investments in the United States. In particular, the expense ratios of most Canadian mutual funds were two to three times those in the United States. The Movers found a U.S. investment manager to manage their accounts in the United States and a Canadian investment manager to manage their brokerage account and RRSPs in Canada. However, this arrangement caused a few issues for the Movers. First, the Canadian and American portfolios weren't being coordinated, and duplicate asset classes and expenses were prevalent throughout. Second, the Canadian investment manager was unaware of the U.S. tax implications of his investment approach and ended up causing an unexpected ordinary tax liability on the Movers' U.S. return. Third, their U.S. investment manager was in violation of securities rules because he was rendering investment advice to a Canadian resident without being registered in Canada. And fourth, because the necessary paperwork wasn't filed with their financial institution in the United States, the Movers had 30% withholding on all investment sales and dividends in the United States. We helped to consolidate all of their accounts under our institutional custodians because we are registered to manage investments in both Canada and the United States. We were able to offer a coordinated investment solution that mitigated their tax situations in both countries and prepared them for their eventual move back to the United States.

APPENDIX E

COMPREHENSIVE CASE STUDY: RETIRED COUPLE

Ed and Nettie Yankee hired Transition Financial Advisors to assist them in making a smooth transition to Canada (this case is based on a real-life fact pattern, but all names and numbers have been changed). Following are the financial planning issues, obstacles, and opportunities our planning process revealed for the Yankees. This is intended not to be blanket advice applicable to all situations but to increase your understanding of the many things that must be taken into account when considering a move to Canada. Each person's situation is unique and requires a custom analysis to determine the best course of action. As any good transition planner should, we review the following eight areas of planning: customs, immigration, cash management, income tax, financial independence, risk management, estates, and investments; each is part of a comprehensive financial plan.

BACKGROUND

After many years of "sunbirding," Ed and Nettie decided to move permanently from Florida to Alberta to spend the rest of their lives. They had some reservations about leaving their friends but decided that being closer to their children and grandchildren in Canada was more important. They recently wound up and sold their business for U$3.5 million and thought it was time to move to Canada. Aged 64 and 62 respectively, married with three grown children and four grandchildren, both Ed and Nettie are Canadian citizens, with Nettie being an American citizen as well and Ed being a U.S. green card holder. The Yankees have a net worth of approximately U$7,750,000, comprised as follows.

TABLE E.1

YANKEES' NET WORTH

Asset	Fair Market Value (C$)	Cost Basis (C$)	Titling
American brokerage account	4,000,000	3,750,000	Joint
IRA	900,000	—	Ed
IRA	600,000	—	Nettie
RRSP — Canada (C$100,000)	100,000	—	Nettie
Checking/savings accounts	150,000	150,000	Joint
Principal residence (Florida)	1,000,000	775,000	Joint
Alberta home (C$650,000)	650,000	450,000	Joint
Autos (2)	100,000	100,000	Joint
Personal/household/ jewelry	250,000	500,000	Joint
Total	7,750,000		
	900,000		Ed
	700,000		Nettie
	6,150,000		Joint

LIFE PLANNING

We started by determining where Ed and Nettie were "going," where they "were" now, and how they were going to get "there." The "plan" allowed individual financial decisions to be placed in context and ensured that limited resources were channeled toward achieving their plan. Following is a summary of their intentions.

- Ed and Nettie wanted to move permanently to Alberta to be closer to their children and grandchildren, severing their tax ties with the United States (if possible) but spending the winter months in Florida close to their friends.
- Now independent of work, they wanted to remain financially independent in Canada.
- The Yankees wanted to pass their estate on prudently to their heirs in both Canada and the United States, with a portion going to their church in the United States.

CUSTOMS PLANNING

The Yankees wanted to keep their home in Florida, along with a vehicle, for their visits in the winter months. We encouraged them to make arrangements for its care when they were gone for extended periods of time and to set up the automatic payments of any utilities, property taxes, etc. Likewise, they needed to make the necessary arrangements for the vehicle licensing and so on. Ed and Nettie elected to hire a reputable moving company to take care of all the details of moving their personal goods to Canada, including the development of a full inventory of goods to present to the Canada Customs agent upon entry. To establish a defensible value for tax purposes, we advised them to get appraisals on their Florida home near the time they left for Canada.

Although "empty nesters," Ed and Nettie still had two babies: Dollar the collie and Loonie the yellow Lab. In preparation for their move, we suggested that they have both dogs examined by a vet and get a health certificate to assure their good health. At the same time, the vet gave each dog a rabies shot and provided a letter confirming this treatment. When it came time to move to Canada, the Yankees had no problems taking their dogs through Canada Customs.

IMMIGRATION PLANNING

Since Nettie is an American citizen, she sponsored Ed for a green card when they first entered the United States 20 years ago. However, since they are both Canadian citizens, returning to Canada should pose no immigration problems. They had no set schedule for when they wanted to move, so their plans accommodated the lengthy time it took to wrap up their business and consolidate their assets. Ed was aware that, after holding his green card for three years, he was eligible to apply for U.S. citizenship. However, he intended simply to go back to Canada with his green card. We explained the "use it or lose it" rules: that is, he had to demonstrate use of his green card by living in the United States and not being absent for extended periods of time. Further, he'd have to continue filing tax returns in the United States regardless of where he lived to demonstrate his use of the green card. With this information, Ed decided he'd just hand his green card in when he went back to the United States. We informed him of the new expatriate rules he would still have to file tax returns under the alternative tax regime for the next 10 years. Once realizing this, he decided to become a U.S. citizen and file U.S. returns for the balance of his life, even when living in Canada.

CASH MANAGEMENT PLANNING

To expediently move their financial assets to Canada, the Yankees selected a discount currency exchange firm to exchange all of their available U.S. dollars into Canadian loonies. These funds were wired into the Yankees' investment account in Canada, so we were able to begin investing them the next day. This approach also avoided the required government paperwork surrounding the transfer of large amounts of cash to Canada.

To ease their move, the Yankees closed all of their checking and savings accounts except the one they'd use for convenience to pay their U.S. auto and property expenses as well as when they were down for the winters. They also filed the necessary paperwork to have their Social Security checks deposited directly into their checking account so their automated bill payments would be covered for their American home and auto expenses.

INCOME TAX PLANNING

Key Assumptions
- Ed CPP C$5,000, Nettie C$2,500
- Social Security: Ed U$12,000, Nettie U$6,000
- Capital gains jointly: C$75,000 (C$25,000 short term)
- Interest jointly: C$42,000

- Dividends jointly: C$83,000 (C$70,000 qualified dividends)
- Standard deduction used for U.S. scenario
- No exchange rates used (to show the net tax effect of the move)
- No tax planning included

TABLE E.2

2013 TAX COMPARISON

Canada	Ed	Nettie	C$	United States	U$
Federal	$10,464	$8,488	$18,952	Federal	$24,415
Alberta	4,023	3,263	7,286	Florida	0
Total	**$14,487**	**$11,751**	**$26,238**		**$24,415**
% of income			11.7%		10.8%
Health insurance			0		$4,800
Grand total			**$26,238**		**$29,215**
			11.7%		13.0%

In the Yankees' situation, the move resulted in annual tax savings of $1,823 in 2013 (using an exchange rate of C$1 = U$1). However, when health-care expenses are factored in, they end up ahead in Alberta by C$2,977. Both Ed and Nettie were dismayed to find that Ed would now be subject to the OAS clawback (so would Nettie in the future if her income increased), decreasing their income every year in Canada, so that leveled the playing field further. Furthermore, since the full amounts of OAS and CPP are taxed in Canada, the Yankees had an even larger income reduction. We were able to decrease some of this differential by structuring their portfolio to integrate with their overall tax and financial plan. Through proper tax planning and preparation, we were able to mitigate their Canadian and U.S. tax liabilities even further and still meet their Canadian income requirements while maintaining their investment risk tolerance objectives.

U.S. FILING REQUIREMENTS

With Nettie being a U.S. citizen and Ed a green card holder, they were shocked to find out they'd have to file U.S. federal tax returns (married filing jointly) when living in Canada and have to declare their worldwide income, including the income that had been accruing in her RRSPs. For Nettie, the embedded gains were more difficult to determine in her RRSP because she is a U.S. citizen. She began working with her brokerage firm in Canada to establish a history in the account so we could determine the tax implications upon withdrawal.

CANADIAN FILING REQUIREMENTS

Ed and Nettie would each need to file a Canadian "start-up" return by April 30th following the year of their move to Canada. On this return, they'd have to declare their worldwide income from the time they took up tax residency in Canada. Since they'd also have to file a U.S. return, competent tax preparation would be key to avoid the potential for double taxation. Our analysis indicated there would be embedded gains of C$250,000 in their U.S. brokerage account. To their surprise, the Yankees were informed that these embedded gains would be wiped out for Canadian tax purposes because there is a "step-up" in basis upon taking up tax residency in Canada. Moreover, since they would file separate tax returns in Canada, we recommended that they equalize their estate before taking up tax residency in Canada to maximize their income splitting and reduce their taxes. We assured Ed and Nettie that their IRAs in the United States would maintain their tax-deferred status in Canada.

INDEPENDENCE PLANNING

In reviewing the Yankees' projections, we determined that a move to Canada wouldn't hamper them from maintaining their desired lifestyle for the balance of their lives. Further analysis revealed a high probability of success in their projections; in fact, they'd have surplus funds to allow for some lifetime gifting to heirs, philanthropy to their church, or enhancing of their lifestyle. Furthermore, their projections revealed that they didn't need to take much risk in their investment portfolio to achieve their financial objectives.

The Yankees were thrilled to find out they'd retain their current Social Security benefits if they moved to Canada. Nettie had concerns about her IRA in the United States. From a tax standpoint, we advised her that it retained its tax-deferred status in both the United States and Canada. She would have to commence the required minimum distributions when she turned 70½, and they would be fully taxable in both Canada and the United States. We encouraged her to change the beneficiary on the IRA from her estate to Ed so he could maintain the tax-deferred status of the account in the event she predeceased him.

RISK MANAGEMENT PLANNING

One of the primary reservations Ed and Nettie had in moving to Canada was about re-entering the universal health-care system. We alleviated their concerns by telling them that in Alberta coverage would commence immediately, and they should apply for it immediately upon their return. Finally, because they were U.S. citizens and had established 40 quarters of coverage before moving to Canada, they would qualify for free Medicare Part A when they turned 65, saving them U$10,224 in premiums in 2014. They questioned whether they should continue to pay for Part B, which cost them U$3,526.60 annually, and we confirmed that, because they intended to reside in Florida for an extended period of time each year, they should pay in to Part B so they wouldn't need to get underwritten for any travel health insurance. With medical coverage assured on both sides of the border, they had the ideal situation.

ESTATE PLANNING

Given the size of Ed and Nettie's estate and because Ed — at the time of our initial planning — wasn't a U.S. citizen, comprehensive estate planning integrated with their financial plan was critical. Several years ago, the Yankees had put a full trust-centered estate plan in place, including a QDOT, so that no estate tax would be owing at Nettie's death if she predeceased Ed. However, with the new unified credit amount, Ed and Nettie have no estate tax owing under current laws. Ed and Nettie were shocked to find out that they would still be subject to U.S. estate and gift taxes when they moved to Canada since they were U.S. citizens or green card holders. Furthermore, they had no idea that trusts in Canada aren't "flow-through" entities, as they are in the United States, but are taxed as a separate entity at the punishing Canadian trust tax rates. As a result, they moved all of their assets out of their trust into their personal names and dismantled their U.S. trust before taking up tax residency in Canada. An additional complication was the fact that Ed and Nettie had an heir remaining in the United States who would receive a substantial inheritance at their passing. We referred them to a competent Canadian attorney very familiar with U.S. citizenship issues for those living in Canada who drafted a Canadian will with testamentary trusts to preserve their estate. Given the surplus indicated by their financial projections, Ed and Nettie decided to increase their lifetime gifting and make greater charitable gifts as well. Since the Yankees wanted their gift to go to their church in the United States, we informed them that their gift would remain income tax deductible in Canada under the Canada-U.S. Tax Treaty. Depending on how the U.S. estate tax rules change over the next few years, and if any of their heirs move between Canada and the United States, a complete review of their estate plan would be needed.

Another shock occurred when we told the Yankees about the deemed disposition at death tax in Canada. In their situation, it was negligible in 2013 because the bulk of their existing capital gains were wiped out upon their return to Canada. The only thing taxable at this point was Nettie's RRSP and any embedded gains that accrue up to the point of the second spouse's death.

INVESTMENT PLANNING

Ed and Nettie asked about transferring their IRAs to an RRSP in Canada. We told them there is a strategy to do so with a 15% tax, but it wouldn't apply in their situation as U.S. citizens or green card holders living in Canada. Their American investment manager, unfamiliar with Canada-U.S. transition planning issues, was eager to get the proceeds from the sale of their business working for them. She wanted to invest their brokerage account in a number of municipal bonds and variable annuities. After consulting with us, the Yankees decided to leave their current investment manager because she didn't realize that both municipal bonds and variable annuities are fully taxable in Canada. This would have unnecessarily increased their Canadian tax and lowered the return on their investments. Since the Yankees had a need for Canadian loonies to fund their future lifestyle, it was important to get Canadian loonie investments into their portfolio. We made arrangements to transfer the bulk of their cash to Canada through a discount brokerage firm and invested it in a low-cost Canadian loonie investment portfolio with global diversification.

DISCLAIMER

This book presents general information, including the author's investment philosophy. This information is not intended as personalized investment advice and should not be relied on by any individual as the basis for investment decision making. Readers are encouraged to discuss their specific investment needs, goals, and objectives with a qualified investment professional.

Additionally, this book contains legal and tax information related to relocating from the United States to Canada. While the information contained in the book is deemed reliable, the author does not intend to provide comprehensive legal or tax advice. Readers are encouraged to seek the assistance of qualified legal and tax professionals regarding their specific legal and tax needs.

INDEX

GET THE EBOOK FREE!

At ECW Press, we want you to enjoy this book in whatever format you like, whenever you like. Leave your print book at home and take the eBook to go! Purchase the print edition and receive the eBook free. Just send an email to ebook@ecwpress.com and include:

- the book title
- the name of the store where you purchased it
- your receipt number
- your preference of file type: PDF or ePub?

A real person will respond to your email with your eBook attached. Thank you for supporting an independently owned Canadian publisher with your purchase!